The Blantyre House I

LESSONS FROM A MODERN-DAY WITCH HUNT

The Blantyre House Prison Affair
Lessons From a Modern-day Witch Hunt

Published by
WATERSIDE PRESS LTD
Sherfield Gables
Sherfield-on-Loddon
Hook RG27 0JG
United Kingdom

Telephone 01962 855567 UK Landline low cost calls 0845 2300 733
E-mail enquiries@watersidepress.co.uk
Online catalogue and bookstore www.watersidepress.co.uk
Direct mail orders Waterside Press Ltd, Domum Road, Winchester S023 9NN

ISBN 978 1904380 313

Cataloguing-In-Publication Data A catalogue record for this book can be obtained from the British Library

Cover design Waterside Press Ltd. Main photograph of HM Prison, Blantyre House.

Printing and binding CPI Antony Rowe Ltd, Chippenham and Eastbourne, UK.

North American distributors International Specialised Book Services (ISBS), 920 NE 58th Ave, Suite 300, Portland, Oregon, 97213-3786, USA
Telephone 1 800 944 6190 Fax 1 503 280 8832 orders@isbs.com www.isbs.com

The Blantyre House Prison Affair

LESSONS FROM A MODERN-DAY WITCH HUNT

Tom Murtagh OBE

Foreword **Martin Narey**

WATERSIDE PRESS LTD

Acknowledgements

I am grateful for the support and tolerance of my wife, Frances, whose strength and wise council have kept me going in the difficult times and my feet firmly on the ground throughout my career. The help and understanding of my family all through that long career, and in writing this book, is deeply appreciated.

I am saddened that my good friend Ron Gooday did not live to see this project completed but his contribution and that of Ed Davidson were invaluable.

I would like to record my appreciation of the help and advice I received from Bryan Gibson, my publisher. My thanks also go to a number of other individuals who helped me but prefer not to be identified; which in no way diminishes my appreciation of their contribution.

Finally I want to record my gratitude to both Martin Narey (former Director General of HM Prison Service) and Phil Wheatley (the current Director General) for their loyalty and support throughout this whole affair. Martin was being 'put through the mill' with me at the same time and his thoughtful and quiet encouragement in the difficult times was reassuring. This is re-affirmed by his agreeing to write the Foreword to this book, for which I am most grateful to him.

Tom Murtagh
April 2007

Dedication

To the memory of my son

Nigel

who inspired me to write this book.

Some Key Abbreviations and Terminology

ATM Automated transaction machine (i.e. usually meaning a bank cash dispenser).

BOV Board of visitors. A committee made up of volunteer members of the public appointed by the Home Secretary to each prison in a purely monitoring role. They have no executive role or management responsibility and HMP Prison Service managers have no accountability to them. Since 2003 called the Independent Monitoring Board (or IMB).

C and R Control and restraint. An approved method used by prison staff to control violent and disruptive prisoners without causing injury.

CSAP Correctional Services Accreditation Panel.

DG Director General of HM Prison Service.

DDG Deputy Director General of HM Prison Service.

Establishment Generic description often applied to any HMPS premises, such as a prison or YOI.

General search A planned speculative full search of premises and/or people but with no specific target.

Governor Any grade of prison governor: but usually qualified so as to denote rank, e.g. 'assistant governor'. They may work in a particular prison or at HMPS headquarters.

Governor in charge (or 'in charge governor' or often 'governing governor') The governor who is in overall charge at a given prison/establishment.

HAC Home Affairs Select Committee. A committee of members of the House of Commons, i.e. that monitors home affairs.

HMP Her Majesty's Prison: as in HMP Blantyre House; HMP Wormwood Scrubs.

HMPS Her Majesty's Prison Service.

KPI Key performance indicator.

NIPS Northern Ireland Prison Service.

NOI Northern Ireland Office (the equivalent of the English Home Office in Northern Ireland).

Open prison One without a secure wall or perimeter fence and within and sometimes outside of which prisoners are allowed to wander subject to requirements of, e.g. security and control.

PGA The Prison Governors' Association. A staff association that represents some prison governors.

POA The Prison Officers' Association. A staff association that represents most prison officers.

Resettlement prison A prison specialising in preparing and assisting prisoners who are approaching the end of a long sentence to gradually reintegrate into the community.

Rubdown search A search carried out on a fully-clothed person requiring the palms of the searcher's hands to be rubbed over that person's body and the removal of his or her shoes (like the standard airport search on passengers).

Semi-open prison A special type of open prison but with a higher than usual category of prisoners and with special security requirements—that emerged partly as a consequence of the story told in this book.

Strip search A search involving the removal of clothing, initially from the upper body and, when replaced, from the bottom half including shoes and socks.

Young offender centre Name given to the equivalent of a YOI, in Northern Ireland.

YOI Young offender institution, i.e. for those aged 18-21.

The Blantyre House Prison Affair

CONTENTS

Acknowledgements   iv
Dedication   v
Some Key Abbreviations and Terminology   vi
About the author   viii
Foreword   ix
Preface   xiiii

CHAPTER

1   Sad Reflections   19

2   Career Choices   22

3   Fresh Start   41

4   The ATM Scam   58

5   The 'Charity Work' Debacle   66

6   The Chaucer Unit   77

7   Downhill Spiral   90

8   Operation Swynford   115

9   Aftermath   128

10   The Home Affairs Committee Investigation   156

11   A Modern-day Witch Hunt?   182

Some Items Found During the Search   202
References   205
Index   207

About the author

Tom Murtagh spent his entire adult working life within HM Prison Service and the Northern Ireland Prison Service, completing almost 40 years' service in 2002. After beginning in England at Wormwood Scrubs he moved to Northern Ireland at the height of The Troubles. He spent three periods at The Maze Prison, including as Head of Security and later as Deputy Governor. He is a former Principal of the Prison Service College in Northern Ireland and served as Governor in charge of both Armagh Prison and Hydebank Wood Young Offender Centre in Northern Ireland and later Dover Young Offender Institution (YOI) in England. For most of his time in Northern Ireland he was a known terrorist target and frequently under police protection. He returned to England in 1988, mainly for security reasons. He became area manager for East Anglia in 1992 and later held a similar position in Kent, then for the Kent, Surrey and Sussex area. A former chair of the Prison Governors Association in Northern Ireland, he was awarded the OBE for services to the Prison Service in 1990.

The author of the Foreword

Martin Narey is chief executive of Barnardo's—the UK's leading children's charity. Until 2005, he was Chief Executive of the National Offender Management Service (NOMs) and a Permanent Secretary at the Home Office until he left that department for the voluntary sector in 2005. He began his career in the National Health Service before moving to HM Prison Service in 1982 where he soon became recognised for his commitment to transforming and motivating prison staff, clarity of vision and his determination to drive through improvements in prison conditions and the way that prisoners are treated, including via a Decency Agenda that led to significant improvements and reforms. In 2003 he was awarded an Honorary Doctorate by Sheffield Hallam University where, in 2006, he was made a Visiting Professor. He received the Chartered Management Institute Gold Medal for Leadership in 2004.

Foreword Martin Narey

I did not get to know Tom Murtagh until just a couple of years before the Blantyre House controversy. We are not, and never have been friends in the true sense of the word. Although I like and admire him, we have never had a drink together, our wives have never met.

He came from a very different part of HM Prison Service. I was a fast stream assistant governor, naïve and idealistic on appointment and spared the grind of many years on the prison landings. I had moved swiftly to the top of the Prison Service. Tom, a lot older than me, had worked himself up from the bottom. He had been a 'Wormwood Scrubs Screw' and he took a longer route to senior management including an extensive—and courageous—spell in Northern Ireland at the height of The Troubles.

Our paths did not cross properly until 1998 when I joined the Prisons Board as Director of Resettlement. We did not get on initially and had one or two clashes. By this time Tom was the area manager in charge of prisons in Kent. I was in the habit of dealing directly with his governors as I sought quickly to re-introduce rehabilitative activity and to spend effectively the cash obtained by the Prison Service in the Spending Review of 1998. I lived in the midst of Tom's area and would frequently seek to make deals directly with his Governors. In particular, I began to spend time with Eoin McLennan Murray, the caring governor of Blantyre, and Eoin and I did become friends. Tom would remind me not to issue instructions to his staff. Encouraged by a view of Tom as a dinosaur, I continued to do so.

On Christmas Eve 1998, I phoned Mike Conway, another graduate entrant and contemporary of mine, and then the governor of Maidstone Prison, to tell him I was to be the next Prison Service Director General. Tom, Mike's Area Manager, was in the office when Mike took the call and he, Tom, added his—I thought—sheepish congratulations to Mike's. I remember thinking that Tom was unlikely to welcome my appointment. But at the same time I reflected that, late on Christmas Eve, when nearly everyone had stopped for the holiday, Tom was still in one of his prisons.

Others must have noted that Tom and I might not be a marriage made in heaven and a few weeks into my Director Generalship, Sir David (as he then was) Ramsbotham's Deputy at HM Inspectorate of Prisons asked for a private conference. He had a list of two names, people he and Sir David thought I should 'move on'. Tom's was the first of those names. I declined to take that advice, started visiting Tom's prisons, and began to notice how fast he was improving things. And in particular I noticed how he was gripping the new rehabilitative agenda, leading in the management of drug abuse as well as giving prison psychology a more influential role. He began to make a key contribution in developing a renewed resettlement strategy for the whole Prison Service. While

Tom was not the darling of the conference circuit, and while he did not speak out eloquently about rehabilitation, he was making it happen. I began to recognise him as an intelligent and outstanding manager.

Meanwhile, I began to take a close interest in Blantyre House. It was the nearest prison to my home and I found Eoin, the governor, to be idealistic and sometimes inspiring. He treated prisoners with respect, placed absolute trust in them and the atmosphere in his prison excited me. I wanted there to be much more of the humane approach prevalent at Blantyre elsewhere in the Prison Service.

But, much as I liked a great deal about Blantyre House, and long before I became Director General I had begun to form one or two doubts. I knew that prisoners were frequently released at weekends to carry out community work. On a glorious day in the summer of 1998 my family and I visited Goudhurst, a pretty little village, close to Blantyre. The village fete was in full swing and a large number of prisoners, freed on licence for the day were assisting. Eoin had told me that the success of the day release scheme was founded on an absolute intolerance of alcohol and that every prisoner on returning to Blantyre had to take a breathalyser test. Those who failed were transferred the same evening to another gaol. But on that sunny afternoon, in the absence of any staff from the prison, I noted that some of the prisoners were drinking. It was clear they knew they were not going to be tested when they returned to the prison. That suggested some staff were colluding.

After my appointment as DG, my doubts about Blantyre began to grow. David Ramsbotham convincingly told me that while he had no firm evidence he believed that prisoners from prisons on the Isle of Sheppey might be buying transfers to Blantyre. An audit of community work placements at Blantyre revealed a singular absence of much in the way of real work. And most troublingly, I discovered that there was at least one prisoner at Blantyre whose placement in a resettlement prison, at a very early point in his sentence, was inexplicable and indefensible. I began to worry.

You have to be political to run prisons effectively. You need always to be aware of the potential for escapes, riots or other embarrassments to prompt public, media and Ministerial anger. In the mid-nineties, notorious escapes from Whitemoor Prison and Parkhurst had nearly brought down the then Home Secretary, Michael Howard and did bring down the then Director General. My understanding with Jack Straw (Howard's successor) was that he would obtain the funding for me to make imprisonment more constructive as long as I did not allow prisons to embarrass him as they had embarrassed so many of his predecessors in office. I knew that a major security scandal would bring to a halt the promising re-emphasis on rehabilitation, decency and humanity.

I urged Eoin and his committed Board of Visitors to ensure there was a proper balance between trust and security at the prison. I reminded them of the capacity of a minority of prisoners to manipulate the freedoms they enjoyed and to abuse the trust placed in them. Tom began, quite properly, to manage Eoin more closely, never doubting his, Eoin's, commitment, but sometimes doubting his judgement.

But things got worse. We began to receive worrying police intelligence about the activities of some prisoners when on day release. Things began to drift and, with Tom's blessing I began to take a more direct role. I thought an immediate way to fix Blantyre, recognising Eoin's compassionate leadership and the caring approach of many of the staff was to try and make it a flagship establishment for the custody of children. The Youth Justice Board were excited by the prospect and I decided to visit Blantyre to share the possibility — in confidence — with Eoin and the Board of Visitors. Shortly afterwards, before I had even discussed the possibility with him, Paul Boateng (the Prisons Minister) was put under pressure by the Home Affairs Committee, and anxious that he might be accused of undermining a resettlement prison, vetoed the idea.

In retrospect, my personal involvement, and wish for Eoin to succeed, probably made Tom's job in managing him more difficult. Later on there would be suggestions that Tom was a bullying and domineering manager. But, in reality, Tom should have intervened much earlier and moved Eoin to a new post. He almost certainly desisted from doing so because he knew I wanted Eoin to be successful.

Eventually, with emerging and extremely troubling evidence of significant criminal activity by serving prisoners at Blantyre and my growing conviction that some staff might be corrupt, I briefed Paul Boateng, and authorised Tom to remove Eoin, and — before prisoners and staff could hide evidence of wrongdoing — to have the whole prison meticulously searched. I remain entirely convinced — on the basis of the compelling evidence we had gathered — that, without that intervention, Blantyre prisoners might have been at the centre of a controversy, probably involving large scale drug importation, which would have threatened the reputation of the whole Prison Service, returning it to the mid-nineties emphasis on 'security, security and security'.

But it was impossible, in the weeks and months which followed, to secure any sensible discussion of the events and their justification. Attempts by me to share intelligence about what might have been happening at Blantyre House were thwarted by a constant leaking of discussions. A private meeting with the local bishop was reported in *Private Eye* the same week. When I invited members of the Board of Visitors to my home, to impress upon them the necessity of my actions, our discussions were later shared over the telephone by a member of the board with a notorious prisoner in another prison (I listened to the tape with some astonishment). My home address was revealed to the same prisoner by the board member, who I know to be a good and decent man, but who had forgotten that we were dealing with prisoners given long sentences for sometimes grave crimes, and that they could not always be trusted.

This is Tom's story. It is a personal account and does not claim to offer a detached view. But I believe it to be an honest and accurate account of an extraordinary affair. It is a cautionary tale about the need in managing prisons — however much one is committed to giving prisoners a second chance — to remain realistic about the potential for a small number to abuse the trust placed in them. And just as significantly, to remain aware of the potential for staff to be corrupted by powerful and wealthy prisoners. It is deeply ironic, after having my concerns about staff corruption roundly dismissed at the time, that just before I left the Home Office in 2005, I read a report from a Metropolitan Police Commander which criticised the failure to fight corruption when it was exposed at Blantyre at the turn of the decade.

This is the story of how, in the weeks and months following the removal of the governor of Blantyre House Prison — arguably an entirely internal matter for the Prison Service — an unholy alliance of Sir David Ramsbotham, the Board of Visitors, the Prison Reform Trust and others (who did not know, and could not be told, about investigations at Blantyre by at least two police forces and Customs and Excise) convinced a misguided Home Affairs Committee to vilify Tom whose actions in managing Blantyre not only preserved all that was good about the Blantyre regime (and it has gone from strength to strength since) but may have saved my then job and perhaps that of the Home Secretary.

Preface

This story might seem to have all the ingredients of a good novel but regrettably it is not fiction. This is a factual account, from my perspective on the inside, of events that occurred between 1998 and 2002 centred on a small Kent prison, Blantyre House. It describes how a small but sophisticated group of prisoners seemed able to influence the Governor, many of his staff and some members of the prison's Board of Visitors to an extent that they appeared to lose a proper perspective of what prisons are about. The group's authority became so strong that, in some instances, a handful of prisoners appeared to be empowered to make what should have been management decisions, leading to a situation in which basic security procedures were ignored or even discontinued.

The Governor was not carrying out HM Prison Service (HMPS) instructions in managing the prison and, it seemed, was at times wilfully disobeying clear orders from myself, at that time the HMPS Area Manager in Kent, Surrey and Sussex and his immediate boss. This situation created an environment in which a small number of people who until then might fairly be described as career criminals — and who in some instances might still be pursuing that career — and who should thus not have been at Blantyre House at all, were able to engage in criminal activity when on temporary release from the prison.

Eventually, this situation deteriorated to such a degree that the Governor had to be moved without notice and the prison subjected to a general search. This action prompted an unbelievable and unprecedented response which ultimately lead me, the Director General of the Prison Service, Martin Narey and the Prisons Minister, Paul Boateng, to the committee rooms of the House of Commons. There the Home Affairs Select Committee (HAC), seemingly beguiled by prisoners and supporters of the former Governor, subjected the three of us to harsh and, in my view, quite baseless criticism for the, again in my view, clearly correct action that we had taken with the benefit of full and underlying knowledge of the events and considerable pause for thought.

●　　　●　　　●

Blantyre House is a small resettlement prison holding just 120 prisoners. Its role is to assist prisoners who are approaching the end of a long sentence gradually to integrate themselves back into the community as law abiding citizens. The resettlement process, in its latter stages, involves prisoners working in the community. Blantyre is one of only three small prisons carrying out this role in England and Wales (although resettlement work is done in many other prisons). Because of this it is important that the unique opportunities offered by these scarce facilities should be targeted at those most in need and most likely to benefit from them. The resettlement process involves a fair degree of risk taking on the part of any Governor and by the Prison Service. However risk taking has to be carefully managed through selection and assessment, constant monitoring and a level of trust in the prisoner. Though the primary role of such a prison is to facilitate resettlement, that objective has to be pursued with equal regard for public safety issues and HMPS's ultimate responsibility to carry out the sentence of a court.

Because of their more relaxed regime and the level of freedom on offer to prisoners at such establishments, in comparison to the norm, resettlement prisons can be an attractive proposition not just to a prisoner who is set on going straight but also to career criminals. The 'wrong type' of prisoner might see a fully blown resettlement regime as an easy option, providing an opportunity to continue and cover for further criminal activities. Constant care had therefore to be taken to ensure that the selection process was not corrupted and that the privileged regime offered was not abused.

The history of Blantyre House shows that at the time of the events which I describe in this book, a number of sophisticated career criminals (at least on the basis of their records or background so far), with no discernible resettlement needs nor, seemingly, intention of altering their lifestyle on release, had somehow found their way there. Once in situ, some of them abused the freedom offered by the regime, including (according to police and other intelligence) so as to pursue criminal activity. Among the prisoners who managed to get to Blantyre House was the infamous Kenneth Noye, who was then serving a long prison sentence for offences linked to the notorious Brink's-Mat gold bullion robbery, which at the time ranked as the biggest robbery in UK history. As I describe in the book, while working out in the community, he again fell under suspicion; and there is some evidence that he formed close relationships with some individual prison officers. Certainly, following his release, a prison officer was arrested on suspicion of assisting a criminal gang in an ATM scam. I also describe this in the book because it forms part of the general backdrop to the whole story. Six men—not including Noye—were convicted and sent to prison for that conspiracy in November 1996. Noye was named by the police as being involved and in his book *Kenny Noye: Killer on the Road* (2002) Wensley Clarkson purports to describe the extent of that involvement. In 1999, Blantyre House appeared to contain a worrying number of comparable individuals, many in the early (rather than later) stages of a long sentence. None of them could have got themselves there without the agreement of prison staff, either at Blantyre or at other prisons.

Following the ATM scam trial, I commissioned an investigation into the involvement of a middle-ranking prison officer at Blantyre House. It resulted in the dismissal of that officer, but the findings also highlighted a number of areas of concern requiring action by the Governor to ensure that such abuse could not be repeated. On a wider basis, it led to the setting up of an area based permanent anti-corruption investigative department that became more commonly known as 'The Chaucer Unit'. Frequent and worrying reports continued to come in to

Chaucer, alleging that a small number of corrupt officers were facilitating the transfer to Blantyre House of prisoners in exchange for sums of money. Though the sources differed, the substance of these reports was remarkably similar.

Prison officers are required to treat prisoners fairly, decently and with humanity—and in most prisons relationships are good and often friendly. But over-friendly relationships sometimes lead officers to loose their proper professional perspective such that they begin to over-identify with the prisoners. This, in turn, can make them blind to obvious abuses that may undermine security and control. Some more sophisticated prisoners are particularly skilled and adept at preying on this fact and developing false relationships. The phenomenon is known within HMPS (and beyond) as 'conditioning'. An analysis of some of the most serious breakdowns in prisons over the years, including the mass escape from The Maze Prison in Northern Ireland in 1983 (which I describe in *Chapter 2*), have owed their success, at least in part, to the conditioning of staff. Governors always have to be alert to such dangers, particularly where the interface between staff and prisoners is less formal. Resettlement prisons are no exception to this and might be said to be especially prone to such risks.

●   ●   ●

In the summer of 1998 I became aware of an apparent breakdown of the controls on the temporary release of prisoners from Blantyre House and commissioned a full investigation. This disclosed that a group of some 20 prisoners were being given an unprecedented amount of freedom to go and come as they pleased under the guise of raising money for charity. Almost all those involved were what I would describe as career criminals. The investigation also highlighted other serious failures at the prison and recommended that the Governor face disciplinary charges all of which I shall outline. I decided to take a less formal approach and to set in train a corrective action plan, agreed with the Governor, and based on the recommendations of the investigating officer.

Initially it seemed that the Governor was working to implement this plan but it gradually became clear that this was not the case. A small number of sophisticated prisoners, so it seemed, continued to enjoy undue favour and protection and were exercising considerable influence throughout the prison. Some were being allowed inappropriate levels of freedom outside the prison and appeared to be enjoying lifestyles inconsistent with their status as serving prisoners. At least one of these was a reputed former close associate of Kenneth Noye.

In the year up to April 2000 the Governor was ordered to make changes, and to exercise greater control and more sound judgment in his management of the prison. This, I believe, he failed to do and by the end of 1999 he appeared to be openly disobeying orders and ignoring national Prison Service instructions. He invited some Members of Parliament who were members of the HAC to the prison and appeared to be seeking their support in resisting my orders. During this visit the HAC members spoke to prisoners and appear to have developed some kind of enduring relationships with a few of the more influential ones. Then, by the spring of 2000, reliable intelligence suggested that a small number of prisoners were involved in serious criminal activity when on temporary release from the prison. The fear was that the prison was the base for some of this activity, all drugs related. The Governor was thus removed on 5 May 2000 by the Director General of HMPS and a full search of the prison carried out that evening. In addition, an HMPS internal investigation into the management of the prison was immediately begun.

Thus followed the unprecedented series of events that led to the House of Commons and what I can only describe as the bizarre behaviour of certain members of the HAC, seemingly under the inordinate influence of serving prisoners, ex-prisoners, the former Governor and his supporters (who included the then Chief Inspector of Prisons, Sir David (now Lord) Ramsbotham and members of the Blantyre House Board of Visitors). Rather than wishing to uphold the authority of HMPS, various attempts were made to excuse the former Governor's behaviour and the breakdown of control at the prison. The HAC accused the DG, Martin Narey, of an error in judgement and me of trying to destroy the ethos of what they described as 'this uniquely successful prison'—because of my supposed, but untrue, opposition to resettlement.

Worse than this, even before starting their investigation or hearing the facts one member of the HAC was alleged to have openly stated his intention to 'make those responsible for the removal of the Governor and the search pay'. They tried to place the blame on me and to have me sacked; but this move was unsuccessful as other people in more powerful positions in Government knew the facts—and the Government later refused to act on the more telling of the HAC's conclusions. But the weight of the publicity damaged my reputation in the eyes of those who were not aware of the facts. The stress to my family and close colleagues of the HAC pursuing this misguided agenda was enormous and, to me, unbelievable. Yet the HAC was covered by Parliamentary privilege; and I had no real recourse; even being denied the opportunity to explain matters.

The decisions made by the DG and myself in relation to Blantyre House, the removal of the Governor and the subsequent search were sound in my view. Though they had led us before the Select Committee, most of the criticisms levelled at us—both in the media and later in evidence to the HAC—were not based on any direct evidence of the facts. In my view, for whatever reason, much of what was said, printed or given in evidence was misleading and underpinned by falsehoods. The substance of the case against us, it seemed to me, was based entirely on a manipulation of the facts. However, in what follows, I will outline the evidence and information that is in my own possession and leave it to you, the reader, to reach your own conclusions.

•   •   •

The account that you are about to read should also serve to highlight the ease with which a few powerful individuals, maybe under subtle pressure from criminal elements, can subvert the system to the highest level. I hope it also exposes the lack of protection that exists for any individual who finds himself or herself at the mercy of a Parliamentary Select Committee, not bound by the rules of natural justice nor fairness that apply to all other judicial or quasi-judicial proceedings. Select Committees are accountable to no one; and the events that I describe in the book might be thought to raise deeper questions about our often revered Parliamentary processes. I wrote what follows only after a great deal of soul searching, but I believe that it is a story which needs to be told.

All royalties from this book are being donated by the author to the

National Association for the Care and the Resettlement of Offenders (Nacro)

Nacro is the leading voluntary organization in England and Wales working to resettle offenders and prevent crime. Founded in 1966, Nacro is a registered charity that provides direct services to around 80,000 people each year, both offenders and young people at risk of offending. Nacro annually accommodates over 3,000 people in its housing projects, trains 14,000 people in its employment and education centres, works with 14,000 young people in its preventive youth activity projects, advises 21,000 serving prisoners through its prison-based resettlement workers and advises over 20,000 people through its Resettlement Plus Helpline.

In addition Nacro has specialist teams providing consultancy, training, monitoring and evaluation services in the areas of youth crime, prisoners' resettlement, mentally disordered offenders and race equality in criminal justice. Nacro also campaigns and works with a range of government departments to influence their policies towards the resettlement of offenders and crime reduction.

Paul Cavadino Nacro Chief Executive
169 Clapham Road
London SW9 0PU

CHAPTER 1

Sad Reflections

I approached retirement in 2002 feeling that it would hopefully be a new and exciting phase in life for my wife Frances and me. Though I had enjoyed and thrived on my work in HM Prison Service over 38 years, the latter years as the Area Manager for Kent, Surrey and Sussex were stressful. We looked forward to being able to slow down and do the things we enjoyed together. I planned to write an account of my experiences in Northern Ireland during the height of The Troubles between 1973 and 1988. We both loved to travel and hoped to see more of the world. Retirement would also enable us to see more of our children and grandchildren and particularly to spend more time with our youngest son, Nigel, who was terminally ill, in the final stages of primary progressive multiple sclerosis. He was then permanently hospitalised in Belfast. Prior to retirement we shuttled regularly between London and Belfast to spend time with him.

Nigel was deteriorating fast and his consultant neurologist told us that one of the frequent chest infections he suffered could be fatal. When I retired I spent a lot of time at his bedside and got closer to him as a father than I could have imagined. His quality of life was minimal but he fought hard to stay alive. Though suffering greatly he never once complained and though he could do nothing for himself he always saw the funny side of any situation. I was with him when he died just before Christmas 2003. He had fought for life to the very end. Frances and I are proud of all our children but I was inspired by Nigel's spirit and determination to face his terrible plight with courage and dignity.

I had enjoyed a long and successful career in the service but the last two years were soured by events when I was unfairly and publicly criticised by members of a Parliamentary Select Committee in relation to events that had taken place at the small resettlement prison in Kent, Blantyre House, which at that time was under my management control as the Area Manager. On 5 May 2000 the Governor of that prison was transferred to another post at short notice and a successor installed. That evening a team of officers was brought in to carry out a general search of the prison and the 120 prisoners held there. There were sound operational reasons for these events and the decisions made by the Director General (DG) of HM Prison Service, Martin Narey. However, not all of these reasons could be rehearsed in public.

In the period immediately following these events friends of the former Governor, including some in powerful positions, embarked on a media campaign against me. Many of the people involved had no apparent knowledge of the background to these events so their campaign was mostly based on disinformation. It appears that pressure from this group, which included criminal elements, encouraged the Home Affairs Select Committee (HAC) to get involved and to carry out an investigation. I quietly welcomed their intervention at the time, thinking that the facts would emerge and put an end to the controversy. How naïve I was to think this way. The 'investigation' was farcical and their whole approach to these important issues an insult to natural justice. The HAC's conclusions, publicised in the national media, cast blame on me for the events that occurred, which they suggested were prompted by personal animosity between myself and the former Governor. The Government later rejected all of their findings relating to me. However a full and accurate account of what led up to the events of 5 May 2000 has never been made public even after that high profile HAC investigation. Because of this I have felt a cloud over me ever since, in spite of the strong public support I received from the DG, Martin Narey, and the then Prisons Minister, Paul Boateng MP.

Closure of the matter between the Government and the HAC did not wipe out the slur that I felt on my character. The hurt was compounded by the fact that the majority of the most damaging fabrications were made under the protection of Parliamentary privilege which meant that I had no means of redress. As a senior public servant at the time I was also constrained in that I could not make any public response to the inaccurate and frequent untruths.

Over my long service I had witnessed some unsavoury events and had no illusions about some of our politicians, but in other circumstances any deviousness or treachery was usually to protect their own skins or to gain advantage. In this case this did not apply.

The HAC seemed to pursue an agenda which they had set for themselves without regard for the facts. Some people might argue that those involved were deceived by untruths and disinformation - but such excuses would be, in my view, an insult to the intelligence of the HAC members concerned. On the other hand if, as they claim, they took full account of all the evidence and balanced it in reaching their conclusions, then their perception of management responsibility and public accountability is strangely at variance with the norm. Whatever the truth of the matter, I began to wonder about the inner workings of one of our more hallowed institutions and about how citizens or public servants can be treated. Ultimately, however, I had the full support of the then Home Secretary, Jack Straw, his Prisons Minister, Paul Boateng, the DG of HMPS, Martin Narey, his deputy (and my direct boss), Phil Wheatley (now director general), and members of the senior management of the Prison Service. Unlike some other much publicised cases involving other Select Committees my operational and political bosses did not abandon me and I am grateful to them for that.

Though disillusioned by these events, my natural instinct as a public servant was to let the matter drop. I felt that the people who really mattered knew the truth. However, in the latter part of 2003, Sir David (by then Lord) Ramsbottom, the former Chief Inspector of Prisons, published his book *Prison Gate* in which he revived the matter and repeated a series of misleading and potentially damaging comments about me in an account of the events of 5 May 2000 that I shall try to correct in the chapters that follow.

After Nigel's death I thought hard about the whole affair and recalled a conversation with him when he still had some speech. He knew I was saddened by events at the close of my career and said, 'Dad, fight these people at their own game, tell the true story'. When I reminded him that I was bound by the Official Secrets Act his response was, 'Fuck the Official Secrets Act! You have given your life to the Prison Service, you and Mum nearly lost your lives because of it, so to hell with them.' Maybe he was right! We as a family had suffered because of my career, particularly in Northern Ireland. I had survived a number of murder attempts, culminating in one by terrorists to kill both Frances and myself with a bomb under her car in 1988. My unwillingness to be intimidated by them had marked me out and their determination to get me had affected our family since 1980.

Prior to my unfortunate experience with the HAC I had confidence in the Parliamentary system in all its parts. Though I had been aware of controversy about the way some committees had conducted business in individual cases, I thought, as I suspect most people do, that their work was subject to the same rules of natural justice that apply to the rest of society. Though I thought I understood the issues surrounding the supremacy of Parliament and its privileges, the discovery that this was not the case, that they seemed unconstrained by the law in respect of individual human rights and (most worryingly) that there seemed to be no avenue of redress available to an individual who unfairly fell victim of their excesses was a big shock to me at the time and has been a constant worry since then. Power in a democracy brings with it a heavy responsibility but that power cannot be unfettered and must be accompanied by some checks and balances to protect citizens against abuse. That essential element seemed to be missing in so far as my experience of the HAC is concerned. I survived the experience but since then it has constantly troubled me but there was no avenue through which I could effectively raise these concerns or shine a light on this aspect of our public institutions.

As Nigel had suggested, perhaps it was time to fight back. I had already consulted a top firm of London lawyers about what I might be able to do to salvage my reputation. Successful litigation might give me considerable satisfaction but it would be long and stressful and might not ensure that the full story was told. I decided to avoid the further heartache which that route would bring to my family and just tell my side of the story. So here it is.

CHAPTER 2

Career Choices

I originally came from the village of Lurgangreen located a few miles outside the border town of Dundalk in the Irish Republic where my family had a small farm. The oldest of six children, I enjoyed a happy childhood in a supportive family environment. There was a strong learning and work ethic within the family which all of us picked up. We were given the best possible education opportunities and worked hard to achieve success. It was that influence that enabled all of my siblings to do well in their chosen careers.

Because of the limited career opportunities that existed in Ireland at that time I decided to move to London in 1964. I had recently married my wife Frances and we were about to start a family. Shortly after our arrival in London my application to join HM Prison Service was successful. It is fashionable to claim that one's motivation in joining the service was born of a desire to work with and help people. Mine was not. My interest was simply the fact that it provided me with a stable work situation and family accommodation until I could find a more suitable job in my own time. After completing my initial training I was posted to Wormwood Scrubs prison.

Wormwood Scrubs

At that time Wormwood Scrubs was the largest prison establishment in the system with four large accommodation units or halls, known as wings. Each performed completely different functions within the Prison Service estate. 'A-wing' held young prisoners (under 21) serving prison sentences and also contained a small separate unit holding adult prisoners who were undergoing psychiatric treatment. 'B-wing' was the Borstal Allocation centre. All young men sentenced to borstal training came there for assessment before being allocated to individual Borstal Training establishments on the basis of their perceived needs. 'C-wing' was an adult short term prison holding more than 500 prisoners. 'D-wing' held long term prisoners serving sentences from four years up to life imprisonment. Each of these units had entirely separate regimes (daily schedules) and the nature of the work provided a wide and variable experience to staff. The Prison Service encouraged and assisted in the personal development of young staff at that time and I was supported in pursuing higher education.

The Wormwood Scrubs experience had a formidable impact on my early development in HM Prison Service. I enjoyed working there and soon decided to settle for a career in the service. The diverse nature of its parts and the general ethos of the place differed so much from the harder line attitudes that were prevalent in most of the other large adult prisons in the system at that time. We were encouraged to treat prisoners with dignity, and by and large relationships were good. Many of the middle and senior management staff, including most of the older prison staff, had come out of the armed services and this was reflected in the disciplined way the prison functioned. However, it did not hinder the development and maintenance of a more enlightened regime. Prisoners were encouraged to make good use of their time by pursuing the educational and vocational training opportunities that were available.

In the six years I spent there I never once witnessed any act of unnecessary force or abuse of authority by staff against any prisoner. Things changed later and I was shocked and saddened by the culture of violence that developed there in the mid-1990s, which I utterly condemn. During these formative years in the 1960s, however, I learned the meaning of professional behaviour in my dealings with prisoners and its importance in doing our job. These standards were carried with me and developed as I progressed in the service. I saw prisoners as human beings who for one reason or another had got themselves into this situation. Many were the products of the environment from whence they came and the criminal sub-cultures that had developed within that environment. Others lacked the educational or interpersonal skills to survive. Quite a number had mental health problems and should not have been in prison at all. A small percentage seemed just evil but even then it was difficult to be sure that the behaviour of this group did not have a more rational explanation. From an early stage I accepted that the prison system had a wider responsibility than keeping prisoners in custody; we had to do all that was reasonably possible within the parameters of the sentence of the court to assist them to resettle in the community as law abiding citizens after their release.

There were of course aspects of my early experience in the service that were not so pleasant. As a young man recently moved to London I was shocked and deeply hurt by the degree of prejudice against me as an Irishman from many of my officer colleagues. The offensive and insulting nature of some of their comments and the obvious prejudicial behaviour of some of my superiors would not be tolerated today. I was so saddened by the ferocity of this prejudice in the initial months that I considered leaving but decided not to give in to them. I was grateful for the support of some colleagues at that time. After a number of months, when presumably they got used to my presence, the problem subsided. However the experience stayed with me and made me determined to act against this type of behaviour whenever it occurred. Thankfully the situation has changed and HM Prison Service now has a very clear policy on prejudice of any kind, whether it is related to race, gender, religion or other improper grounds— involving staff or prisoners—and acts very decisively against it if it occurs. Under the leadership of Martin Narey as Director General that policy was later developed to the extent that the service would not recruit anyone who had a connection with any organization or political group that advocated racism of any kind, and many individuals were dismissed from the service for racist behaviour.

In 1968 I was encouraged to prepare for the promotion examination to the new rank of Senior Officer which had been created on the recommendations of the Mountbatten Report into the escape of the Russian spy George Blake from Wormwood Scrubs. I saw my career developing through the uniformed supervisory grades with the ultimate objective of becoming a Chief Officer. The Chief Officer at that time had similar status to the Regimental Sergeant Major in the Army and was seen as the pinnacle of their career by most prison officers. The Prison Service management structure had a non-uniformed element above Chief Officer, known as Governors. The Governor grades were mostly recruited directly, starting as Assistant Governors and with a separate career structure up to Governor Class 1 (often in charge of the biggest and most difficult prisons). A small number of uniformed officers were selected to join them but I had little interest in that avenue of promotion at that time. However that was to change.

One Saturday evening in the late 1960s I sat with a group of colleagues and our wives in the staff social club at Wormwood Scrubs, of which I was Honorary Secretary. A drunken middle ranking Governor imposed himself on our company. Ignoring his boorish behaviour we tried to be polite. He clearly had a high opinion of himself and a not so high opinion of us. During the conversation, he boasted about how good he was and how he was destined for the top in the service. I admired his self-confidence and tried not to be offensive. However when he insultingly suggested that we lacked the intelligence, education or management skills to become Governors, I took offence. I invited him to leave our table but not before I had rather foolishly challenged him, declaring I would out-achieve him career wise. Most people in our company that night ignored and forgot about this incident but I did not and I have him to thank for fuelling my ambition. Within 15 years I had achieved equal rank to this man and within a further two-and-a-half years I passed him as I was promoted to a higher grade.

Ashford Remand Centre

In 1970 I was promoted to Senior Officer and posted to Ashford Remand Centre in Middlesex. This was an establishment holding young men (under 21) who were remanded in custody awaiting trial by the courts. Its structural design was not exactly suited to its purpose as a prison. This, together with the degree of overcrowding that existed made it a difficult environment in which to work and not a pleasant one for the young men committed to custody by the courts.

One of my main tasks there was to manage the Legal Aid Department. In that role I talked to every prisoner coming in and advised them of their rights in respect of their court appearances. Those people who were not legally represented were assisted in obtaining the services of a solicitor of their choice. In most cases I had to complete the necessary documentation for them as many of the prisoners lacked the literacy skills to do so. I was also responsible for managing a wing at the centre and in conjunction with my Senior Officer colleagues, took turns in charge of the centre outside normal office hours. The

Governor in charge at that time was Bill Brister, whom I still consider to be the best Governor with whom I have worked in the service. He had excellent management skills and I learned much from him about leadership. Bill left Ashford on promotion to become the Director of Security and Operations in the Northern Ireland Prison Service (NIPS) and some months after his departure he asked if I would consider applying for an Assistant Governor post in that service. I was already pursuing promotion to Assistant Governor in the England and Wales Service but a post in Northern Ireland would enable us to move closer to our families in Ireland. Frances and I decided that I should apply.

THE NORTHERN IRELAND EXPERIENCE

I went through the selection process successfully and joined the Northern Ireland Prison Service in September 1973. Assistant Governors from the England and Wales, the Northern Ireland and the Scottish services were trained together on a staff course at the Prison Service College in Wakefield. My tutor on the course was Phil Wheatley, who in 2004 became Director General of HM Prison Service and with whom I worked closely in the latter stages of my career. When I completed the staff course I was posted to The Maze Prison on the outskirts of Belfast (also known as Long Kesh).

Because of my origins in the Republic of Ireland some people were surprised by my decision to join the Northern Ireland Prison Service. I had no such misgivings. I am a prison service professional and as far as I was concerned I was joining another of Her Majesty's services where my skills and experience were needed. Though I was raised in the Republic, I was now a British citizen and apolitical as far as the situation in Northern Ireland was concerned. Whatever had gone before, I felt that the Government was then addressing the problems in a fairly even-handed way. Northern Ireland was a part of the United Kingdom and that was clearly the wish of the majority of people who lived there. As far as I was concerned violence had no place in a democratic society and could not be justified from any side in the conflict. Furthermore it seemed to me that none of the terrorists groups had any real mandate for their actions and little support outside their own enclaves. The Northern Ireland Prison Service had traditionally been fairly well integrated and prison staff initially seemed to be viewed as non-combatants by most of those actively engaged in the political conflict. Although it was going through a major upheaval when I joined it the service still retained a professional ethos.

The Maze
At that time The Maze prison was a unique establishment with a capacity to hold up to 2,000 prisoners. The population fluctuated but was generally made up of about 500 detainees held under the Special Powers Act 1922 and later under the Northern Ireland (Emergency Provisions) Act 1973 who were accused of being

involved in terrorist activity and about 800 convicted and sentenced prisoners whose offences were deemed to be 'politically motivated' and who were afforded 'Special Category' status. There was also a separate facility holding up to 80 young offenders. Prisoners were accommodated in Nissen huts in compounds, each holding approximately 80 prisoners. There were 22 such compounds. Detainees were held in a sector divided from the convicted population. The prison bore a strong resemblance to a wartime prisoner of war camp. The resemblance was not just structural as the outer perimeter was controlled by the military. HM Prison Service staff were responsible for the safe custody of prisoners, the day-to-day running of the prison and general security.

Prisoners were divided roughly into four separate paramilitary groups: the Provisional IRA and the Official IRA, which were Republican; the UDA and the UVF, which were Loyalist. Each group was held in a separate compound and organized themselves along paramilitary lines. Their leaders liaised with the prison's management and staff on behalf of the individual prisoners within their groups.

Following the introduction of internment, the status of detainees presented additional problems for the Prison Service whose traditional role was to hold prisoners committed by the courts either on remand or sentenced and whose status was clear. Detainees had not been charged with any criminal offence and the decision to place them in custody was political rather than judicial. Because of this their rights in custody were extensive in comparison to remanded/untried or convicted prisoners. This was reflected in their entitlement to daily visits, large food parcels, handicraft materials and more.

NIPS was experienced in holding and caring for unconvicted and sentenced prisoners. However in 1972 the then Secretary of State for Northern Ireland, William Whitelaw, acceded to the demands of prisoners who were claiming 'political status'. In granting them 'Special Category' status he insisted that it should not constitute 'political status'. However this was exactly how it was perceived by the prisoners and the public in general. Within months the consequences of that decision, which was primarily intended to facilitate the segregation of the different paramilitary groups, were that the paramilitary organizations took over control of many parts of the prison. Prisoners were only granted special category status if they were 'claimed' by one of the four main paramilitary groupings at that time. These groups took control of their compounds and set up paramilitary command structures. Prisoners could not be located in any compound unless the leaders agreed to take them. Though it was never intended to be thus, within months convicted special category prisoners were enjoying similar privileges to those available to detainees. Inside their compounds the paramilitary leaders were almost autonomous. The staff role was relegated to that of security. In many areas prisoners tried to deny officers access to the compounds and individual prisoners would only talk to staff through their 'officer commanding'. Though there was an interface between prisoners and staff at the perimeter of the compound most communications were between the Assistant Governors and the prisoners' leaders.

In 1965, before The Troubles started, the average prison population in Northern Ireland was 400, housed between the main prisons at Crumlin Road in Belfast, the borstal at Millisle and the women's prison at Armagh. The total number of prison staff in Northern Ireland was no more than 300 at that time. Innovative programmes were available to prisoners and in many areas this small service was well ahead of its sister services in the rest of the UK. However in 1969 at the start of The Troubles the prison population escalated to in excess of 3,000. Most of the additional prisoners were high risk terrorists and detainees. To accommodate them the prison estate was expanded with the opening of new prisons at Castledillan, The Maze, Magilligan and HMS Maidstone, a naval ship converted to a prison ship and brought to Belfast harbour in 1971. The new prisons at The Maze and Magilligan consisted of Nissen hutted compounds.

The service had to expand all aspects of its operations to accommodate this mushrooming population. To overcome the initial difficulties in recruiting and training suitable staff, prison officers were seconded from the two UK sister services on detached duty. Difficulties were compounded by a high turnover of local staff as a result of intimidation and the regular changeover of detached duty staff which affected continuity, diluting and eventually destroying the admirable culture that had existed in the Northern Ireland Prison Service prior to The Troubles.

It was into this situation that I came in 1973. Until then I had developed knowledge and skills appropriate to the traditional prison environment. Those skills would be inadequate if I was to function effectively in this new and challenging environment. In conventional prisons power is vested in the management and staff. Prisoners are a group of individuals and are treated as such. Though relationships and regimes in some prisons may disguise this fact it is never-the-less true. In The Maze the consequences of William Whitelaw's decision to create Special Category status quickly led to a new dynamic in relationships. Allowing paramilitary groups to organize themselves in their respective compounds led to a similar hierarchal structure developing within each organization which quickly straddled their respective compounds across the prison. We no longer dealt with individuals but with cohesive and disciplined groups, some of whom were dedicated to challenging and destroying the authority of the state and all of whom were committed to challenging the authority of the prison's management. Individually and collectively the power of these groups was formidable. Irrespective of their perceived political status and the consequences of the decision to grant it, legally they were convicted prisoners with the protection appropriate to that status. We were therefore a civilian prison service responsible for the safe custody of convicted criminals who had been afforded the perceived status of soldiers and freedom fighters and allowed to organize themselves as such. In effect this amounted to us holding opposing armies within the prison.

I had to learn new skills quickly. My initial job was to take charge of the Phase VI sector of the prison which contained six compounds. All four main paramilitary organizations were represented there. In addition to the compound leaders, this area also held the overall leaders of the four factions. I quickly found myself dealing with compound leaders on localised issues and with their senior leadership on wider matters. Entering a steep learning curve, I had to get a sound grasp of the main issues in the Northern Ireland conflict, while developing my negotiating and leadership skills and a sharp political awareness very quickly. Attempts were made during training to address these needs but they only touched on the issues. I took a conscious decision to pursue a programme of personal development through private study and participation in all available development courses which, together with developing experience, enabled me to function effectively in this very challenging environment.

The expansion of the Northern Ireland Prison Service created many problems, not least the need to find enough senior Governors to take charge of the prisons. Some experienced Governors were already in the service but the scale of the expansion could not reasonably be managed by them alone. It therefore became necessary quickly to promote individuals to management grades to which they would not previously have aspired. Though some of these people were obviously over-promoted and limited in their contribution, others became strong and inspiring leaders even if on occasions their more subtle management skills might be found wanting. I learned a lot from these men about operational management in a situation of conflict and disruption. I also learned from others how not to run a prison.

The legal obligation on the Governor and prison staff to manage the safe custody of prisoners was unaffected by the granting of special category status. They were still expected to maintain control, discipline and security within the prison, and carry out security procedures. In the environment that existed at that time this was very difficult. Prison staff lived in the community amongst the families and associates of the prisoners and were constantly threatened and intimidated. Officers who were determined to do their duty properly were often singled out by the paramilitary groups and they and their families were threatened with death. Many middle and senior managers, from the comfort of their offices, issued orders to staff which they knew prisoner groups would resist. Faced with resistance or threats many staff backed off and orders were not carried out.

I soon learned that I had to give strong and high profile leadership to staff if I wanted things done. They needed support at the interface and where prisoner resistance was predictable I would go there to issue the order to staff in the hearing of the prisoners or their leaders. This enabled me to test the resistance of prisoners and to take such steps as were necessary to impose the will of the

Governor should they resist. This approach also diverted blame from the individual officers, enabling them to do their job without added pressure. The lessons I learned over this time about the importance of high visibility and high profile management remained with me. It was also during this period that I developed the direct and forceful management style and the often self-effacing sense of humour for which it seems I would become well known within HMPS.

A feature of The Maze Prison at that time was the frequent outbreaks of violence by prisoner groups, both toward staff and between their different factions. What would have been considered a major riot and be talked of for years in the other UK services became a regular occurrence in The Maze. These incidents had to be managed and controlled by Governors. Initially the Army was used to suppress riots but prison staff had to deal with the initial stages of such events and their aftermath. Later these incidents were handled by prison staff themselves, with the Army only providing back up. Governors had to develop strategic management, tactical and leadership skills to contain and manage these events and I soon learned to take them in my stride. I was involved in many such incidents, all of them frightening to varying degrees.

By far the most serious of these occurred on 15 and 16 October 1974 when a major riot by Republican prisoners led to the destruction, by fire, of most of the prison. On this occasion I took charge of a small group of 40 officers, in riot clothing, protecting the main gate and control room from a marauding group of up to 500 prisoners. Some of my officers were seriously injured during the incident but their courage in the face of such overwhelming odds was admirable. I was lucky to have an exceptional Principal Officer as my second in command and he deserves most of the credit for our effectiveness in holding the lines. On the basis of my report of this incident and his role, he was awarded the Queen's Gallantry Medal.

Shortly after the events of October 1974 a group of high risk prisoners successfully escaped, having tunnelled out of their compound. Following the investigation into the escape I was appointed Head of Security at The Maze with a brief to set up an effective department and ensure that there were no more escapes. I selected and moulded together a small team of officers who would gather and collate intelligence on all matters that could impact on the security and control of the prison. In selecting my team I did not only opt for those perceived to be amongst the cream of the staff. The group included a number of staff previously labelled unreliable. From my experience of these individuals I suspected that their less than perfect performances owed much to boredom and a lack of leadership at middle management level. The team quickly developed and embraced a common purpose and without exception all of its members blossomed. Many would later progress their careers to a higher level in the service. Together we monitored, evaluated and where necessary revised security systems throughout the prison. The success of this department is perhaps best measured by the fact that there were no escapes during my tenure in the post but intelligence did enable us to foil quite a few and to identify and dispose of the services of a number of corrupt staff. Among the escapes foiled was one by the current Sinn Féin leader, Gerry Adams.

Towards the end of 1974 Lord Gardiner was commissioned to chair a committee that would look at detention. He recommended that detention be ended but his report was also very critical of the original decision to grant Special Category status and he recommended that it too should be ended. The report also recommended that the Government undertake a building programme to provide suitable accommodation for prisoners that would enable staff to be in control. This recommendation was accepted and a building programme was immediately started. Cellular accommodation was built on a site adjacent to the existing compound prison at The Maze. Accommodation of a similar design was also built at Magilligan prison.

The announcement by the Secretary of State that Special Category status would be ended brought fierce resistance from all the paramilitary organizations, both inside the prisons and in the community outside. There was widespread rioting in both the Republican and Loyalist heartlands of Belfast and elsewhere in the province. In March 1976 the Provisional IRA's Belfast brigade, in an effort to put pressure on the Government to abandon its plans, issued a warning that prison officers and their families were 'legitimate targets'. A few weeks later the first prison officer was shot dead at his home by the IRA. Many more would die as prison staff stood firm in implementing the Government's policy.

The first prisoners convicted and sentenced for offences after Special Category status ended began to arrive in the new accommodation at The Maze in the latter part of 1976. A campaign of resistance to wearing prison clothing and conforming as normal convicted prisoners began immediately and heralded what turned out to be years of protest attended by the deaths of both prison staff and prisoners. As Head of Security I was an obvious target for the terrorists and I was warned of this by the police.

Northern Ireland Prison Service College

In 1977 I was promoted and appointed Principal of the Northern Ireland Prison Service College. The need to recruit and train officers to meet the needs of the service meant that training centre instructors were working flat out with no break between course intakes. No development training was being provided for any grades. Shortly after my arrival I carried out a training needs analysis of all grades in the service. As a result of that exercise a programme of training courses was developed to meet the separate needs of the various grades and groups, including management training for all staff on promotion. I took over tutorial responsibility for the training of Assistant Governors in the Northern Ireland Prison Service in conjunction with the college at Wakefield. I involved myself in the development of most courses and participated, at least in part, in presenting them. This was a very rewarding period in my career during which I was able to make a substantial contribution to developing the professionalism of the service. The nature of the task also enabled me to develop my own knowledge base and the interaction with students helped to broaden that base.

The Maze again

I moved from the college on promotion in 1980 to undertake a short term project setting up a professional personnel department at The Maze as Head of Personnel and third in charge of the prison. My arrival corresponded with the tragic hunger strike during which ten prisoners were to die. Republican prisoners were continuing their protest for the restoration of Special Category status that initially took the form of refusal to wear prison clothing or to work. Wrapping themselves in blankets they escalated the protest by spreading excrement on the walls of their cells. Their 'dirty' protest was to last for a long time and end with the hunger strike. During this period prison officers carried out their duties in this unpleasant environment and specialist teams of officers cleaned the cells in sequence with prisoners being regularly moved into clean accommodation. After an initial period refusing food, hunger strikers were transferred to the prison hospital where they were cared for by the medical officer and prison hospital officers. The level of care given was of the highest quality and many of the officers involved were deeply affected by what they were witnessing. The medical officer seemed to have been very distressed. Sadly he later took his own life.

Armagh Prison

When I completed my work at The Maze I was appointed Governor in charge of Armagh Prison. Armagh was a high security local prison mainly holding women prisoners. There was one wing holding low risk adult male prisoners providing the essential services to the prison. A small group of female Special Category IRA prisoners were held in accommodation separated from the main population. These included the Price sisters who were convicted of the Old Bailey bombings in London and sentenced to life imprisonment. A-wing held sentenced and remand female prisoners who claimed membership of the Provisional IRA. Their recognised leader was Mairead Farrell who was later to die with two of her colleagues at the hands of the SAS in Gibraltar. B-wing contained a mixture of Republican, Loyalist and ordinary non-aligned convicted female prisoners.

Some of these prisoners had also been engaged in a 'dirty' protest in support of their male colleagues in The Maze and a small number had been on hunger strike. Like The Maze, Armagh Prison's recent history of IRA prisoner disruption had had its effect on control, discipline and the general morale of the staff. My brief on taking up the post was to restore control and ensure that the prison operated in accordance with Prison Rules.

It was clear from the start that IRA prisoners were intimidating officers, some of whom were backing off from doing their job properly. At that time, in NIPS, only female prison officers were allowed to work with female prisoners.

Most of the officers were keen to carry out their duties properly but many feared, not without reason, that they would not be supported. The situation would have to change and quickly. I assembled the staff and explained how I wished them to operate. It was made clear that officers acting professionally and exercising control in accordance with the rules would be fully supported. Many good female officers had lost confidence and were nervous. I realised that they needed some initial high profile support to rebuild confidence. Within a short space of time they regained that confidence and became more assertive in carrying out their duties. The changes being made did not go unnoticed by the IRA and prompted immediate allegations of mistreatment of their prisoners.

The extent to which standard security procedures had ceased to be carried out at Armagh through intimidation of staff and even of Governors was highlighted to me, within weeks of taking charge, when I was made aware that basic reception searches on new prisoners coming into the prison, a procedure common to most closed prisons throughout the world, were not being carried out. This procedure should have been in operation in Armagh Prison as it held very high risk prisoners but I discovered that it had been quietly discontinued a couple of years earlier because of resistance by paramilitary prisoners.

All prison Governors in Northern Ireland had to consider the political consequences of every one of their decisions. I realised that re-imposing correct procedures would meet with strong prisoner resistance within the prison and could lead to rioting and disruption on the streets. The situation was drawn to the immediate attention of headquarters in a discussion that embraced the political and operational aspects of the options available to us. Later that day I received a telephone call, from a very senior level, ordering me immediately to implement proper procedures. I believed this was the correct course of action. IRA prisoners violently resisted the searches and in most cases, regrettably, the staff had to use force. The IRA and its supporters immediately began a worldwide campaign alleging torture and degrading treatment of female prisoners. I have never witnessed the searches being carried out but they were frequently witnessed by female members of the Board of Visitors (BOV) and senior female managers who assured me that the officers were acting professionally.

The intensity of the campaign against this standard search procedure placed pressure on both ministers of state and those of us tasked with ensuring the security of the prison. Prison officers faced violent resistance from prisoners and many were assaulted in the process. Ministers and senior officials faced frequent questions in Parliament, lobbying by pressure groups and MPs sympathetic to the prisoners. In answering a Supplementary Question to one such Parliamentary Question, the Minister's reply was wrongly interpreted as attributing the policy to me as the Governor. This enabled the IRA and its supporters to personalise their campaign against me. As time passed, though opposition to the searches continued, its intensity lowered and re-introduction of searches was by and large consolidated in the prison.

Having successfully achieved this I would now experience what seemed to be a devious and irrational betrayal of both myself and my staff by Ministers and senior civil servants at the Northern Ireland Office. I was called to a meeting at headquarters with the then head of the service and his senior officials where I was told that the Secretary of State now 'wished the reception search procedure at Armagh Prison to be the exception rather than the rule' and that this should be implemented immediately. I was shocked by the direction I was receiving, having re-introduced the procedure on clear orders from a senior level at HQ. How was I now going to command the loyalty and confidence of my staff, put them through the trauma of implementation only for Ministers to concede to pressure from terrorist organizations? What impact would this have on good order and discipline as this was a standard procedure carried out at all other prisons?

Because of the manner in which this sudden change of direction was being handled I asked for a verbatim record be taken of the meeting. This was refused. Having clearly stated my views on this sudden change of direction and its likely operational consequences, I told the head of the service that, as I was being ordered to ignore a standard operational security procedure I could only comply with the order if it was put clearly in writing. My resistance was obviously irritating to all those assembled except the Director of Security and Operations who openly supported my assessment of the impact and my insistence on written instructions to suspend normal reception searching. I also asked for a clear instruction on the level and frequency of searching to replace it.

When it was clear that attempts to force me to make the changes on the basis of a verbal order were not going to be successful, I was told that a written instruction would be issued. I eventually received a short and carefully crafted letter informing me of the Secretary of State's wishes. It was extremely vague on the level and frequency of searching that should replace it other than that change should be phased over a prolonged period. I recognised the importance of this instruction and ensured that copies were placed in safe places should they be needed in the future. Though I was not the source, its existence and content became known to Julian Amery MP who used it to embarrass the Secretary of State, James Prior, during the House of Commons debate on the Chief Inspector of Prison's report into The Maze escape of 25 September 1983.

Within weeks of the decision to reintroduce the searches I was visited by a senior police officer and advised that the Provisional IRA Army Council had issued instructions for me to be killed. He urged that I take the threat seriously. At the time I travelled daily between my home and the prison in Armagh, a distance of approximately 35 miles. Within days I was provided with an armour plated car. My home was also fortified against attack. On quite a number of occasions during my three years as Governor of Armagh Prison, police foiled

IRA plans to murder me. There were times when I had to move out of my home and live for periods in army camps. I also had to move house. Throughout this period my wife and family were subjected to horrendous pressure and stress.

A small number of prisoners convicted of terrorist offences were young married mothers. Some had received long sentences and this was having a devastating effect on their husbands and children. A few of them seemed to be distancing themselves from the disruptive elements in the prison. At that time the service operated a scheme that allowed selected prisoners to have periods of Christmas and summer leave to maintain family ties. This system had been in place for many years prior to The Troubles but did not apply to prisoners convicted of terrorist offences. I raised the question of allowing some of the young mothers who were behaving themselves access to this privilege with the Security Minister on one of his visits to the prison and he agreed to consider it. It was evident that some senior officials were not in favour of my suggestion. I was therefore surprised to receive a call, giving the idea a 'green light' but suggesting that failures would reflect on my judgement. The scheme was a success and quite a few female convicted terrorists eventually participated and complied in full with the conditions of their temporary release.

Armagh Prison was my first prison command and in spite of the difficulties it presented to me and my family, it was an experience I would not wish to have missed. For a male, managing a female prison presents different problems to those encountered in male establishments. The added dimension of the paramilitary influence and the serious safety issues affecting me outside the prison contributed to my personal development as a Governor and my ability to operate effectively under considerable stress. Because of the political situation that existed in Northern Ireland, Armagh and The Maze prisons required a high degree of political sensitivity in their management and this brought me into frequent direct contact with Ministers, senior officials from the Northern Ireland Office and some high profile political and religious leaders in the community. This enabled me to develop a greater political awareness, but it also allowed me to experience the true nature of some of these prominent people who frequently differed from their public persona and not always for the better.

Northern Ireland Prison Service Headquarters
In 1983 I was again promoted and appointed Assistant Director, Security and Operations at headquarters. There I had the pleasure of working with and learning from some very experienced and respected individuals. As well as operational management issues, I worked closely with ministers and learned to value and respect the skills of civil service colleagues from whom I gained new expertise. Though I enjoyed working in headquarters, after nearly three years there I became bored and keen to get back in the field. The Deputy Governor post at the new Maze cellular prison became vacant and I expressed an interest.

The Maze a third time

As Deputy Governor of The Maze Prison I was responsible for its day-to-day management, its 800 prisoners and approximately 2,000 staff. The Governor was Des McMullan, an affable man with whom I had worked in the past when he was Deputy Governor of the 'Old Maze Prison' in the mid-1970s. Like me, Des had come up through the ranks. He was popular with colleagues and the staff in general. I enjoyed working with him. Our management styles complemented each other and generally he gave me a free hand. Shortly after my arrival we became aware that he was to be the next Director of Security and Operations at headquarters. He was frequently away from the prison attending courses and meetings in preparation for his new job which meant that I was in charge for much longer periods than was the norm.

Since my last stint at the prison it had been through the traumas of the dirty protest and the end of the hunger strikes. It had also suffered the worst mass escape in British prison history in 1983 when 38 IRA prisoners took control of their cell block using firearms, knives and other cudgels and made their way to the main gate in the kitchen food lorry. By the time they were discovered they had reached the gate. A small group of officers on duty there tried to stop them and in hand to hand fighting managed to apprehend 13 of them. But 25 prisoners managed to escape. During this incident one officer was shot in the head. Others were stabbed and beaten with cudgels. Officer Jim Ferris, who was on duty at the gate, received three stab wounds to the chest and died from a heart attack brought on by the trauma.

Though many of the prisoners were apprehended after the escape, this was a major failure of security at the prison and cost the Governor his job. Though there is little doubt that the failures were serious, many professionals familiar with the facts believe that a large part of the blame lay at a higher level and that the Governor was the 'fall guy'. As with the Armagh reception search affair, I was present at a meeting when he was ordered to introduce a work regime for very high risk paramilitary prisoners that would inevitably lead to a breakdown of control. Again these changes were being driven by senior officials for purely political reasons.

Following the escape, security was tightened and stricter controls introduced. When I returned as Deputy Governor in 1986 I had expected to see these controls still in place and to find an efficiently secure prison. On my second day back it became apparent that this was not the case. The concessions made by Ministers to Provisional IRA prisoners at the end of the hunger strike, which were now also enjoyed by Loyalist groups, seemed to have been a grave mistake. Though the Government's stated intention was to treat them as ordinary convicted prisoners, the concessions made to them predictably enabled them to recreate the Special Category environment that had, in my own view, rightly been removed. It seemed that the deaths of my colleagues in enforcing that policy had been in vain. It was the prisoners' ability to recreate that environment that had been a key factor in enabling them to organize the escape. I found that both the IRA and Loyalist prisoners had again managed to erode most of the controls introduced following the escape. Through intimidation, their wings were now 'no go' areas for management grades above the rank of Principal Officer.

Both the prisoners and the staff seemed surprised when I insisted on going into the wings. For the remainder of my time there my energies were focused on restoring security procedures and raising the profile of some middle and senior managers to support officers on the front line. My insistence that managers should do their job properly was not popular with some and met with resistance from the prisoners. My early experience in dealing with Special Category prisoners had convinced me that standards could only be maintained through high profile management where officers felt supported and this situation was no different. A short time after my departure from The Maze I learned that control there had again been eroded.

Hydebank Wood Young Offender Centre

I became Governor of Hydebank Wood Young Offender Centre, Northern Ireland in September 1987. I was glad to be back in a normal prison environment. This was a purpose built institution for young offenders between the ages of 16 and 21. It had opened in 1979 and was well equipped with wide open spaces ideally suited to its role. It replaced the Borstal institution at Millisle when that closed and retained much of what was good about Borstal training in its regime and general ethos. The centre was firmly focused on training and resettlement supported by an extensive education and vocational training programme, reinforced by an incentive based system of progression. Because it was the only such facility in Northern Ireland, a number of the young men sent there had connections with paramilitary groups. Some of these young offenders caused problems but the majority participated fully and gained from the experience.

Prior to my arrival, Hydebank Wood had developed a reputation for difficult industrial relations, disruption and resistance to change. Though there is little doubt that its reputation was well deserved, my initial impression was that its staff were highly professional and well motivated but lacking in strong management leadership. In its absence the vacuum had been filled by a militant trade unionist who had built a power base. In the first couple of months after my arrival I had to undermine that power base and win the support of the staff. I believe that I achieved this goal and began to move the work of the centre forward. Interim objectives were met and together with my team we drew up longer term plans. I knew that things were going well and I was enjoying my work. I hoped to be allowed to stay there until my objectives were achieved.

Around this time I was elected chair of the Northern Ireland Prison Governors Association and led negotiations with the Northern Ireland Office on a number of serious matters affecting my colleagues. I also began discussions on the amalgamation of the association with the Prison Governors Association in England and Wales.

A brush with death
Throughout the previous ten years I had been aware of IRA plans to murder me. A number of attempts had been foiled but I knew that even at Hydebank Wood I remained a target. Because of this I travelled in an armour plated car to and from work and on all predictable journeys. As far as possible I tried to vary my movements and times. I also carried a firearm for my personal protection.

On the morning of 4 October 1988 people in the service were shocked to hear of the murder of Prison Officer Brian Armour who had been killed by a bomb exploding under his car, after leaving his home. A number of prison staff had already been murdered but we in the Prison Service never got used to these events. We were always shocked by the loss of a colleague. Brian had been a decent and well respected man who was the vice-chair of the Northern Ireland section of the Prison Officers Association. He had been in the service for 14 years and left a wife and two children.

Frances and I had been planning some home improvements and that evening we decided to visit some bathroom equipment showrooms the following morning. It was at this short notice that I decided to take the day off. During the evening and throughout the night the weather was horrendous with almost continuous torrential rain and flooding on many roads.

On the morning of October 5, Frances took her car out of the garage and went to the local newsagents. She drove a blue Honda Accord and I drove a red Ford Escort which was armour plated. I would not normally drive or travel in her car. On her return from the newsagents we had a quick breakfast and left to go shopping. Frances had left her car outside our front door on the steep downward sloping drive. Although I should have done so, I did not check the underside of the car for any device. Nobody knew I would be in the car and foolishly I thought that the IRA would not attack my wife. We came out of our drive and immediately through a badly flooded section of the road near to our home before driving through the busy centre of Lisburn to visit a showroom on the outskirts of town. When returning home we stopped at a large department store also on the outskirts.

On entering the store I was immediately approached by the wife of a prison officer and a former neighbour saying, 'I have just heard your name mentioned on the radio. They said that there is a bomb under your car that has not exploded.' As I was not in my own car I thought it related to a colleague whose name sounded similar to mine. However as we left the store I thought it wise to check the vehicle. From a distance I could see a shape on the underside of the car, below the driver's seat, not consistent with the normal profile of the vehicle. Frances stayed by the store entrance and I called out to other shoppers in the car park to move away. Then I went to the vehicle to make a closer inspection. A lunch box sized container was attached to the underside and from my experience I knew it was a bomb. Having cleared the area, I contacted the police. They told me that the Provisional IRA had alerted a local radio station about the bomb and that they had been searching for us for over an hour. During this period the radio station put out regular calls to us and to the public with details of the vehicle. We would normally have been listening to the radio but on this particular morning we were discussing bathroom equipment. Perhaps it was best that we did not hear. I knew these devices were detonated by a mercury tilt switch when armed and even the process of stopping and getting out would have been very traumatic.

There had been a number of attempts to murder me and we had lived with this threat for many years, even having to move home on occasions. This was the closest the IRA got and it was clear that they planned to kill us both. The reality of the situation came home to me in the car park and I experienced a surreal vision of a person placing the device knowing that it would kill or maim my wife. However I was quickly snapped out of this state by the sight of Frances emotionally disintegrating in front of me. We were both placed in a police car and driven to our home where, incredibly, TV crews were already encamped.

We were understandably traumatised by the experience, as were our children, three of whom had been made aware of the situation by the local radio station or the police. Before we knew of the bomb they too were out searching for us. We received many messages of support, some from people we did not even know. But we received little support from the Northern Ireland Office. On the afternoon following the incident an untrained staff welfare officer arrived at our home. This junior civil servant, though well meaning, could give no constructive assistance either to me or my family and I declined her offer of help. No realistic post-incident support was ever offered to us in Northern Ireland.

After a difficult day and a sleepless night my wife and I both reported to our respective places of work the next day. That morning I was called to headquarters to meet with the Director of Security and Operations. As I waited for him in the office of the Deputy Director, I met an army technical ordinance officer (bomb disposal) also waiting to brief him on the nature of a bomb he had disarmed from under a car the previous day. He did not know that it was my car and proceeded to describe what he said was a 'miraculous escape'. The bomb had armed and the mercury tilt-switch had established a contact. However a small amount of rust on the contact got very wet when we drove through the flood and probably acted as temporary insulation, stopping detonation of the bomb that contained three pounds of semtex explosives. It was only when he described the likely effect of such an explosion and saw my reaction, that he became aware of who I was.

An unexpected and disappointing aspect of these events was the fact that some people we had thought were close friends did not even call us on the telephone. Some had regularly socialised with us each week but following this incident they broke off contact. This was probably because of a fear of danger by association, particularly as the Provisional IRA issued an immediate statement that they would return and they would not miss the next time. Frances and I were deeply traumatised by the incident as were all our children. However both of us and our three sons returned to work immediately and tried to get back to normal. Our young daughter, Yvonne, who was still at school, was badly affected by events but also tried to disguise it. She had contended with this kind of stress for many years. I recall an earlier occasion, at our previous home, when the family had been told of an imminent attempt to murder me. Security advisors visited our house to see whether security could be improved and a group of them were standing outside the house when Yvonne and her friend, coming home from school, rounded the corner onto our road. She could not see me in the group and assumed the worst. Yvonne became physically sick and trembled uncontrollably. This continued even after she could see me and was aware that I was safe. Prior to this I had known that my family were suffering as a result of the situation, but the extent of this was only brought home to me by this event.

It would have been easy to submit to these pressures and leave but taking such a course was giving in to intimidation by terrorists. Like some colleagues I was not prepared to do this. I took the view that by not submitting to intimidation, I was denying the terrorists their strongest weapon. Senior managers had to stand firm and give leadership to staff who were also suffering similar dangers and pressures. Not all of them did but it is because of this that I lived with the situation for so long. Sadly, I would later learn that Principal Officer Christopher Hanna had been arrested in connection with the car bomb murder of Prison Officer Brian Armour and the attempted murder of Frances and myself. Hanna had been in charge of the first block I visited on my return to The Maze Prison where I discovered the extent to which security and control had been eroded. He had been corrupted by IRA prisoners in his block and provided them with the detailed intelligence on Brian—and on us—to enable them to launch these attacks. Hanna was sentenced to life imprisonment and sadly died in prison.

Shortly after the events of 5 October 1988 and the statement by the Provisional IRA that they would return I was again called to a meeting with a senior official at headquarters. I was told that the police were seriously concerned about my safety and that of my family and that I should consider 'easing' the situation by returning to the England and Wales Prison Service for a period to allow the situation to settle down. I thanked him for his offer but declined as I did not want to leave Northern Ireland. Over the next couple of weeks I was again spoken to by senior officials and a senior police officer and placed under considerable pressure to change my mind. After discussions with my wife and family we agreed that I should move. My wife and daughter would accompany me. Our three sons, who at that time still lived at home, were adults and each separately would buy their own homes. The effect of the move was to split the family and with the benefit of hindsight it caused further long term distress to us all.

It was unclear at that time how long we would be away but because our home was now marked by the incident we had to sell it. As with the previous home moves for security reasons, our house was not saleable on the open market and had to be disposed of under a special scheme. We therefore never obtained market value and gained only limited equity on these homes.

Having agreed to return to the England and Wales Prison Service, I attended the 1988 Prison Service Conference at Blackpool where I met both the Director General (DG), Chris Train, and the Deputy Director General (DDG), Brian Eames, to discuss the move. Both were very kind and welcoming and tried to accommodate my needs. I had worked with the DDG in the 1960s at Wormwood Scrubs where he was Deputy Governor. It was suggested that I might join his team at headquarters in London. This was a position supporting him in the operational management of the service and could involve directing, or at least advising, in-charge Governors (sometimes called 'governing governors').

I had been away from the England and Wales service for 16 years and the only contact I'd had with Governors in that service was through attendance at the Prison Service College and short attachments with HM Chief Inspector of Prisons Team and the Northern Regional Office Operational Assessment Team. I did not consider this enough to establish credibility and win the confidence of senior Governors. I asked him if I could be considered for a post in a prison preferably in the south of England. A number of possibilities were discussed and it was agreed that I would be appointed Governor of the Young Offender Institution at Dover. I moved there on 30 November 1988.

I left Hydebank Wood with a heavy heart. Though I had been Governor for just one year I knew that a lot had been achieved in that short time. But there was much more to do and I knew that the management team and the staff could develop it as a centre of excellence. I also felt guilty that I was deserting a team who had worked well and supported me. I hoped that if the situation settled down I could come back there. On the other hand, after the briefing I received, Dover was also an attractive proposition for me in that I was told that it too was going through a difficult time. There had been a history of racial tension and violence among inmates. Industrial relations were also described as 'difficult'. My challenge was therefore clearly identified for me before I arrived.

CHAPTER 3

Fresh Start

For the previous ten years I had lived with the constant threat of death hanging over me and I had learned to cope with the stress involved. My wife and children had also lived with this situation. Strangely, this way of life can become 'normal' after a time as what 'normality' means to most people is forgotten. We went about our business and social life with the inconvenience of the situation but tried not to let it inhibit us unduly. I had developed a coping philosophy which accepted the inevitability of dying at the hands of terrorists, 'but not today'. When on occasions the situation did get to me Frances was my rock. Though clearly suffering herself, she would point out the benefit of a philosophical approach rather than the increased danger to my health from getting 'stressed out'. The nature of this warped perception of 'normality' is perhaps best evidenced by the fact that two of my sons followed me into the Northern Ireland Prison Service.

My 'temporary' return to HM Prison Service in England and Wales, we reasoned, would enable us to get back to some degree of real normality, at least for a time. I would no longer need to be in a constant state of alert, to carry a firearm or to drive around in an armoured plated car. We could live a normal life and go wherever we wished as and whenever we pleased. With me off the scene, there would be less pressure on my sons who were staying in Northern Ireland. But on my arrival in England I soon discovered that the nature of the perceived threat to my life was greater than we had thought and I now had an armed police escort accompanying me everywhere I went. This was to continue for a long time and though I greatly appreciated the protection this afforded, and the professionalism and friendship of the officers involved, it was also restrictive and I was relieved when an alternative protection strategy was agreed and implemented. My family's experience of 'normality' still differs from that of most people.

The Young Offender Institution at Dover

I arrived at the young offender institution (YOI) at Dover in December 1988 at a time when HMPS was implementing a new 'Fresh Start' national agreement which had been negotiated and agreed with all the staff associations. This agreement covered a wide spectrum of issues, from changes to the staff grading structure to industrial relations disputes procedures. It also ended overtime working for prison officers which, until then, had been a substantial element in their pay and had played a prominent part in the running of prisons for many years. This aspect of the agreement was to be implemented over a fixed period of years through an annually reducing contracted hours agreement. A new and important element in Fresh Start was that the national framework agreement was to be implemented by each establishment through a negotiated local agreement, within the national framework, that best met local needs. A key objective of the national agreement was for local difficulties to be, as far as possible, resolved at local level.

There had been difficulties in reaching agreement at Dover prior to my arrival and only one prison took longer to complete the task. However an agreement had been signed by my predecessor. I carefully studied it on my arrival. It was obvious that it was not in the spirit of the national agreement, would inhibit change and would make implementation of other key elements of Fresh Start impossible. My initial impression, later confirmed by the chair of the local Prison Officers Association (POA) branch committee, was that they, the POA, drafted the terms of the agreement signed by my predecessor. I made it very clear that I was not prepared to accept this and formally notified them that I was withdrawing from some aspects of the agreement. There followed a difficult industrial relations period. The staff association had become accustomed to passive and submissive management and were having difficulty coming to terms with this difficult Irish Governor.

However, it was not just the POA who were having this difficulty, which I felt had a cultural basis. I noticed on my return an aspect of the England and Wales service's culture, probably originating from its closeness to the Civil Service, whereby disapproval or disagreement was expressed in coded terms and if the antenna was not receptive to the signal it was not noticed. Many senior managers seemed to shy away from confronting even their juniors and open disagreement with or challenging of ideas from above was rare. I considered this to be an unhealthy situation which invariably undermined the effectiveness of a management team. It was this cultural difference that perhaps caused most initial discomfort to my team at Dover but the realisation that I expected equal frankness in return from them eventually encouraged greater team spirit.

The situation at Dover was in stark contrast to that which I had left at Hydebank Wood in respect of facilities for prisoners. Dover YOI was situated on the Western Heights in what had once been a Napoleonic fort built to counter the threat of a French invasion. Some of the buildings that were still in use dated back to those times. It was also an English Heritage site which was taken over by HMPS from the Army in 1952. It became a borstal institution in 1957 and on the subsequent abolition of borstal training it became a YOI. There were five living accommodation units: four of which provided dormitory accommodation with up to six inmates per dormitory and one unit providing single cell accommodation. The institution could hold approximately 316 young men. I was immediately struck by the shabbiness of the accommodation and the general untidiness and dirty state of the establishment and took immediate steps to get a redecorating programme up and running in each unit. I also demanded much higher standards of cleanliness throughout the establishment. In some areas the fabric of the buildings was in a bad state of repair and I sought funding to correct this with some degree of success.

Like Hydebank Wood, Dover was clearly focused on assisting its young offenders to resettle in to the community and equipping them to get jobs on release. An extensive educational programme supported a variety of vocational training options. Young men progressed through the system and, when considered suitable, worked outside in the community or undertook community based projects supervised by staff. A number of lads completed the Prince of Edinburgh Award Scheme and selected groups took part in Outward Bound schemes, one of which was under sail.

My initial assessment of Dover was that it lacked firm leadership and direction. Like Hydebank Wood, the vacuum was being filled by the POA whose power base was strong enough to block new initiatives. This had to change. The local branch was led by its chair, Prison Officer Ken Broad. Ken had a fearsome reputation and was a traditional trade unionist. He was understandably protective of his power base and did not, I think, take kindly to my insistence on change. I too had been a staff association representative when I was a prison officer and had more recent experience as chair of the Northern Ireland Prison Governors Association. As a Governor and a trade unionist I had learned that a win-win approach to resolving conflict was the most constructive strategy in industrial relations. This was an alien concept to Ken and his colleagues who saw industrial relations as a monthly meeting with management during which they would seek to block or delay management initiatives and the occasional skirmishes in between when operational decisions by management were not to their liking.

The normal informal interaction between staff representatives and management did not happen and it appeared that any dialogue between a manager and an official, however informal, was discouraged. In contrast, my approach to industrial relations was exactly the opposite. I viewed all staff as part of the team and welcomed the input and views of their representatives at any time. To that end I continuously engaged in informal discussion with staff and their representatives.

Because the POA officials continued to resist change I embarked on a strategy to weaken their base with staff in an effort to change the industrial relations culture. Having outlined my plans for improving the performance of Dover I began holding monthly meetings with the whole staff group to explain policy and plans, to review the effectiveness of changes already introduced and to take on board the views of staff. These meetings were informal. After a nervous start they became frank and constructive. I deliberately held these meetings just days prior to the scheduled meetings between myself and the POA. Until then a regular feature of the formal meeting had been a report from the POA on the 'low' morale of staff accompanied by a list of grievances. My own regular dialogue with the staff enabled me to challenge this from a position of strength. After a couple of months Ken came to my office and asked me not to schedule meetings with staff just before our meeting with his committee in exchange for greater informal participation. I agreed.

Within a few months of my arrival the relationship with the POA was on a more constructive footing. My relationship with Ken and some of his colleagues was good and there was a developing mutual respect and trust. Ken was much more constructive than before and remained a strong and perceptive advocate for his members. We developed a strong professional relationship and also became good friends. Without compromising on his principles, Ken and his colleagues were of considerable assistance to me in improving the performance of Dover. That progress was acknowledged by HM Chief Inspector of Prisons in the report on his inspection in April 1990.

Early in 1990 I was honoured to receive an OBE for services to HMPS. This was a great surprise as I had never expected it and it was unusual in the public service as I was still relatively young.

Although I had served the first ten years of my career in the Prison Service of England and Wales, my management style and skills were honed within the culture of the Northern Ireland Prison Service at a time of great difficulties. Effectiveness required a high profile and strong leadership. My style was therefore plain speaking, forceful and directive but also supportive of my staff in achieving our goals. This was not a common style at that time but it is more prevalent today as HMPS has become more performance based.

The first real signs of the cultural change in HMPS that was to follow came in 1990 when the senior operational management structure of the service changed. The four Regional Directors were replaced by Area Managers who would be responsible for much smaller and more manageable areas of the service. They would have a much higher profile in setting objectives for individual prisons and monitoring their performance. Area Managers were part of headquarters and reported to one of two Operational Directors. My own newly appointed Area Manager was John Hunter. He visited all the Kent prisons at least once per month. John was a strong character with wide operational experience with whom I enjoyed working. Towards the end of my time at Dover and in the year following my departure dramatic changes to the culture of the service began to take place and its new direction was more reflective of my views.

NO GOING BACK

In 1991 I was invited by senior headquarters managers to stay in the Prison Service of England and Wales where, they suggested, I would have good career prospects. My family and I had hoped to return to Northern Ireland but equally I was enjoying working in England. Before making a final decision I sought advice on my security situation from both the police and the prison service in Ireland.

They offered me conflicting views on the degree of risk but the police advice strongly discouraged any return at that time. We decided to stay at Dover.

The Strangeways Prison riot in 1990 and a number of copycat incidents in other establishments forced prison issues into the media headlines for weeks. Lord Woolf, then Lord Justice of Appeal and later Lord Chief Justice, led an enquiry into the Manchester riot and his report (written in part by His Honour Judge Stephen Tumim the former Chief Inspector of Prisons) reflected the unacceptable situation in prisons. Overcrowding was widespread particularly in local prisons. Regimes and the quality of life for prisoners were unacceptable. Many prisons were experiencing control problems. Escapes were also at an unacceptably high level. Woolf's recommendations addressed the need for HMPS to prevent escapes and maintain control of prisons but also refocused it on its obligation to treat prisoners with humanity and firmness and to assist them to return to the community as law abiding citizens. His recommendations were welcomed at all levels and particularly by Governors who saw it as reinforcing the reformative and resettlement aspect of the work of prisons. I have never met a prison Governor who did not believe that resettlement and rehabilitation were essential elements of the work of prisons together with carrying out the order of the court. I share that view and, like my colleagues, I was optimistic about the direction that HMPS appeared to be taking.

Following Woolf, the Home Secretary commissioned a review of the management of HMPS by Admiral Sir Raymond Lygo, a former Chief Executive of British Aerospace. In his report Sir Raymond described the service as 'the most complex organization I have encountered and its problems some of the most intractable'. Years of under-investment and poor management had taken their toll and he recognised that 'if the service was to achieve the direction and unity for which successive reports called, it must be allowed to operate much more independently of day to day ministerial control and more separately from the Home Office'.

Since the abolition of the Prisons Commission in 1963 HMPS had been a department of the Home Office, managed at the most senior level by senior civil servants with no operational experience. Lygo recommended that the service become an executive agency similar to the Passport Office and that it be given clear direction and the autonomy necessary to produce a better and more efficient service. He recommended that the DG should have freedom to manage day to day operations without ministerial involvement, should provide high profile leadership and should be appointed by open competition with the post open to candidates from the private sector. The main thrust of Lygo's recommendations was accepted. It seemed that exciting times lay ahead.

Area Manager, East Anglia

In September 1992 I was again promoted and appointed Area Manager for East Anglia. I was sad to leave Dover where I had made some enduring friendships and I will always remember that period of my career as being a rewarding and happy one. The East Anglia Area consisted of six prisons including Bullwood Hall (a closed women's prison and young offender institution). Hollesley Bay was an open male adult prison with a closed YOI (Warren Hill) on the same site and managed as one institution. The other four prisons were larger, more secure male adult prisons, two of which were local prisons at Norwich and Chelmsford. Highpoint and Wayland were large category C male prisons holding prisoners mostly from the London area. Managing a group of prisons, particularly at a time of major change, would present a new challenge for me.

The Area Manager's role, defined in its job description, was to:

> line manage the Governors of the prisons in their area, provide support and encouragement to them, set performance targets through annual business plans, monitor performance and take corrective action when necessary, allocate annual budgets to each of the prisons, communicate new policy and strategic direction to key stakeholders, Governors and other key management staff in Establishments, ensure that the requirements of the Prisons Board were clearly understood, and provide operational knowledge and advice to Headquarters that would inform the development of policy and where appropriate to brief and advise Ministers.

Area Managers were also required to liaise with other criminal justice agencies and were responsible for all prison casework in their area. They were the appeal authority for the staff disciplinary system and, at that time, for prisoners in respect of the prison disciplinary system (known as 'prisoner adjudications')—and also had a key role in managing industrial relations particularly with regard to the resolution of disputes. Area Managers reported directly to an Operational Director who was a member of the Prisons Board.

For years Governors of prisons had been like the captains of ships tied up in port. Domestic chores had to be done but the lack of targets and challenging standards added little in the way of stress to the role. There were, of course, exceptions and some Governors created the challenges for themselves, developing innovative regimes. However in many other cases the Governor was seen as a local dignitary and many spent their time living that role and doing little in their prisons.

The task of implementing Fresh Start at local level presented an opportunity for constructive progress but in many prisons the management teams failed to maximise the opportunity because of local POA opposition. This in turn made implementation of other essential aspects of the national agreement more difficult. Overtime, on which the service had depended for so long to maintain regimes in prisons before Fresh Start, was phased out. At the end of the process Governors were required to maintain the quality of regimes and wrapped up in this was a substantial reduction in operating costs. This together with a requirement for Governors to deliver the agreed targets in their prison's business plan signalled HMPS's entry into a new era where the nature of governing a prison would quickly change and where increased outputs, reduction of resources, higher standards and value for money would become the norm.

The demands on Governors and senior managers would be severe and some would not cope with the pressure. They were accustomed to a budgeting process where funding was allocated on the basis of what had happened in the previous year. Little distinction was made between the efficient and the inefficient or regard taken of the quality of output or whether it offered value for money. In the initial stages of this process many Governors were helped by a reducing prison population as a consequence of the provisions of the Criminal Justice Act 1991, which introduced a new sentencing framework complete with an emphasis on community sentences, fines and statutory restrictions on the use of custody.

The process of change began under the leadership of Sir Joe Pilling when he was Director General of HM Prison Service. However it was his successor, Derek Lewis, who had the greatest impact. Derek was the first Director General appointed from the private sector, where he had an impressive management record. He led the service through the transition to agency status and into a more business like culture. Though his time as DG was marked by some major operational disasters that eventually led to his, in my view, premature departure, he succeeded in altering the culture of the service and laid the foundation for a more focused and performance centred approach to the management of prisons. His relationship with the Home Secretary, Michael Howard, was a key factor in his leaving HMPS but many observers felt that it was a lack of understanding of ministers and politics that contributed to his downfall. However by the time of his departure HMPS had embraced Sir Joe Pilling's clear and meaningful mission statement[1] by setting itself firm objectives that had to be achieved. Derek's successors, all of whom were Prison Service professionals, built on the foundations he had laid, becoming more performance orientated and providing greater value for money.

I followed a well respected and able area manager in East Anglia and most prisons were in good shape. My task was also made easier by the fact that most in-charge Governors (sometimes called 'Governing Governors') were good managers. However it was immediately clear that the tension caused by trying to achieve meaningful targets with reducing resources was having an increasingly stressful impact on all of them. Though experienced in managing prisons on a day to day basis their training did not prepare them for this new situation. Reactions to the demands being placed on them varied individually from confronting the task to ignoring it in the hope that it would go away. In the past there had been initiatives that Governors were required to implement which had

---

[1] Her Majesty's Prison Service serves the public by keeping in custody those committed by the courts. Our duty is to look after them with humanity and help them lead law-abiding and useful lives in custody and after release.

been ignored by a few and no action had been taken against them. A small number now thought they could do the same. It became obvious that strong high profile management of the area was essential. I needed quickly to develop an in-depth knowledge of each prison, the strengths and weaknesses of individual Governors and their senior management teams. This was demanding of my time and consistently saw me working 15-hour days during the first couple of years in East Anglia.

Budgets were allocated through Operational Directors to Area Managers, who in turn set the budget for each prison based on its business plan. Governors then decided how best to achieve their targets and where savings could be made. In the early years the stress of the process was clearly taking its toll. Like my fellow Area Managers I spent much of my time helping Governors through these difficulties. A firm line had to be taken in insisting that objectives were met but it was equally necessary to be supportive and watchful for the signs of dangerous stress levels.

Governors had until now operated with a high degree of autonomy and the new pressures fell heavily on their shoulders. There was as yet no exchange of best practice between prisons and individual Governors were simultaneously 're-inventing the wheel' in terms of efficiencies. As an organization we needed to take a corporate approach to delivering the business and I invited my Governors to join me in developing this approach. Though the responsibilities still rested with the Governors to achieve their respective goals, they were encouraged to share problems and solutions and exchange details of best practice. My objective was to create a situation where no Governor would feel alone or isolated and where he or she could talk through a problem with a colleague without me being involved if they so wished. Within a short time the group developed that corporate identity and this was reflected in the performance of the area. As well as achieving targets, mutual support and the pursuit of excellence in a good humoured atmosphere had become a key feature of the team. Only one Governor was unable to cope with the changing demands and retired. The remainder went on to develop their skills and thrive in the new culture.

The creation of a corporate identity and the development of a team approach amongst Governors became a feature of my style as an Area Manager for the remainder of my career. However as the service became more performance driven I felt it needed to be developed further. Prisons are large and complex organizations, each with their own unique culture and problems. Achieving change can be very difficult for one individual even with the vested authority of a Governor. Just as the development of a corporate identity was effective in the area, Governors needed the same level of commitment and support from their management teams. They needed skilled managers capable of providing that support. Regrettably these were not always available.

Many senior and middle managers also made the adjustment to the new culture of HMPS but equally a few did not. Some were so much into the old culture of their prisons that they were more part of the problem than the solution. Logic suggested that such individuals should leave the service or be transferred elsewhere, but in reality moving them on or out was not that simple. For many years performance appraisal reports on these individuals failed to address or reflect their limitations. Options were therefore limited to raising their performance, disposing of their services as poor performers, which was time consuming and an anchor on progress, or shuffling the pack and moving them to another prison. Though we used all of these options I was convinced that the performance of prisons could only be improved by teams built around the Governors, with members selected on the basis of their skills. Though commonplace in the private sector, this was difficult to achieve in HMPS at that time.

Area Manager, Kent

In 1996 the boundaries of most operational areas were changed and the managers of the old areas were stood down. Area Managers were now selected by open competition and had to pass stringent qualifying tests. All the successful candidates would become Assistant Directors and members of the Senior Civil Service. I was lucky to be successful and was pleased to be appointed Area Manager for the Kent area on the retirement of my old boss, John Hunter.

There were eleven prisons in the new area. Like East Anglia, about half of the prisoners held there came from Greater London. The area included my former establishment at Dover and two women's prisons at Cookham Wood and East Sutton Park. Rochester Prison was a multi-functional establishment holding young men on remand, immigration detainees and adult sex offenders in separate units. It also operated a resettlement unit in one wing where selected prisoners approaching the end of their sentences were permitted to work out in the community in preparation for release. Similar units were operating at Canterbury and Aldington Prisons. The area also included four category B (higher security) prisons: Swaleside and Elmley on the Isle of Sheppey, Maidstone and Canterbury. Aldington was a category C (medium security) closed prison and Stanford Hill an open prison. Blantyre House was a category C (medium security) closed prison with a specialist resettlement function for selected long term prisoners. I was able to take all my East Anglia support team with me to Kent. This avoided the need to rebuild and allowed me to start with an efficient and loyal team who understood and supported me.

Kent prisons were at a similar stage to those in East Anglia in coming to terms with the new culture of the service. Governors were finding the challenge difficult but most were adjusting successfully. Maidstone Prison was proving to be the exception. All was not well in that the Governor was finding it impossible to achieve the efficiency and performance targets set for him. His predecessor had had similar difficulties and had a breakdown before taking early retirement. He, the replacement Governor, too now fell ill and retired on medical grounds. The prison had claimed two Governors in the space of one year and was not making any progress. After taking advice I appointed a previously successful Governor. Though he initially made progress, he was soon experiencing the same difficulties as his predecessors. Unable to achieve change in spite of valiant efforts, he too became ill and left the service after only a few months at Maidstone. The performance of the prison and its reputation as a minefield for Governors was a real cause for concern. We were about to appoint the fourth Governor in two years and the selection required careful thought. I needed a strong and skilled manager to take on the job and after listening to the concerns of the Board of Visitors, whose views I greatly respected, I asked the Director General to approve the appointment of Mike Conway. Mike was then Deputy Governor of Elmley Prison in Kent. He had all the qualities the job required. We began the process of building a management team capable of supporting him. Under his leadership Maidstone overcame its problems.

The Prison Service was now becoming a completely performance orientated organization. In addition to addressing efficiencies, the business plan included a list of key performance indicators (or 'KPIs'): operational targets set annually that included reductions in escapes and assaults, increased prisoner activity hours and time out of cells for prisoners and increased but more focused education programmes etc. The introduction of powers to carry out compulsory random drug tests on prisoners supported a target to reduce the number of prisoners testing positive. Though efficiency savings were demanded on an annual basis, extra funding was being provided on a 'ring fenced' basis for specific programmes that confronted prisoners with their offending behaviour. Offending behaviour programmes, some devised locally and some centrally, had been provided for many years but their effectiveness had not been confirmed. Most of these were discontinued and resources moved to CSAP accredited programmes. Standards of delivery of new programmes were strictly monitored and where standards were not maintained management action was taken to correct the problem.

Area managers and prison Governors were by now facing similar pressures to those faced by senior managers in large private sector organizations. My job was to line manage my Governors and ensure they were delivering services to the highest standards. Again I operated a corporate model within the area and a culture of mutual support. I also adopted a policy of assisting Governors to build effective management teams around them. There were occasional difficulties which were quickly sorted out, but the area functioned well, and in the performance league tables of the Prison Service was consistently in the top two. Our model for the management of the drug treatment programme was adopted by the whole service as was our partnership approach to colleagues in what is now the National Probation Service and other criminal justice agencies.

I considered it important that the adverse impact of budget reductions on regimes and security should be minimised. One advantage of the area's corporate approach was that it facilitated an exercise that would enable us to critically evaluate the possibility of reorganizing or clustering the delivery of services without reducing standards. Rochester and Cookham Wood Prisons shared a site in the village of Borstal (the home of the original establishment of that name). Swaleside, Elmley and Stanford Hill Prisons also shared a site on the Isle of Sheppey. These prisons operated independently of each other in terms of services. Each had their own large kitchens, healthcare departments, works/maintenance units and administration departments. It seemed sensible to me that we should look at all of these areas. The Governors concerned, with the assistance of specialists, carried out feasibility studies including detailed impact analysis and where it was considered appropriate, produced business cases in respect of each service.

It was immediately clear that centralising the delivery of maintenance and works services at both the Rochester and Sheppey sites was feasible, cost effective and, properly managed, could improve delivery standards that could be guaranteed through a service delivery agreement. Catering was centralised with Rochester servicing the needs of the small prison at Cookham Wood (sited less than 100 metres away) and Elmley Prison provided a similar service to Stanford Hill (sited about 800 metres away). The existing Cookham Wood and Stanford Hill kitchens were about to be replaced and consolidation of these services made an initial capital saving of approximately £2.6 million in addition to the reduced running costs of the new arrangements.

Though managed separately, doctors from Rochester Prison already provided healthcare services to Cookham Wood Prison. Healthcare was formally centralised. All eleven prisons in the area operated separate pharmacies or bought in pharmacy services from other agencies. New legislation required higher standards than currently existed and some of the pharmacies were operating illegally. Raising standards would be very costly and would have to be funded from within the existing area budget. We decided that the most cost effective approach was to create a central area pharmacy based at Rochester which would be fully resourced to legally service the needs of all the Kent prisons by means of modern technology and an in-house courier service.

The concept of 'clustering' services was embraced by Kent Governors and further examples followed, mostly driven by the Governors themselves. Some other Area Managers also took this approach which was fully supported by headquarters as good management practice. However this view was not shared by HM Chief Inspector Sir David Ramsbotham, who to my mind seemed to become critical even before he had acquainted himself with the full facts, pressures and competing interests as I and those fellow Area Managers who were committed to clustering as a means of more effective management saw them. Again, without knowing every detail, some members of the Boards of

Visitors of the prisons involved also expressed their concern about the effects of the clustering of services on their respective prisons.

Outside the management line, HM Prison Service is one of the most regulated and inspected of organizations, even for a public service. The problem is compounded by a lack of coherence to, or control of, the boundaries on those appointed to these roles. It is essential in the interests of the public and of the service itself that its work is independently monitored. However it is equally important that this monitoring does not inhibit its proper management. There must be a clear separation between the monitoring/inspecting role and those responsible for operational management and development of policy, though it is important that all views are taken into account in developing such policy. Unfortunately some of those people with monitoring roles try to exercise executive authority that they do not have, and on occasions they were allowed to do so without any accountability for the consequences. As an Area Manager and Governor I would not allow that to happen in my area and this brought me into conflict with some people who did not take kindly to being reminded of the parameters of their respective roles.

Each prison in the UK has a Board of Visitors (now, since 2003, called an Independent Monitoring Board or 'IMB'). These boards are independent watchdogs whose members are drawn from the local community and appointed by the Home Secretary. Their role is to monitor the welfare of staff and prisoners and the state of the premises and to report annually to the Home Secretary. Members have unrestricted access to all parts of the prison. Though they do not have a management role, they can raise prisoner and staff concerns with management, the Governor, the Area Manager, and ministers. In the event of a serious incident in the prison the chair of the board is informed and a member invited to observe. A small number of board members found it difficult to accept that they were neither managers nor a management board and this sometimes led to conflict. Where there is an absence of strong local management, problems inevitably follow. Boards should be representative of the community. However new members, though appointed by the Home Secretary, were generally selected by the boards themselves. In some areas recruitment of volunteers is difficult and can lead to members drawing in their own friends or worse, a phenomenon that exists in relation to many walks of life, recruiting in their own image, sometimes called 'cloning'.

The boards in both the East Anglia and Kent areas were formidable and properly functioning in the majority of prisons. But there were exceptions. A properly functioning board is, in my view, a most effective protector of the public interest and the welfare of the prisoners and staff. During my career as a Governor and Area Manager I had come to value and respect the boards I worked with, even though we might occasionally have been in conflict. A few, generally the more formidable members, became valuable sources of advice and in some cases, good friends.

The best known independent monitor—in the broader sense of that word—is HM Chief Inspector of Prisons. The independent inspectorate was established in 1980 on the recommendation of the May Committee. It functions under section 5A of the Prisons Act 1952 (amended by section 57 of the Criminal Justice Act 1982). The remit of the Chief Inspector, as defined by Sir David Ramsbotham himself in his book *Prison Gate* (2003), is:

> To inspect or arrange for the inspection of the prisons in England and Wales and to report to the Secretary of State on them, in particular to report on the treatment of prisoners and conditions in prisons.

The Secretary of State may also refer specific matters connected with prisons in England and Wales and prisoners in them to the Chief Inspector and direct him or her to report back on them. Importantly, in 2006 Sir David, now Lord, Ramsbotham led a strategic and successful revolt in the House of Lords against Government moves to abolish the separate HM Inspectorate of Prisons and to subsume it within a new, overall, Criminal Justice Inspectorate.

There have been five Chief Inspectors appointed since that position was first established, in 1981 with the appointment of William Pearce who served for just one year before his death. He was succeeded by Sir James Hennessy (1982-7), His Honour Judge Stephen Tumim (1987-1995), Sir David Ramsbotham (1995-2001) and Ms Anne Owers CBE (2001 to date). There was a gradual build up of support staff including inspection teams and specialist advisors. I had the privilege of working with the inspectorate as a guest inspector in the mid-1980s. That experience convinced me of the importance of their role and the potential benefit to the Prison Service and the wider community. When I worked with them I was struck by their professionalism and by the fact that the Chief Inspector could attract the cream of the service's Governors to his team without difficulty. During the tenure of Judge Stephen Tumim there seemed to be a shift away from straightforward traditional inspection to the beginnings of the campaigning inspector with a high profile in the media. Tumim clearly had a genuine desire to improve conditions for prisoners and he embarked on various successful campaigns to achieve them. I was in support of much of what he achieved.

In 1994 a Prisons Ombudsman (now the Prisons and Probation Ombudsman) was appointed by the Home Secretary as an independent point of appeal for prisoners. For the purpose of investigations, the Ombudsman has full access to Prison Service information, documents, prisons and individuals including classified material and information provided to the Prison Service by other organizations such as the police. Vice Admiral Sir Peter Woodhead was the first Ombudsman. He quickly established the credibility of his office with the Prison Service. He was succeeded by Stephen Shaw, a highly respected prison reformer who retained and built on all that had been achieved by Sir Peter.

Agency status and the introduction of operating standards led to the creation within Headquarters of a separate Standards Audit Unit with audit teams visiting and auditing performance standards in each establishment. Though this was an effective vehicle for ensuring consolidation of good operating standards, Governors were often the subject of both an operating standards audit and an inspection by HM Chief Inspectors of Prisons within a short time frame, the findings of which could be in stark conflict with each other. The role of Standards Audit has now changed.

THE BEGINNINGS OF CONFLICT

During my service in Northern Ireland I had worked closely with quite a number of army regiments involved in supporting the Prison Service. I had also been a frequent guest in the Officers' Mess of many of them. This gave me some insight into the psyche of the typical army officer who I saw as highly trained and professional. I thus viewed with interest the appointment of the retired army general, Sir David Ramsbotham (now Lord Ramsbotham) as Chief Inspector of Prisons as successor to His Honour Judge Stephen Tumim. I reasoned that in view of Sir David's background he would bring a new, focused and maybe less theatrical element to the inspection process. But his much-publicised walkout from Holloway Prison on the second day of his first inspection seemed to raise questions about this. Were his tactics contrived to highlight the problems that were known to exist at Holloway I wondered, or could there be some other explanation? He would later more or less confirm to a Prison Service conference that the walkout had been rehearsed. Whatever the reason behind it, the approach was to be reflected in certain other events during his tenure as Chief Inspector when, to my mind, there was a tendency to make what I and other HMPS personnel saw as exaggerated and sometimes inflammatory comments, which he would quietly modify, withdraw or accept as having been wrong in the first place.

My first direct experience of Sir David came early in 1997. My attention was drawn to the preface of the first draft of an inspection report on Chelmsford Prison. When I was Area Manager of East Anglia, Chelmsford was one of my prisons but I had been in Kent for almost a year at this time. The draft preface, which was circulated widely at the highest levels in the Home Office and Prison Service—but not officially to me—shocked and horrified me. In it the Chief Inspector called for a high level Civil Service investigation into the propriety of my actions in the allocation of the budget for Chelmsford Prison. It implied that I had misused a large sum of public funds and that I had shown favouritism to Eva Butler, the Governor at that time, by reducing the budgets of other East Anglia prisons to a greater extent than Chelmsford. His comments were a serious slur on my professional and personal integrity and were completely unfounded. There was no impropriety and budgets had been allocated on a proper basis. The suggestion that I had shown favouritism in the budget allocation to Chelmsford was wholly incorrect, the reality being that I had applied a seven per cent reduction in the Chelmsford and Norwich budgets and only 3.5 per cent to the other prisons in the area. An examination of the facts suggested that the inspectors did not fully understand the budget allocation system of HMPS and did not try to clarify their concerns during the inspection. The budget had been correctly allocated and subsequent decisions made by the Governor regarding it were also wholly legitimate.

I asked for an immediate meeting with Sir David. Legal advice was sought as the document could damage my reputation. It was also possible that it might find its way outside the circle into the public domain. I was told that there was little I could do as his reports, even in draft form, enjoyed Parliamentary privilege. I met with him in his office a few weeks later, together with a colleague from the Prison Governors Association (PGA). By then he should have known that the preface was inaccurate but I felt that he was responding in a dismissive way to my complaints. I would describe it as bordering on arrogance. I asked for a written apology to be circulated to all recipients of the original draft, but I left his office without any clear commitment in that regard. Eventually I did receive a brief letter seemingly acknowledging that he had got it wrong. As it was unclear whether he had circulated copies to recipients of the draft, I made sure that it was copied to them. From these initial dealings I formed the opinion that I should tread warily.

It had become the practice for Chief Inspectors to use the preface of their inspection reports to highlight issues arising from an inspection and frequently to link them, if sometimes tenuously, to a wider agenda, something that Stephen Tumim had become quite adept at. It was an effective mechanism as many sections of the media tended to concentrate on the preface. Sir David Ramsbotham did the same, but his essentially provisional first drafts might include statements, some of which were inaccurate, incorrect or unfair, which he would eventually delete or modify before publication proper.

Because of his forceful nature, I saw great potential for him to achieve considerable change for the better and to be fair he has contributed to or even led on arguments for change in some areas. But all too often it seemed to me the message was lost following the early soundbite or dramatic headline. He had operated at a very high level in the British Army, but seemed oblivious to the political constraints on HMPS in terms of both policy, funding and staff instructions. However, I did agree with his assertion that funding for all public sector prisons should be based on a realistic costing of the resources required to deliver target outputs, similar to that in operation in the private sector. He appeared to draw on his military experience in commenting on and criticising the management of HMPS and to my mind would frequently oversimplify problems or solutions. For example, the armed forces are assisted by the military discipline, punitive powers and culture that are a part of that system. Prison officers are civilians and successful management requires more than barking orders. Furthermore, the army spends most of its time training and preparing for deployment and is in a state of readiness rather than permanently active. HMPS has to deliver on a daily, come rain come shine basis and cope with whatever comes it way. The DG or a Governor cannot say, 'Our prisons are full, we cannot take any more prisoners' because HMPS is obliged to take all those committed by the courts irrespective of the availability of accommodation, staff or other resources. He was, of course, right to point out our failures and highlight our shortcomings, but in my view he occasionally went beyond that, intentionally or otherwise, an effect of which was to undermine individual managers working within the approved policy of HMPS. I believe that I was on the receiving end of this kind of approach on a few occasions but was denied any public right of reply due to HMPS and Civil Service conventions. It was different in terms of more private communications but could still be a matter affecting the reputation of a particular member of HMPS.

In 1999 while I was Area Manager for Kent we were in the process of completing feasibility studies into the clustering of maintenance and catering services on the Isle of Sheppey. The BOV at Swaleside were understandably concerned that standards should not slide and reflected these concerns in their annual report to the Home Secretary. Reports were copied to Sir David, at his request. In June of that year he wrote to the chair of the board describing me as 'obsessed with clustering every available activity'. He went on to suggest that operational efficiency was not my objective and that he (Ramsbotham) was against clustering which he considered a 'bad thing'. This seemed to be a clear attempt to undermine my management of the area and to encourage resistance. His letter was eventually drawn to my attention by the chair of the BOV, with whom I had a good relationship. I wrote to Sir David protesting at what I considered to be his inappropriate interference with my management of the area. In a letter dated 5 February 1998, he replied that his primary concern was the treatment of prisoners and went on to say:

> Marrying the un-marriageable purely for resource reasons may be the immediate answer to demands for cutting costs, but is not the right answer in the long term. No Area Manager in the country has produced more suggestions for clustering different activities than you have, and it is something you brought with you from your previous post as I recall from attempts to merge Chelmsford and Bullwood Hall.
>
> My comments to Chairmen of Boards are exactly what I would discuss with them if I was speaking personally. They know, and I know that my comments are my own and like any recommendations that I make in my reports have no other weight than that. I do not hesitate to make the minister aware of my views, nor will I. My aim remains to press for what I regard as best for the Prison Service, and if at times that means my saying things in public which I believe to be in the best interest of the Service, which may be uncomfortable for Ministers, that is my responsibility.

In what I saw as sarcasm he added:

> Incidentally, in view of the time it has taken, and the number of people involved, I suspect there is no-one in the Prison Service in Kent who does not know of your ambitions for Rochester and Cookham Wood, and whenever I have been asked by anyone I have always made my implacable opposition to this well known, and will continue to do so.

Since my clear objective was to avoid impacting on the quality of regimes for prisoners in running the area with a reduced budget and I was successfully doing so, his comments seemed inconsistent with the facts. In identifying areas where costs might be reduced, feasibility studies had been carried out and some were rejected as unsuitable or likely to have an adverse impact. His comment about services at Chelmsford and Bullwood Hall was one such case. Feasibility studies take time and where there is a case for change it must be carefully managed with all parties brought along. His comments relating to Rochester and Cookham Wood were presumably referring to this process, but what was happening was no secret. Sir David was aware of why I and other colleagues were engaged in this process and that it had the support of HMPS headquarters. But though he had no executive authority, it seems that he thought he knew better than its senior management about how HMPS should be run. In short, he disagreed with us. Though strong on criticism his comments ignored the realities of life at the time and offered no constructive alternative options to me or my colleagues.

CHAPTER 4

The ATM Scam

In 1995, when I was still Area Manager of East Anglia but also temporarily in charge of the Kent Area, I received a telephone call from Brian Pollett, the Governor of Blantyre House Prison. He informed me that a prisoner named Martin Grant had approached the Chaplain and told him that he believed he was being drawn into a criminal conspiracy at the work placement to which Grant had been allocated as part of his resettlement programme. The Governor immediately alerted the police. After an initial interview with Martin Grant the police asked the Governor to continue allowing him to attend the work placement and report back daily to them. Brian's call sought guidance on how he should respond to the police. As it was Prison Service policy to assist police in cases of this kind, providing adequate safeguards were in place to protect the public, I advised him to co-operate with them.

The initial information suggested that Martin Grant, a graduate electronics engineer, was being drawn into a criminal conspiracy by a gang who were planning to use his specialist skills to help them steal large sums of money, via ATM machines, from the bank accounts of ordinary people using cloned bank cards. As the investigation progressed it became clear that this was a major criminal conspiracy involving a gang of well known dangerous criminals who were planning a multi-million pounds scam. If they succeeded it would be bigger than anything in British criminal history, including the notorious Brink's-Mat robbery, with which a connection would eventually be established. It also involved the corruption of prison officers, one of whom was suspected of playing a key role in helping the gang. From the police investigation and a subsequent internal investigation commissioned by myself, the extent of the conspiracy emerged.

Kenny Noye

The name of Kenny Noye became infamous following one of the UK's most notorious crimes, the vicious murder of Stephen Cameron in a road rage incident off the M25 at Swanley in Kent on 19 May 1996. Noye is now serving a life sentence for that killing with a tariff that means he cannot be considered for parole until he has served 16 years. However this was by no means his first brush with the law. In the late 1970s Noye had already acquired a reputation as what most police officers and prison officers would describe as a 'professional criminal' or 'career criminal' and had become very wealthy, seemingly and to a large extent on the proceeds of crime. He was well known to police in his regular haunts in south east London and in Kent, where he lived in the village of West

Kingsdown. His image was that of a ruthless, violent but clever individual who avoided getting his hands dirty by direct involvement in robbery or other violent crime, preferring to use his accrued wealth to finance such projects and fence the proceeds, ensuring a substantial slice of them went to him. Allegedly by the early 1980s he had established contacts with organized crime in the USA. Noye is also suspected of having raked in millions of pounds from the smuggling of Krugerrands into the UK and their being melted them down to extract the gold, avoiding VAT payments on it.

The Brink's-Mat robbery
On 26 November 1983 an armed robbery took place at the Brink's-Mat security facility near Heathrow Airport. The robbers got away with 3,670 kilos of gold, then worth £26,369,000. They also took cash and diamonds worth a further half-a-million pounds. This was the biggest ever haul from any robbery up to that time and a major police investigation was launched. A week later the police arrested one of the security guards, Tony Black, who eventually made a full statement. Within a very short time the police believed they knew the names of all those involved. Micky McAvoy, Brian Robinson (brother-in-law of Tony Black, the security guard) and Tony White where quickly arrested. At their trial at the Old Bailey in October 1984, Tony Black, Micky McAvoy and Brian Robinson where convicted and received long prison sentences. White was found not guilty. The police believed that the robbery had been carried out by a six-man gang and they were convinced that John 'Little Legs' Lloyd was one of them. Lloyd was a friend of Noye's and a criminal well known in London's East End. Following the robbery, Lloyd disappeared, returning nearly ten years later when it is believed that the Crown Prosecution Service decided there was insufficient evidence to take action against him.

Because the proceeds of the robbery had not been not recovered, the police investigation continued. As a known professional criminal Noye was of interest to the police who kept him under surveillance. He was suspected of involvement in handling the proceeds of the robbery but the police where unable to establish how. Eventually they became suspicious of comings and goings at his home and through surveillance were able to identify a number of individuals whose involvement seemed to point to a smelting operation. Since the movements invariably originated from Noye's home, it was placed under observation. The secluded nature of the property and the high level of security he had created made it difficult for police to reconnoitre the area before executing a search warrant. On 26 January 1985, two police officers where ordered to carry out a covert reconnaissance of the property. Detective Constables Fordham and Murphy scaled the perimeter fence into the grounds. One of Noye's rottweiler dogs detected them and began barking. DC Murphy was able to move back and get out but John Fordham was apprehended by Noye and his associate, Brian Reader. Noye stabbed the police officer repeatedly with a knife. DC John

Fordham died from his wounds. In the follow up search police found evidence to link Noye to the Brink's-Mat gold.

He was charged with the murder of DC John Fordham. At his trial he admitted stabbing the police officer but claimed to be acting in self-defence and was found not guilty by the jury. He was later convicted of offences related to the Brink's-Mat gold and other criminal activities and was sentenced to 14 years in prison in July 1986. In May 1987 he received a further sentence of four years' imprisonment for receiving stolen property which was to run concurrently with the earlier sentence.

Noye was a Category A prisoner indicating that he was believed to have the resources to escape and presented a risk to the public. He spent the initial stages of his sentence in Wandsworth Prison before being moved to Frankland Prison, a high security prison in the North East of England. Like many career criminals, Noye was a model prisoner who worked the system to his own advantage. He developed good relations with prison staff and if he could corrupt any of them he would. The staff at Maidstone Prison were surprised at his unannounced arrival there at a stage in his sentence which might reasonably be considered premature. After a period at Maidstone he managed to get himself moved to Blantyre House Prison, also in Kent.

Blantyre House is a specialist resettlement prison where selected long term prisoners, who are approaching the end of their sentences and are considered to have genuine resettlement needs, are sent to prepare for a return to society. After a period prisoners there are helped to find jobs and go out to work in the community on a daily basis. The regime is designed to encourage prisoners to take responsibility for their lives, to rebuild relationships with their families and to leave prison on release with a job. By its nature a resettlement prison provides prisoners with a greater degree of freedom than a normal prison would and the balance between freedom and trust is finely set with a level of security to protect the public. There are three such specialist prisons in England and Wales, the others being Latchmere House near Richmond, Surrey and Kirklevington Grange near Darlington in the north-east of England. Access to resettlement prisons is based on strict criteria that should have excluded known professional criminals like Noye. This man had considerable presumed wealth, had shown no outward indications that he intended to change his lifestyle and was unlikely to stay in any normal employment after his release. These prisons, of course, are attractive to career criminals in that they present them with both a relatively pleasant environment and an opportunity to continue their criminal activity whilst still serving their sentence. How Noye and others of his ilk got there is open to debate but corrupting prison staff would not be beyond him and remains a possibility.

Blantyre House is located relatively close to Noye's family home in Kent and if he had had genuine resettlement needs it would have been an ideal location for him to participate in a resettlement programme. It is therefore difficult to understand why, after a period there, he was allowed to transfer to the other resettlement prison at Latchmere House, which is much further away from his home. However, it can be speculated that the fact that the regime at Latchmere House was considered more liberal than that at Blantyre House may have been a factor. Whatever the reason, his transfer should not have been allowed and could not have taken place without the agreement of staff at both prisons.

In his book *Kenny Noye* (2002) Wensley Clarkson describes Noye's lifestyle at Latchmere House and the fact that he spent approximately 18 hours each day out of the prison. During these absences there was no opportunity for prison staff to keep tabs on his movements or activities. However, unknown to both Noye and the prison staff, the police were keeping an eye on him. While at Latchmere House he allegedly set up a £50,000 cocaine deal with his old American Mafia contacts. Unfortunately for him the deal was being monitored by the American Drug Enforcement Agency whose agents were amazed to discover that he was engaged in this serious criminal activity while still serving a prison sentence.

It has been claimed by Clarkson that Noye was tipped off that the police were onto him by a corrupt detective, Sergeant John Donald. Donald, then a member of the South East Regional Crime Squad was later convicted of charges relating to the taking of bribes and passing of information on police drug operations to a number of career criminals. He was sentenced to imprisonment for eleven years Alerted to the situation, Noye is alleged to have pulled out of the drugs deal but his criminal activities led to his transfer back to the higher security Swaleside Prison in Kent, where he wasted no time in feathering his nest and developing 'close' relationships with a few staff and prisoners. Clarkson also describes Noye's developing interest in the drug culture and his investment in it through a new-found friend, Essex based drug dealer, Pat Tate, whom he met at Swaleside. Noye is alleged to have financed the purchase of ecstasy which was distributed by Tate after his release. Noye himself was released from prison in 1994. In 1995 the death of schoolgirl Leah Betts, after taking an ecstasy tablet, sparked national outrage. Clarkson claims that the drugs concerned were supplied by Tate and he alleges that Noye helped fund their purchase. Tate was later murdered with two colleagues in what appeared to have been a contract killing.

The ATM scam
To return to the phone call I received from the concerned Governor of Blantyre House in 1995, Martin Grant had been convicted of the attempted murder of his wife and child and sentenced to 16 years imprisonment. He was not a career criminal but he would have had contact with many of them during his sentence in the high security prisons. There is no evidence that he had previously used his knowledge and skills for criminal purposes but he had clearly come to the notice of others who would. He was advised to apply for a transfer to a lower security prison as part of a progressive move in preparation for release. Though a likely candidate for a resettlement prison, even he was surprised by the speed of the

move. From his account of events there seems little doubt that individual members of staff in more than one prison 'helped' the process.

John 'Little Legs' Lloyd was well known to Kenny Noye. He was the common law husband of Jean Savage, who in 1992 had been jailed for five years for handling £2.5 million of Brink's-Mat money. Early in 1995 Noye is alleged to have met with Lloyd in a south-east London pub to discuss Lloyd's plan for a major cash card cloning scam that he expected would net millions of pounds. He was seeking backers to set it up and allegedly had already got the support of Billy Hayward, another well known south-east London criminal and a friend of Noye's. Realising the potential of the scam Noye wanted in. He is alleged to have given financial backing to Lloyd and his gang and practical help in recruiting the expertise required.

During his period at Blantyre House Noye had allegedly developed relationships with a few members of staff in key positions. One of these was alleged to be Principal Officer Gary Catton who had considerable influence on the temporary release and working out schemes. He also had influence on the selection of prisoners to go to Blantyre House. Catton had arranged for Martin Grant to work at a van hire business owned by Paul Kidd. Grant told investigators that Catton originally instructed him to help Kidd sort out some computer problems relating to Kidd's business. However he was soon being drawn into more sinister matters and he told investigators that he became aware of the involvement of Noye, Lloyd and other heavyweight villains who wanted to use his skills to develop the technology to carry out the scam when he met with them and discovered who was involved. It was at that stage that Grant became frightened. His concerns must have been obvious to the gang who, he told investigators, tried to get him to toe the line by implied threats to members of his family, supported by evidence that they knew where they lived. A subsequent intelligence report suggested that Grant was also visited at the prison by another well known criminal, who 'encouraged' him to continue and arranged for him to be paid £50,000.

Grant found himself between a rock and a hard place. He did not want to get involved in this criminal conspiracy but was also aware of Noye's apparent influence over key staff at the prison, particularly Catton. Grant told investigators that Noye produced copies of official prison documents, relating to him, containing details and addresses of his family. Because of this he felt unable to trust the staff and could not tell them of his fears. This was why he confided in a part-time Chaplain. Shocked by the suggestion that some of his staff had been corrupted, the Governor worked on the basis that there was substance to Grant's fears and alerted the police and myself.

With our agreement, Grant continued to work at Paul Kidd's van hire firm but was regularly debriefed by the police who were keeping close tabs on the progress of the conspiracy. In July 1995 police searched the Kent home of Noye's friend and alleged co-conspirator, Billy Hayward, and found 70,000 blank cash cards and 28 computer disks. Hayward and four others were immediately arrested. A short time later Principal Officer Gary Catton was also arrested. The police had insufficient evidence to charge Noye, though they claimed to have been aware of his involvement in investing money in the project. In November 1996, John 'Little Legs' Lloyd and six of his associates, including Paul Kidd, were found guilty and jailed for their part in the ATM scam.

Principal Officer Gary Catton was not charged by the police, however he was charged with serious breaches of the HMPS code of discipline for prison staff following an internal investigation lead by John Podmore, Governor of Swaleside Prison. Catton was charged with serious misconduct on eight counts and was dismissed from the service. The evidence against him suggested that he had a relationship with Noye and had been in contact with him and his wife Brenda. Their phone numbers were found on his personal organizer. Throughout this time I continued to receive worrying intelligence concerning the possibility of wrongdoing and corruption and took appropriate measures to keep this under close review.

Following the arrest of the gang there was genuine fear for the safety of Martin Grant as it was believed that a contract had been placed on his life. For more than ten years since the arrests he has been in protective custody and subsequently on the witness protection scheme, where he still remains. Given the nature of this gang he is likely to remain at risk for the rest of his life.

The Chaucer Unit

During the initial disciplinary investigation, which I had commissioned, John Podmore and his team interviewed Grant at length. His description of events and what he had witnessed, together with the evidence of other witnesses, pointed to the presence of other corrupt staff at Blantyre House, two of whom were named. His evidence also indicated more widespread corruption amongst a small number of officers at other prisons within the area and in the wider Prison Service. However nothing could be done against these individuals without evidence to support disciplinary action.

In February 1997 John Podmore reported to me on the progress of his investigation and the worrying picture that was emerging about the extent of staff corruption. He was particularly concerned at allegations that some prisoners were 'buying' their places at resettlement prisons. His terms of reference had restricted his investigation to Blantyre House and therefore did not allow him to pursue allegations in respect of other prisons within the area.

On my instructions John briefed all the in-charge Governors on the emerging evidence when we met for an area Governor's conference at the Chaucer Hotel in Canterbury. Collectively we agreed that these allegations had to be fully investigated and that amended terms of reference should be issued to enable him to follow up any allegation of corruption or serious misconduct within the area. Furthermore the Governors agreed to provide additional officers to resource

John's team properly to carry out its increased task. I issued revised terms of reference, together with guidance on how they were to operate. This central investigation team became known as the 'The Chaucer Team', taking their name from the venue of their formation. Following their initial success and with the agreement of the Governors in the area their remit was further extended and the unit became a permanent resource. Investigators were trained by Kent Constabulary and in addition to its investigative role the unit, in conjunction with security departments in prisons, undertook an intelligence gathering and collating role.

In mid-1996 Governor Brian Pollet moved from Blantyre House on promotion. It was the norm for Area Managers to identify potential candidates to fill Governor in-charge posts and to confirm appointments in consultation with the Operational Director and the Director General's office. I was considering a number of candidates including a bright young man who had recently spent a period as Staff Officer to the Director General, Derek Lewis. I had first met Eoin McLennan-Murray when I was in East Anglia where he was a junior member of the management team at Highpoint Prison. On the basis of what I had seen of him I recommended that he be appointed Governor of Blantyre House.

Before taking charge Eoin had a period of handover with the outgoing Governor. I also briefed him on what I required, all of which was already contained in the establishment's business plan. He was made aware of all matters relating to the criminal conspiracy and continued to be briefed on the emerging information about prison staff, including their names. The Chaucer Team would continue to monitor intelligence but the Governor was expected to keep tabs on suspect staff. Where possible he would introduce systems to reduce the possibility of abuse and ensure that suspect officers were not placed in positions that afforded them the opportunity to engage in corrupt activities.

In comparison with other prisons under my command, Blantyre House was by far the smallest, with no more than 120 selected prisoners held there at any time. However its scale did not diminish its importance nor the key role it played in helping prisoners to resettle as law abiding citizens.

HM Prison Service at that time did not have a clear policy on resettlement prisons. The three specialist prisons had evolved through the foresight of their Governors. Small resettlement units had also sprung up in or attached to other prisons and provided a similar service. I had units at Rochester, Canterbury and Aldington Prisons in addition to Blantyre House. The importance of facilities like this cannot be over emphasised and their scarcity made it important to make proper use of them by ensuring that only those with genuine resettlement needs and a commitment to change were allocated to them. Resettlement prisons differed from other, more secure prisons in that an integral part of their objectives was to encourage the activation and demonstration of self-discipline through increased trust and responsibilities. This required a degree of trust and freedom of movement, which in turn brought risks which had to be balanced with the service's responsibility to carry out the order of the court and to protect the public.

The public as a whole may sometimes seem to have little sympathy with offenders and are not tolerant of what they may perceive as 'holiday camp' type prisons. However professionals in the field recognise that the process of resettlement is critical in helping some individuals to change their behaviour. The continued existence of these facilities is dependent on public confidence in the Prison Service and requires the service to ensure a proper balance between meeting the needs of the offender and protecting the public. I believe strongly in the value of resettlement and the need for such a balance.

Blantyre House now had a new, bright young Governor. His awareness should have been heightened by his knowledge of the earlier events and he should have been ensuring that there would be no recurrence. I visited Blantyre House regularly following his appointment. Under his leadership the performance of the prison in achieving its targets was good. I was impressed with him and reflected that in his annual appraisal reports. I believed him to be well motivated and committed to the objectives of the service. He was an intelligent and articulate individual, well able to manage the prison and to argue his corner with me when necessary. I felt that he was a bright prospect.

CHAPTER 5

The 'Charity Work' Debacle

The performance led culture of HM Prison Service placed constant pressures on all managers, particularly Governors. As Area Managers were accountable for the performance of their prisons we too shared these pressures. Kent prisons had their share of problems but the nature of our corporate commitment was such that they were quickly addressed as they arose. When the performance of a prison fell below acceptable standards support was always forthcoming from other Governors. High standards were expected from my Governors and their management teams but equally they were fully supported to the best of my ability. I think that I must have acquired something of a reputation as a tough, robust manager with a direct style, but the Governors knew that this was only part of a façade. Though avoidable failure would not be tolerated, I tried at all times to be fair and supportive. The degree of humour and banter that was an integral part of the management culture at all levels, especially between Governors and myself, together with the consistently high performance of the area led me to believe that the balance was right. I was lucky to have such a strong and able team of Governors and I was pleased that I had picked many of them out and assisted in their development.

•　　•　　•

By the late 1990s I was feeling the effects of my 15 years in Northern Ireland and the pressures of managing a large area, with some difficult prisons, through the cultural transition that was now nearing completion. After medical tests I was admitted to St Thomas's Hospital in London in March 1998 where I underwent major heart surgery. On the morning of the fifth day following surgery I was deemed fit enough to go home and recover. The first few weeks were uncomfortable and painful. Frances's distress and worry were obvious although she tried to hide it. Like most men, I was not a good patient but with her care and coaching I became increasingly active in regaining my strength.

I convinced Alan Walker, my Operational Director, and my doctor that I could go back to work in June. Both insisted that my return should be gradual: a few days each week initially. My deputy during the period of my absence had been Adrian Smith who was then the Governor of Elmley Prison. Alan insisted that he should remain at Area Office to assist me for at least a few weeks. This proved to be a wise precaution as I discovered that I was not quite as fit and well as I had believed. I found the first few months very difficult but I did manage to visit each of the eleven prisons during June and July to take stock of how they were progressing.

In early July 1998 when I was still in the gradual return to work phase, I was contacted informally by a senior police officer whom I had known for many years. He told me of his concern at the apparent lack of control over prisoners at Blantyre House and described an incident when two individuals in a van made contact with a group of known and then active criminals who were under police surveillance. A check on these individuals revealed that they too were known professional criminals serving sentences at Blantyre House. I agreed to check this out but felt confident that there would be a logical explanation. However a few days later I received a short intelligence briefing from the Chaucer Unit suggesting that there had been a breakdown in the controls over some parts of the working out scheme and the community projects.

I visited Blantyre House on 15 July 1998. The Governor was away on a course at Cambridge University. His Deputy, Brian Hales, was in charge. My visits to all prisons were normally structured and included an inspection of all areas of the prison, talking to staff and prisoners and then an audit of performance against the business plan. All seemed well and performance statistics were good. Towards the end of the visit I raised the issue of the working out scheme and my concerns at these reports. I had known Brian for a few years and his reaction to these questions caused me to doubt his assurances that all was well. After pressing the matter further I eventually talked by telephone to the Governor. Far from being reassured by these conversations, I gave immediate verbal instructions to the Governor to suspend all external 'charity' activities where prisoner's work places in the community were not static and properly supervised. A worrying picture seemed to be emerging but I was not feeling strong enough to deal with the matter myself. The Governor was told that Adrian Smith was being tasked to carry out a detailed audit and enquiry into the operation of the working out and the community work schemes at the prison. Later that day I issued terms of reference to him.

The audit began immediately. The senior investigating officer was assisted by two experienced Chaucer Unit investigators. From the start one of the main areas of concern was a 'charity scheme' involving about 20 prisoners who were engaged in 'fund raising' activities in the community. The audit was carried out in two parts: an audit of the working out scheme, the charity scheme and other temporary releases; and separately an examination of the operation and legitimacy of 'special funds' in use to support the 'charity' activities. The second part of the audit was carried out by auditors from the HMPS headquarters Audit Department who would report separately.

All prisoners arriving at Blantyre House should have been selected on the basis that they had genuine resettlement needs. The facility was designed for long term prisoners nearing the end of their sentences. Criteria for their selection already existed in terms of stage of sentence and other considerations for eligibility. Following their arrival prisoners would spend a minimum of six months being assessed before being security cleared to leave the prison. This meant that at any time approximately 50 per cent of the prisoners were not allowed to leave the prison. Most of the prisoners going through this process had committed very serious criminal offences.

When he reported, Adrian Smith identified a serious breakdown in the control of the temporary release system. A group of prisoners, most of whom were career criminals, under the guise of performing charity work, were permitted to move around at will in the community driving vans that they themselves had procured. The 'fund raising' activities included buying items which they would subsequently sell at boot fairs and markets. There was also evidence of less clear 'fund raising' activities. Members of this group were given free rein to come and go as they pleased and a minimum of control imposed:

> Prisoners, sometimes in twos and threes appeared to cover considerable distances by private vehicles, often in their home areas, whilst on licence without any apparent staff supervision. The reasons for these temporary release licences and the conditions of release seemed to be decided by the prisoners themselves. The nature of these activities also meant that the persons that these prisoners dealt with in most cases could not be subject to verification. (Smith Report 1998, p. 6, 5.1)

More seriously, (p.7, 1.3) 'there did not appear to be any officially designated person responsible for the oversight and management for these activities'. As a consequence (p.6, 5.1) 'the accounts for buying and selling goods were also under the prisoner's control'.

Prior to these events prisoners at Blantyre House had genuinely engaged in raising funds for a number of charities, including Mencap, the charity for people with a learning disability. Though it is not absolutely clear how this new situation developed it appears that a small number of career criminals persuaded the Governor that they could raise considerably more funds for Mencap. It seems that the Governor, in a spirit of trust, gave his approval. However there was no evidence of him setting any ground rules or tasking any member of staff to take oversight. Many of the prisoners concerned were sophisticated individuals who would use the Governor's seemingly naïve trust for their own ends. At the time of the audit 20 prisoners were regularly being granted temporary release to undertake 'charity' activities at street markets, boot fairs and charity shops. In addition to these activities journeys were being made for the alleged collection of bric-a-brac to destinations in London, Essex and Kent. Destinations were invariably nominated by the prisoners involved. The average duration of the licence for these activities was 12 hours, which on the face of it and without adequate further explanation appeared to be somewhat open-handed. In his report Adrian Smith states (p.7, 1.8):

A sample of three releases reveal that distances of 133 miles, 88 miles and 141 miles were covered and on each occasion the journey route coincided with the home area of at least one of the prisoners involved in each journey.

Furthermore (p.7, 1.9.):

when some of these prisoners were informally interviewed they confirmed that contacts that they met during these journeys were often family or friends.

and (p.7, 1.13):

There was considerable evidence to suggest that 'charity' work may have been used to gain extra licensed release, outside the national instructions, by 'grafting together' different types of release licence to avoid some of the restrictions imposed by the national instruction. This was evidenced by the fact that during the week commencing the 12 July 1998 48 days' temporary release had been granted to a total of 14 prisoners specifically for 'charity' activities.

Two freight containers and two garages had been provided at the prison for these prisoners to store merchandise and equipment. When the audit team sought access to them there was confusion about who was responsible for holding the keys. Some keys were not available and where they were many did not fit the locks. Entry had to be forced. Investigators were told by staff that they did not control or search these areas. A search by an area drug dog team showed an indication that drugs had probably been stored in the one of the 'Mencap' containers. Two mobile phones and £58 approximately were also found in one of the vans.

In examining other aspects of the temporary release schemes Smith found that (p.6, 5.1):

the majority of projects audited were seen as appropriate, with no indications of serious wrongdoing discovered. However the potential for it, we felt was considerable. We also had some concerns over the appropriateness of some projects in terms of the need for them, the 'host' briefing about their role in prisoners' supervision, the needs of some prisoners in terms of resettlement and staff checks to ensure that the prisoners were doing what they had been given a licence for.

Approximately 40 per cent of the work projects were generated by the prisoners themselves and inadequate checks had been carried out on the hosts, their suitability and their relationship to the prisoners. Some were actually friends or relatives of the prisoners and others had criminal records themselves. Smith expressed concerns over the nature of some projects, the lack of adequate audit trails, prior and ongoing checks on the suitability of projects, issues surrounding the use and ownership of vehicles used by the prisoners and the apparent ability of some prisoners to exert control over a number of these projects, which should have been the responsibility of staff.

At the time of the audit 37 vehicles were being used by prisoners, mainly for commuting. He was concerned by the lack of controls over their use. The expense of running these vehicles led to some prisoners having credit, debit and various agency cards in their possession. Some prisoners also had cheque books. He considered this inappropriate for serving prisoners. His report acknowledged the lack of a national policy on resettlement prisons which was leading these establishments and their Governors to plough their own furrows.

Commenting on the nature of the population at Blantyre House during the audit Smith went on to say (p.8, 5.1.):

> At the time of the audit, we had assumed that less adequate, less sophisticated prisoners without financial resources, who required, to varying degrees assistance to reintegrate into the community would be the norm. Instead, in a number of cases we found some very adequate sophisticated prisoners with available financial resources 'sometimes abundant' and others with stable domestic situations to return to on release.

The report went on to recommend that to avoid the perception that the system may be corrupt or corruptible (p.11, 6.9.2.):

> the process of selection should be integrally linked to Sentence Planning Boards and recommendations for selection should emanate from the host establishment in association with the prisoner rather than independently from him.

As to the working out scheme the report concluded (p.7, 5.1.):

> The risks presented by a number of projects were assessed by the investigation team as very high and sufficiently embarrassing to the Prison Service to require permanent cessation of some and re-evaluation of others.

Smith more than confirmed my concerns about what was happening at the prison and I welcomed all his recommendations in respect of corrective actions. This was made clear to the Governor. Before setting out the detail of the corrective action plan Adrian Smith was asked to meet with the Governor to discuss his findings and recommendation in advance of a meeting to firm up the plan, on my return from a period of annual leave.

The financial audit was carried out separately but in tandem with the Smith audit. This report also made worrying reading and concluded (Internal Audit Review of Special Funds at Blantyre House 1998, p.2, i.3.2.):

> From our findings it is clear that there has been no management/official control exercised over the Community Care fund and only limited management/official control exercised over the Mencap fund. This is evidenced by the following:
>
> - prisoners making purchasing decisions
> - prisoners making decisions on donations from the fund and directly handling donations to the fund

- no control over prisoners committing to credit purchases
- no income or expenditure accounts produced
- prisoners making cash payments directly to suppliers with no checks to ensure that payment was made or that cash has been properly applied
- off book transactions undertaken by prisoners without official knowledge or approval
- failure to identify a limited trading loss of between £1.5K and £2K.

The auditors identified a further five serious failures to comply with Prison Service financial management instructions including provision of large cash advances to prisoners and failing properly to check receipts prior to approval. They also highlighted what appeared to be a conflict of interests involving the Governor in respect of the school which his son attended. A prisoner was working there without payment and another, Prisoner A, a convicted armed robber with suspected links to organized crime, organized activities for a fete at the school which seemed to have been paid for from 'charity' funds.

Auditors highlighted a number of irregularities in the management of both the Mencap fund and the Community Care fund and instances of (p. 3, 1.3.3) 'actual or possible misappropriation or misapplication of assets or cash'. The evidence suggested that there had been movement of funds from the Community Care fund to support the Mencap 'fund raising' operation. They formed the opinion that two prisoners, Prisoner A and another professional criminal, had been acting as the principal managers. They were responsible for purchasing decisions and receiving cash or cheques.

The auditors examined a number of fund raising activities by prisoners but in most cases were unable to find any reliable records of income or expenditure. From what records were available they identified a loss of cash and assets of approximately £3,034. This included a trading loss on pine furniture that Prisoner A had purchased from a London based supplier for resale at markets. Some of the supply costs had not been paid.

Commenting on the responsibilities of both the Governor and the Head of Management Services, the author of the report concluded (Internal Audit Review of Special Funds at Blantyre House 1998, p. 4, 1. 5.):

> Based on the findings of our review we consider that, over all, these responsibilities have not been discharged in relation to Special Funds at the Establishment. In particular with regards to the Community Care fund and to a lesser extent the Mencap fund, we feel that insufficient action was taken by both the Governor and the Head of Management Services to ensure propriety and regularity in relation to their financial operation. This failure may have resulted in the loss of cash and assets totalling £3,034 and a diversion of public funds totalling £895.

I received a copy of the initial draft of the audit report, which contained a strong recommendation that both the Governor and the Head of Management Services at Blantyre House should be the subject of formal disciplinary proceedings. The wording of the draft left me little room to manoeuvre in dealing with the consequences of their failures, as I held the view that formal disciplinary action should be used only as a last resort. The Governor seemed traumatised by the experience of both investigations. Though he tried to resist some of the changes recommended by Adrian Smith which he felt impacted on the ethos of the prison, I thought that he would learn from the experience and would be a better Governor as a result. I reasoned that though he had made some serious errors of judgement and had allowed himself to be conned by a few very sophisticated criminals, it was unlikely that he would allow such a thing to happen again. On that basis I argued, not only with the author of the report but with the director of finance, that I should be given more flexibility in dealing with the matter. I felt that the Governor had learned from the experience and argued that formal disciplinary action would certainly damage his prospects in the service and that as an able and intelligent young man he would do better in the future.

Pending a decision on my plea for flexibility, I commissioned a disciplinary investigation under the provisions of the code of discipline for HMPS. This would allow statements to be taken under caution. Evidence gathered in this form would be admissible in a formal hearing and would speed up the process for all those involved. Keith Nesbitt, the Governor of Stanford Hill, was asked to lead this investigation. In briefing him it was made clear that my preference would be to deal with the matter outside the provisions of the code of discipline. Having completed his investigation, Keith concluded that the management failures were so serious in this case that he had no alternative but to recommend formal charges. It seemed that we were going down that road when, to my surprise, Prison Service headquarters agreed to give me discretion on the matter. I decided that I would not proceed with formal charges against the Governor and Head of Management Services but I would reflect their failures in their end of year performance appraisal reports with a rating of 'unacceptable'. This would have the effect of reducing the possibility of promotion for a few years but would be less damaging to their careers in the long run.

I talked to Eoin and his staff member individually and told them of my decision. During these meetings I made it clear that further failures of this kind would not be tolerated. Both were ordered to arrange their attendance on a financial management course without delay. They accepted these conditions and assured me that they would carry out their duties properly in the future. I would later regret my decision to try to protect them in that they both repeated similar failures two years later. But most disappointing of all, Eoin would later wrongly claim that I had not told him that his failures would be reflected in his performance appraisal report, clearly overlooking the fact that in his briefing to the Board of Visitors at their meeting of 3 November 1998 the minutes themselves record (p. 3, para 2):

> the Governor did confirm that no disciplinary action would be taken against him or Margaret Andrews but it will be reflected in their personal performance reports.

Between commissioning the Smith report and receipt of its findings I had ordered the Governor to suspend all 'charity' schemes and placed restrictions on a number of other activities that were causing concern. Eoin tried to resist some of these constraints and argued that he feared that the ethos of the prison would be undermined. His naïveté seemed incomprehensible. In his otherwise laudable commitment to the resettlement ethos of the prison, his personal judgement seemed to have gone out of kilter. Whatever the justifications behind giving trust to prisoners and allowing them leeway as part of the resettlement regime, Eoin seemed to be unable to maintain the delicate but at other times quite plain balance between the resettlement needs of prisoners, the protection of the public and HMPS's duty to carry out the order of the court. As a consequence and behind the scenes we had some quite heated exchanges during which we both expressed our views in forceful terms. Eoin held his own in these discussions but eventually accepted that there would *have to be* change. However when he met with Adrian Smith and his investigators to discuss their findings and recommendations, they sensed that he was openly hostile to some of them and resistant to certain key recommendations of the report.

Adrian Smith and I met with the Governor and his senior team on 14 October 1998. After a full and frank discussion on the findings and recommendations of the report we progressed to identifying and agreeing the way forward. Having agreed to accept all the report's recommendations for corrective action I gave the Governor detailed guidance on the criteria to be applied in assessing the suitability of a work placement. Based on that he agreed to carry out a review of all existing placements and report back to me. Selection criteria were already in existence but were obviously being disregarded. These were to be properly implemented in future. Eoin agreed to produce a time-bound action plan for the implementation of the main recommendations together with details of any resource implications which might result from implementation by October 31.

He wrote to me on 29 October 1998 confirming his acceptance of all of the recommendations and enclosing his corrective plan. There was only one issue on which he sought any concession and that related to Blantyre House staff interviewing potential candidates for transfer there before accepting them. In his memorandum he stated:

> I have amended criteria for admission to Blantyre House as discussed but must insist that my staff continue to interview all prisoners prior to acceptance. The excellent record of minimal temporary release failures and escapes has proven the worth of these interviews. I am concerned that, if prisoners without stable home backgrounds are allocated directly without being interviewed, this enviable record will be compromised.

Given the risk of corruption, I quite naturally had some worries about the integrity of a small number of staff within the prison acting as gatekeepers to

Blantyre House and the scope that this might give for manipulation and abuse of that part of the process. However, Eoin was aware of these individuals and assured me that he would make it work. On that basis I agreed to compromise on this point.

I was not satisfied that proper security checks could be carried out on outside workers and placements with the resources he had and so I agreed to fund one senior officer post to do this work. Because of my concerns that some middle managers at the prison could not be relied upon to do this job properly I insisted that a suitable officer should be recruited from another prison. When appointed, this senior officer would only work on this task and would report directly to the Governor.

There was strong resistance to this arrangement from other middle managers who seemed threatened by this new security officer and particularly his independence from them. This appointment had an immediate impact at the prison and the officer was quickly branded by prisoners and many staff as 'The Terminator'. He was made to feel unwelcome by many of his peers and there was a strong suspicion that some of them were undermining his effectiveness by alerting prisoners on outside projects of his movements. However the Governor appeared to give him his full support.

Some of the investigators on the Smith team privately expressed their concern at the closeness of relationships between some staff and prisoners at the prison. These experienced managers feared that professional lines had been blurred and as a consequence staff over-identified with prisoners and therefore became vulnerable to corruption by them. The presence of so many career criminals whose resettlement needs were questioned by Smith again raised the issue of whether some prisoners might be buying their places at the prison through corrupt staff. Though there was no direct evidence against any member of staff, circumstantial evidence and persistent intelligence reports did lend weight to the possibility. The Governor was aware of the concerns about 'payment for places' and of the identity of the staff named in the earlier investigation. Implementation of the new allocation criteria should have limited the scope for such activities and on that basis the matter was left in the Governor's hands. The support of Area Office and the Chaucer Unit were available to him at any time should he need them.

As the Governor had agreed in writing to implement the corrective action plan it appeared that the prison was moving on. It was now a case of monitoring progress. Blantyre had a history of achieving targets and was a centre of excellence well before Eoin McLennan-Murray became its Governor. There was no reason why this should not continue if greater control was exercised in a few key areas.

During a visit to the prison on 24 September 1998 I met with David Smith, a member of the BOV, and briefed him on the main findings of the audit. It became clear during that discussion that the board had shared my misgivings about the

Governor allowing prisoners to carry out 'charity work'. During their monthly meeting on 7 July 1998 they recorded these concerns asking for a full explanation from the Governor. Their concerns were never brought to the attention of my office or headquarters. The minutes of that meeting only came to my attention two years later when another worrying entry relating to their meeting on 3 November 1998 was also pointed out to me.

Though the Governor had just agreed his corrective action plan following the audit and was presenting as compliant, he seemed to be preparing the ground with some members of the BOV to undermine attempts to regularise the situation at the prison thus exceeding their proper role. At that meeting the Governor gave the board an account of his meeting with Adrian Smith which he described as 'stormy'. He went on to describe the subsequent meeting which I had chaired as 'going much better'. The minutes then record (p. 2, para 6):

> The question of whether or not there is a 'hidden agenda' was fully discussed with the board that are anxious to support the governor in any way possible.

The board asked the Governor for sight of the audit report which he declined, however the record shows that (p. 3, para 1):

> it was finally agreed that the Governor would go through the report with Mr Smith to highlight the areas of concern with a view to (a) [seeing] if he wished the Board to take any action; (b) the timing of such action.

It is not clear what the Governor perceived the 'hidden agenda' to be though it was later to emerge that he seemed to see any attempt to constrain him as part of a conspiracy to undermine resettlement; and anyone seen to be involved in such constraints was automatically stereotyped as being 'against resettlement'. In December he told the BOV that he was gathering evidence to support the concept of resettlement and suggested that this would demonstrate that the regime at Blantyre House was more beneficial to prisoners than that of any other prison regimes looked at. He even brought a serving prisoner to the BOV meeting to support his case. But in truth no accepted research evidence in support of his claim exists. He did produce a thesis, as a project in his masters degree course at Cambridge University, in November 2000, in which he asserted that the regime and culture of Blantyre House were the most significant factors with regard to its lower reconviction rates, in comparison with the national average, rather than the selection of prisoners who were at lower risk of re-offending. Yet he himself acknowledged when presenting that thesis that it contained a number of weaknesses. Now in his various presentations he continued to assert the validity of his conclusions. I know for a fact that his confidence in his own conclusions was not shared by a number of more experienced researchers who saw them as lacking full academic rigour and testing. I certainly do not accept his arguments and had I been aware at the time that the Governor's outward compliance with my instructions was a façade I have no doubt that the then DG, Sir Richard Tilt, would have immediately removed him from his post.

The minutes of his meeting with the BOV also seemed to signal the intent of the board, or at least some of its members, to exceed their remit and actively engage in attempts to undermine the senior management of HMPS. Except for my discussion with David Smith in September 1998 and a few brief and informal conversations with the then chair, Mrs Alexina Roberts, some time earlier, I had not spoken to the BOV. I had not met most of its members and certainly none of them knew me or had any contact with me. However I had one experience of them much earlier in my tenure as Area Manager which may have affected my views concerning their ways of doing things.

When I took up my post as Area Manager for Kent I was made aware of a planning dispute relating to the Prison Board's policy of fitting steel cladding, two metres high, to the perimeter fences of all Category C prisons. Blantyre House was in this category and some members of the BOV actively opposed any attempt to implement the policy at the prison. It seems that some of them might have been involved in orchestrating local opposition using planning regulations as a vehicle for this. The upgrade of the fence was blocked by the local planning authority on grounds that remain unclear. The matter eventually landed on the desk of the Secretary of State for the Environment and a public hearing was set up. It was at this stage that I arrived on the scene and had to lead for the Prison Service at this hearing.

After seeking a legal opinion from a specialist in the field I was amazed to find that planning permission could not, as such, be refused, as it had never been required in the first place! Since my predecessor had agreed to attend the public hearing I decided to keep our powder dry and go along. As the hearing opened, the barrister I had instructed to lead for HMPS raised his challenge. The presiding officer readily accepted his arguments and closed the hearing immediately, leaving us with the suspicion that he already knew permission was not required. Some members of the BOV attended the hearing perhaps intent on obstructing HMPS when objections were called for. They became quite irritated when the hearing collapsed and vented their anger on me personally—despite the fact that the matter should never have reached that stage.

CHAPTER 6

The Chaucer Unit

As described in outline in *Chapter 4*, the Chaucer Unit was set up to investigate corruption and serious misconduct by prison staff in the Kent Area following the ATM scam at Blantyre House. Its first investigation, in 1997, related to the activities of Principal Officer Gary Catton and on the basis of their work he was charged under the HMPS internal staff disciplinary code with eight counts of serious misconduct, found guilty on six of these and dismissed from the service.

The unit also assisted Governors within the area to carry out major investigations on their own behalf within their prisons. This, together with their own workload, enabled the unit members to gain considerable experience and develop their investigative skills. Their professionalism was, as indicated in the previous chapters, enhanced by specialist training they received within the service and from Kent Constabulary. In a number of serious cases they worked jointly with the police investigating matters where criminal charges were considered probable. Their relationship with the Kent Police Liaison Unit was close and of benefit to both services. An important element of their role was to gather and collate intelligence and their various activities enabled them to build a substantial intelligence database.

There was considerable hostility to the Chaucer Unit, particularly from the Prison Officers' Association (POA) and to a lesser extent from the Prison Governors' Association (PGA). The unit's brief required it to operate, at all times, in compliance with the service's guidance for the conduct of investigations and with the procedural requirements of the code of conduct and discipline for HMPS staff. In spite of this their existence seemed to generate irrational fear in some quarters. Invitations to a briefing on their work and operating procedures were issued to some national officials of the POA. The invitations were rejected even when these officials were in the same building as the Chaucer offices.

For many years POA officials had used their wider experience of the code of discipline and its procedures to frustrate investigations and disciplinary hearings. These were not common occurrences at many prisons and the managers adjudicating were relatively inexperienced in comparison to some POA officials. Because of this many managers found difficulty in coping with their obstructive refusal to answer questions and their constant challenges to procedures. As a result procedural errors frequently occurred that were then seized on as fatal flaws warranting dismissal of the charges. Chaucer investigators were well drilled in investigation procedures and in the requirements of the code of discipline. They were not prepared to accept an individual's refusal to be interviewed and would patiently use written questions, which staff were obliged to answer, to get to the facts of a case. Because their investigations were generally procedurally perfect and thorough they made much more effective and confident witnesses at formal disciplinary hearings. This seemed to present a problem to POA officials in defending some of their members. Perhaps this is why they were so hostile to them.

The concerns of the POA at national level were so great that their National Vice-Chair, Terry Bond, raised the matter formally with the DG of HMPS arguing that the unit should be disbanded on the grounds that it was not operating on a proper basis. Though he had been assured as to the probity of operating procedures Richard Tilt, the then DG, asked his Deputy, Tony Pearson, to carry out what he described as a 'health check' on Chaucer. Tony reported that the unit was operating in accordance with correct procedures. Richard Tilt then conceded to the POA a right of appeal to an authority outside the service in cases where an officer was found guilty of an offence after a Chaucer investigation, which may have been an attempt to buy peace in the industrial relations climate of the time. However, the concession was withdrawn, but not before, in my view, one damaging and seemingly perverse decision by the appeal authority. The Chaucer unit was investigating one of the POA's own officials at the time, which may have had some influence on its opposition to Chaucer.

Until the formation of this unit, there seemed to be little awareness of the corruptibility of prison officers. At a Prison Service conference in the late 1990s John Podmore (head of the ATM scam investigation mentioned in *Chapter 4*) raised the issue of staff corruption in a question and answer session chaired by the broadcaster, John Humphries. The panelists included Richard Tilt and Sir David Ramsbotham, Chief Inspector of Prisons. From their comments and a show of hands from the floor the overwhelming view was that HMPS did not have a problem in this area. Many senior managers would not entertain the proposition that relatively unsophisticated prison officers could be manipulated by the ever increasing number of sophisticated professional criminals in our prisons some of whom might have virtually unlimited funds available to them from the proceeds of crime, particularly drugs. Many reasoned that because cases had not come to light the problem did not exist. The reality was that unless you are aware of the potential and look for it you will not find it.

Because of the opposition to their work, Chaucer investigators suffered hostility from some of their colleagues as well as from their own staff association. Individuals were ostracised and on occasions subjected to threats. A number of web sites appeared on the internet on which disgusting and untrue comments about Chaucer members and myself were anonymously made. In some cases it was possible to identify the sources, who by and large were individuals who were under investigation or had already left the service.

Under the leadership of John Podmore, Governor of Swaleside Prison where they were based, and Ron Gooday, their Senior Investigator and a Governor grade colleague, the unit insulated itself from these pressures and got on with its work. The courage of all its members at this time was remarkable and I greatly admired all of the team that included: Governor Steve Spratling; Principal Officers Lance Kennedy, Ed Davison and Mal Thompson; and Senior Forensic Psychologist Jo Capelin for their steadfastness.

Because of the surreptitious nature of some corrupt relationships they are often extremely difficult to prove, even where intelligence is so strong as to leave little doubt as to its accuracy. Investigations can sometimes take months or even years of patient work before they can be brought to a successful conclusion. There is no doubt that corruption does exist to a greater degree than many people like to admit and where there is sound and reliable intelligence it is essential to act. However, corruption is not widespread within HMPS and the vast majority of prison officers are honest, decent and professional.

In the first three years of their existence the Chaucer Unit completed 47 separate investigations, two of which were jointly carried out with the police. As a result of charges brought against them by Chaucer, three members of staff were dismissed from the service. A further nine staff resigned when presented with charges and supporting evidence that Chaucer had gathered against them. Two major investigations were ongoing at that time involving eight members of staff. Until recently, when it was disbanded, the Chaucer Unit enjoyed similar success.

Though Chaucer members had attracted the odium of some people they had also impressed many good staff who recognised the value of the work they were doing. This helped them to build up valuable contacts and sources of information across the Kent area. Within a short period after the audit at Blantyre House a small number of reliable staff at the prison, some of whom were in key positions, made contact with Chaucer. These people were concerned about what had been happening at the prison but until our intervention thought that it had been approved by the Area Manager. I was not aware of these informants at the time but they were to become a valuable source of information to Chaucer.

Within weeks of the completion of the Smith investigation at Blantyre House the name of Prisoner A who I mentioned in *Chapter 5* was again drawn to my attention. He was then on a work placement at an international brokers in the City of London. The exact nature of the work he was doing was unclear but concern was being expressed by some staff at the amount of time he was being allowed outside the prison. They reported that he was leaving the prison very early in the morning and not returning on many occasions until late evening in what was described as a large 'flash' car. The Governor had already been instructed to ensure that all work placements were within a reasonable travelling distance of the prison and capable of being monitored. He had also been told that in the event of a work placement having to be in London then public transport should be used. This would enable prisoners to get into work and return to the prison at a reasonable time.

According to intelligence, Prisoner A had been a career criminal with suspected links to organized crime. He had also featured prominently in the recent shambolic 'charity work' affair which might have seriously damaged, amongst other things, the Governor's own career. As the Governor was now aware of Prisoner A and his associates' abuse of trust in this matter, it was hard to understand why he allowed him to participate in this placement. Eoin was asked for an explanation on my October 1998 visit. His reaction was dismissive of my concerns and made it clear that Prisoner A had his complete trust. He also justified his apparent disobedience of my instructions on the use of cars for London placements by a requirement for Prisoner A to use a car in the course of his work. He did not seem to have given any consideration as to the suitability of the placement, having regard to the instructions given to him. From his body language, Eoin was clearly unreceptive to any interference in what I think he saw as his exclusive domain. Nevertheless it was made clear to him that I was unhappy with the situation which I classed as yet another error of judgment on his part.

Though the Area Manager is the line manager of his Governors and accountable for the performance of their prisons, Governors have considerable vested authority within their prisons and the discretion to make decisions within the framework of national guidance. That discretion includes decisions on the temporary release of prisoners. Because of this and the fact that we had just agreed a corrective action plan in respect of the Smith recommendations I decided not to overrule Eoin, but to keep an eye on the situation.

A short time after this discussion with the Governor a senior police officer from the Flying Squad at New Scotland Yard contacted me regarding Prisoner A. They were clearly interested in him and it appeared that he was under surveillance. At their request I agreed not to stop the outside work project. Within days the Chaucer Unit was also contacted by a different police unit registering a similar interest in Prisoner A and an ex-prisoner with whom he was allegedly in contact. The police suspected that the two were conspiring to commit further serious crime.

The police had requested strict confidence as to their interest in Prisoner A, However I felt that the Governor had to be alerted to the situation as the temporary release was being granted on his authority. The matter was raised with him in November 1998 in his office. As soon as Prisoner A's name was mentioned he became visibly irritated and accused me of victimising the prisoner. When briefed on the situation he seemed to reject any suggestion that Prisoner A could not be trusted. He had been briefed and though he appeared to view the briefing with scepticism, I naturally expected his total discretion on the matter. However within a short space of time Prisoner A's movements on temporary release changed, suggesting that he had been alerted to the police interest. Though there is no evidence or suggestion that the Governor had betrayed the confidence, my suspicions affected my trust in him and I would be much more careful with confidences in the future.

The Governor's seemingly protective relationship with Prisoner A and a small number of what I would describe as career criminals was a constant worry. Other observers expressed similar concerns. Though I frequently raised my worries about the degree of freedom Eoin was affording Prisoner A in particular, he was always dismissive. The view that I was against resettlement and victimising Prisoner A was his constant refrain. It is unclear how this prisoner got to Blantyre House but my concerns about him appear to coincide with those of the Parole Board who did not grant him parole on his initial eligibility date despite his time at Blantyre House. However this did not influence the Governor and Prisoner A remained on the same work placement for about two years before his release. It would later emerge that in that two-year period he had been out of the prison on all but 59 days. On most of those days he was leaving the prison before 7 a.m. and not returning until late in the evening. There is no evidence that he committed any offence during these releases but because of the lack of supervision the extent of his activities can be known only to himself.

At the same time as the police were interested in Prisoner A concerns about the activities of other prisoners on temporary release from Blantyre House were reinforced by the arrest of a prisoner while on home leave in Essex. He was found to be in possession of approximately one ounce of cocaine, two grams of heroin, five ecstasy tablets and £1,500 in cash. He is alleged to have told police that he bought the drugs for £900 while on temporary release from the prison working at the Bluewater Shopping Centre, which was then under construction. The prison appeared to be unaware that this man had a £100 per day drug habit. He was earning £250 per week. Where he found the money to feed his habit, spend £900 on drugs, still have £1,500 in cash and run the car that the Governor had allowed him to obtain I could only speculate on. The circumstances of the case pointed to the possibility that he was involved in drug dealing when serving a prison sentence.

Though I was worried by these events, the recommendations in the Smith report which now formed the basis of the corrective action plan provided an ideal vehicle to regularise the situation. The Governor had to be given time to implement it. Though there was concern about a number of other matters at the prison, the overall performance was good. All of the targets I had set in the prison's business plan were being met and in many cases exceeded. As a resettlement prison Blantyre House appeared to be doing a good job. The worrying aspects that were putting the work of the prison at risk could be overcome by the changes about to be made. In a letter to me dated 29 November 1998 Eoin outlined his corrective action plan covering the 21 Smith recommendations and indicating that implementation would be immediate in most cases with the remainder by 30 November 1998. I was content with that.

However he was clearly peeved by my intervention and it now seems that he grudgingly agreed to implement the changes that were necessary. His Deputy, Brian Hales, was less forthcoming with any opposition. The third in charge was

Dave Newport. He was a former tradesman who had moved up the ranks in that specialist field before reverting to a generalist junior Governor Grade. He had been at the prison for many years and had little relevant experience of other conventional prisons. Dave was totally committed to the Governor's policy and I think hostile to the changes now being made. Consideration was given to transferring him to another prison but as he was approaching retirement it was decided to leave him there.

● ● ●

Since taking over responsibility for the area I had been concerned about the lack of a clear national policy on resettlement and guidance on the management of resettlement prisons. Adrian Smith had highlighted this and recommended that guidance be issued. I raised the matter with the then Director of Regimes, Martin Narey, who agreed to take it on board. Policy development could be a slow process and as headquarters staff were already engaged in other equally pressing policy work, I knew it would be some time before resettlement could be addressed. Because of this and my very real concerns that the whole concept might fall into disrepute through a loss of public confidence if a damaging event occurred, I decided to begin the process of developing the policy myself. I brought together all key interests in the service both at headquarters and in the field. Because of the lack of guidance, Governors of the resettlement prisons were developing their own policies in isolation. All were genuinely committed to resettlement but there was no clear consensus as to how a prisoner's needs should be met and who this scarce resource should be targeted at. As a result resettlement regimes appeared to focus on giving prisoners what they wanted rather than what they needed. The lack of a coherent selection process also appeared to leave scope for abuse.

I chaired the first three meetings of this working group. Once I had stimulated an interest in the subject and established the pressing need for a clear policy, a senior official from the appropriate policy division picked up the baton and led on this project. I became a member of the working group which was extended to include representatives of other agencies. A national policy on resettlement is now in place that embraces all the areas that caused concern.

Full attention could then be given to supervising and supporting the Governors of the other larger and more difficult prisons in the area. Most were operating well, achieving their targets and maintaining good order and control. The main problems affecting Governors still related to reductions in budgets, the need to make savings and to maintain or improve regimes. Concerns were beginning to emerge regarding Canterbury Prison and the viability of its plans to operate within budget. HM Inspector of Prisons carried out an inspection in late September 1998 and was exceptionally glowing in his praise of the regime and its management. When the Governor moved on, the extent of the problem was exposed. A new management team was put in under the control of Jane Galbally, a formidable and highly capable Governor whose calm and caring presentation disguised the iron will that lay beneath.

Governors were demonstrating considerable skill in finding ways to overcome the consequences of budget cuts and in most cases were maintaining all the key elements of the regimes of their prisons. However, in the performance led world that now predominated that was not enough. National operating standards were introduced, covering every aspect of the work of prisons, as a vehicle to maintain and improve performance. Operating standards were policed by a new Standards Audit Unit which visited each prison annually and graded performance in every area. Their findings were published to the service for all to see. This created a strong incentive for Governors to raise performance levels and to ensure that standards were maintained even in circumstances where resources were diminishing.

When Jane Galbally and her team took over at Canterbury she was faced with a prison that was not only massively overspending and overstaffed but also failing to meet basic operating standards in most areas. Paul Carroll was appointed as her deputy. He was an able manager who would complement her with his particular strengths. We met and agreed a corrective action plan that would be challenging to the Governor and would not be popular with staff. The Governor was given a year to achieve these major changes, which would require the re-profiling of the work of the prison and more efficient use of staff. It was inevitable that a substantial reduction in staff would result and this was likely to be resisted by the staff associations. I had expected an intractable dispute that would delay progress toward the necessary changes but was pleasantly surprised when very responsible local officials of the POA reached an accommodation with the Governor. She and her staff set about the task of raising standards in all areas and successfully achieved an acceptable rating the following year.

Meanwhile, the Governor of Blantyre House appeared to be getting on with implementing the corrective action plan and was being given space. However during Christmas week 1998 a letter was received at my office from him regarding a prisoner who I shall call Prisoner K. It explained that this man's wife had recently died from cancer and that he was now the primary carer of his two children. The Governor proposed allowing Prisoner K to go to his home one day each week and sought authority to use the 'Voicetrack' system, which at the time was being tested by the Kent Probation Service, to monitor his movements. This was a very unusual request in that Voicetrack was not an approved system for use in HMPS. It is not for HMPS routinely and regularly to undermine the sentence of the court however compassionate the circumstances and it was very unusual to allow any prisoner to go home for a day each week to care for children, even where he or she was the primary carer. Provision was made to allow primary carers to maintain contact with their children but not to this extent and it was normally focused on mothers in custody for short periods. Arrangements existed for fathers to maintain contact but not normally to the same degree. Because of this I asked my Staff Officer to obtain more information on the prisoner and the background to the case.

What emerged was that Prisoner K was yet another career criminal and an alleged associate of the infamous Kenny Noye mentioned in *Chapter 4*. Readers will recall that Noye was a former Blantyre House prisoner alleged by police to be a co-conspirator in the ATM scam but never convicted and was the killer of PC John Fordham found by a jury to have been in self-defence. He was convicted of offences in connection with the Brink's-Mat robbery and is now serving a life sentence for the murder of a young man in a road rage incident. Prisoner K had been sentenced at the Old Bailey in June 1996 to five years' imprisonment on four counts of corruption and a further two years on two counts of perverting the course of justice. In July 1997 he was again sentenced to a further four years imprisonment for drug offences. All the sentences were to run consecutively.

The corruption charges related to Prisoner K paying a corrupt Metropolitan Police Service detective sergeant £19,000 to obtain bail and offering him a further £40,000 to have police files destroyed or lost. He was also alleged to be a middle man in deals between Noye and the same corrupt detective to obtain information about police operations involving Noye. The drugs charges related to him being found in possession of cannabis resin to the value of approximately £222,000. Following his arrest he exposed the corrupt police officer to investigative journalists in a BBC TV *Panorama* documentary shown nationwide, allegedly in the hope of getting a more lenient sentence. The policeman was eventually sentenced to eleven years' imprisonment. Passing sentence on Prisoner K for the corruption charges, Mrs. Justice Heather Steel said:

> What you sought to do was use your illegally gained wealth to buy your freedom and information about yourself. What you did was to exploit the weakness and greed of the officer you had just met. You appear before this court with a long criminal record and a man who has spent his entire life outside the law.

At that time Prisoner K had 53 previous convictions dating back to 1968 and had allegedly amassed a substantial fortune from the proceeds of crime. I discovered that he had been moved to Blantyre House in June 1998 on compassionate grounds because his wife was terminally ill with cancer. This was arranged to facilitate visits with his wife. It remains unclear exactly who arranged this as visits could just as easily have been facilitated at any of the secure prisons on the Isle of Sheppey. Because of his criminal record and as he was at such an early stage in a long sentence, he was not eligible even for consideration to go to Blantyre House. HMPS has dealt with similar unfortunate situations over many years and where necessary has escorted prisoners to hospitals to be with a terminally ill spouse. Though there was genuine sympathy with his situation a move to Blantyre House was not appropriate in this case.

His presence at the prison does not seem to have come to light during the audit in July but it now emerged that the Governor had, perhaps kindheartedly, allowed him an unprecedented amount of freedom to spend time with his wife prior to her death. During all of this freedom he was accompanied by just one elderly officer. A similar escort from a prison more suited to his security needs would have had at least two officers. He would have been handcuffed at all times except possibly in the ward with his wife. Following the unfortunate death of his wife he should have been returned to Elmley Prison, which was more suited to his needs. Instead he was allowed to remain at Blantyre House and managed to convince the Governor to allow him to go home for a full day every week to be with his children, accompanied by the same elderly officer. This highly irregular situation was justified on the basis of him being the primary carer. The children were actually in the care of their grandmother who was the primary carer. How Prisoner K, given the long sentence he faced, could be considered to be in that category beggared belief. His treatment at this stage was unprecedented in HMPS in my experience.

Because of the seriousness of the situation the matter was discussed with the Director of Operations (South), Alan Walker, who was clearly unhappy. It was agreed that the Governor's request would be refused and that I should meet with him after Christmas to discuss Prisoner K's treatment. In the interim the Governor was instructed not to allow him out of the prison or to lead him to believe that further temporary release would be granted.

The Governor attended a meeting in my office early in January 1999 to discuss the situation. He was clearly unhappy that his proposal had been rejected and that I was again intervening to restrain him. Eoin argued that what he had planned was reasonable given the prisoner's 'primary carer' role and he could not understand how that view was not shared at headquarters. He was equally resistant to the view that Prisoner K should be immediately returned to a more secure prison, arguing that he should be allowed to stay at Blantyre House. He seemed unable to recognise the validity of public safety issues or the Prison Service's own security classification system. After a long and tedious discussion I gave him three options to resolve the matter. The first was that Prisoner K should be immediately returned to a more secure prison suitable to his security needs. Alternatively if he felt strongly that the prisoner should stay at Blantyre House as he was already there, he should make the case in writing for consideration by the Director of Operations. The third option was to carry out a full risk assessment using standard prison procedures and allocate him accordingly.

The Governor was reminded that if he decided to retain Prisoner K at the prison he would remain ineligible for outside activity until he had reached the stage of his sentence at which he became eligible for consideration for resettlement. The earliest date for such consideration was September 1999 but in most cases would not be until six months later. He was also ordered to ensure that this prisoner's visits with his children took place at the prison just like every other prisoner in his situation. He was not to be afforded special privileges as a primary carer and would not be allowed to go home, either escorted or unescorted. Governors had authority to grant temporary release on compassionate grounds in clearly defined circumstances which were well documented and it was made clear that my instructions did not restrict his powers in such circumstances.

I was at Blantyre House the next day on a routine pre-scheduled visit. The Governor was again absent and, according to his deputy, in Cambridge. Performance data indicated that the prison was achieving targets and that the general atmosphere was good. During my inspection of the prison I was told that Prisoner K had asked to speak to me.

I talked to him in the presence of the Deputy Governor, Brian Hales. From the onset of our discussion it was clear that Prisoner K had been fully briefed on what was said at the meeting the previous day. As the Governor was not in the prison it appeared that he had possibly rushed back or at least been in communication with Prisoner K in order to tell him. Prisoner K initially adopted an aggressive manner in challenging my decision to stop his home visits. When he saw that I was not impressed he became more reasonable in attempting to argue his case. I made it clear to him that my preference was for him to go to a more secure prison but if the Governor wished him to stay then the conditions outlined the previous day would apply. Though he was clearly aware of them I again repeated them to him. I also explained the exceptional circumstances under which the Governor might allow temporary release in accordance with national instructions. This was the first time I had met Prisoner K and I formed the impression that he was a clever and manipulative individual who was trying to minimise the impact of his sentence.

●   ●   ●

Immediately following my visits to any prison I always wrote a detailed report on its performance and the events of the day. These reports were always copied to the DDG and the relevant Governor. It also means that I have a written and contemporaneous account that I was able to return to on many occasions when writing this book. An account of my conversation with Prisoner K was recorded in my report on that visit.

I had been in America for most of February but shortly after my return I paid a short unannounced visit to Blantyre House. On my arrival I was surprised to meet Prisoner K leaving the prison to participate in a project in direct contravention of my orders. I was told that there was 'confusion' over what I had said during my last visit. Hales looked me straight in the eye and told me that he heard me tell Prisoner K that he could accompany his son to a parents' meeting at his school. It was also suggested that there was confusion about the instructions that had been given regarding temporary release. Since the details of what I had said were recorded in both the contemporaneous note of the meeting with the Governor and in my similar visit report, both of which were copied to the prison, there did not seem to be any room for misunderstanding. The situation caused me to worry further about the influence of Prisoner K and the way in which he now seemed to be gaining some kind of hold over not just the Governor but Brian Hales and other HMPS managers. I repeated my earlier orders and arranged for the situation to be monitored covertly.

The Governor's questionable judgement, as I saw it, and disregard of my orders was causing me increasing anxiety. This was heightened in late March when I discovered that he had arranged a week-long event in the prison involving 29 teenage children of both sexes working with prisoners. The event involved a well known opera company in conjunction with pupils from a local school and a group of prisoners working together 'to create a promenade piece of music-theatre that will be performed in and around the prison site'. The presence of such a large group of teenage children in the prison for a week could be problematic and needed strict supervision. But it emerged that only one member of staff was being deployed to supervise these activities.

The situation was discussed with the Director of Operations (South) who ordered that the event be cancelled unless it could be properly supervised. This instruction was passed to the prison. In discussions with managers it became obvious that they had no appreciation of the dangers presented by the presence of such a large group of teenage girls and boys working with prisoners at various locations in the prison without proper supervision. They had not considered the understandable public outcry that would have followed if anything happened to any of the children and again they resented the interference. However they took action to supervise the event properly which went ahead.

Matters came to a head in May 1999 on a routine visit to the prison to review its performance in the year ending March 31. The business plan for the year beginning the immediately following April 1 had already been agreed. The prison was performing well in most areas but there was serious concern about a number of matters primarily related to management perspicacity and the integrity of the selection process. Conformity to the instructions issued during the February visit was covertly monitored and contrary to my instructions the Governor had again allowed Prisoner K to go home accompanied by one officer. A review of implementation of the corrective action plan based on the Smith Report also revealed that important recommendations had not been addressed.

I confronted the Governor with all of these issues in an interview that incorporated his annual performance review. The interview was long and contentious with Eoin being dismissive of the issues raised. He claimed that I was undermining the whole ethos of the prison by the restrictions I was placing on him and argued that the regime he was delivering was more effective than any other in the service. He seemed quite unable to recognise that in setting the business plan I was in fact demonstrating my commitment to the objectives of the prison. He seemed to have considerable difficulty in grasping the fact that he was not autonomous of HMPS policies and was accountable through the line for the proper management and performance of the prison in accordance with Government policy and operational instructions. However he did take notice when told that his annual report performance rating would be 'unsatisfactory'. The reasons for this were discussed in detail and they covered the failings identified by Smith, his poor judgment in relation to his decisions about Prisoner A, Prisoner K and other matters and his deliberate disobedience of my instructions. He was told that further failures could not be tolerated and would result in his removal as Governor. We discussed the possibility of him moving to a Deputy Governor post in a larger prison where he could benefit from the support and advice of a more experienced Governor.

It was not within my power to remove him from his job without the authority of the DG of HMPS but I was aware that my growing concerns about him were shared by both the DG and the DDG, Phil Wheatley, who was fully abreast of events. Confronted with the reality of a possible move Eoin undertook to complete all outstanding work and to show greater care in making decisions about releasing prisoners on licence. He agreed to seek my advice on matters of judgment where existing guidance did not cover the circumstances. I decided to give him a final chance.

His attitude and disobedience was creating a strain on our previous good relationship and resulted in some frank and robust exchanges of views between us on occasions. But his persistent disobedience is perhaps a good indicator that he was by no means intimidated by me or easily swayed from his own point of view. Because of this I wrote to him immediately following our interview confirming the substance of our discussion and the consequences to him if he failed to carry out my instructions. The letter, dated 17 May 1999, included the following comments (paras 4, 5 and 6):

> I emphasised to you that I cannot continue to overlook these errors in judgment and that you must ensure that similar mistakes or omissions do not occur in the future. I advised you that, if in doubt, you should seek my advice before committing yourself in circumstances that are not clearly defined by existing instructions and guidance. I believe you should be clear from our discussions that I will have no option but to seriously consider removing you from your post as Governor of Blantyre House if you continue to demonstrate a lack of sound judgment in its management. I have no desire to take such steps but in the interest of the Service and in your own interest I may have to do so.
>
> During our interview we explored whether you might benefit from operating at your current level as second-in-charge in a larger establishment where you would have the benefit of the support and advice of a more senior Governor. You undertook to consider this possibility and we agreed that we would discuss the matter again when you had time to consider the position. In making this suggestion I am mindful of the fact that you are an extremely able and intelligent Governor with much to offer the Service and it is perhaps unfair to you, without the benefit of greater experience at

a more senior level, to have been placed as Governor of Blantyre House with its associated pitfalls of loosely defined parameters.

I will discuss these matters with you on my next visit and we will hopefully agree how best to move forward. In the interim I am content that you remain as Governor but you must be clear that greater thought and consideration must be given to your future decisions.

It seemed that we were making progress. Though the Governor had demonstrated a lack of understanding of the political environment in which HMPS operated and appeared to have no appreciation of the possible adverse consequences of some of his decisions, he now seemed more willing to learn from his mistakes. We would try to make a fresh start.

CHAPTER 7

Downhill Spiral

CHANGE AT THE TOP

The senior management of HM Prison Service was partially restructured in 1999. Martin Narey became Director General (DG) and Phil Wheatley his Deputy (DDG). The Operational Director management level was removed and Area Managers now reported directly to the DDG whose area of responsibility now spanned that of all the Operational Directors.

Like his predecessor, Martin Narey had joined the Prison Service as a junior Governor. He worked in a young offender institution (YOI) and then in a high security prison before moving to a middle grade Governor position at headquarters in 1989. His potential was soon spotted and he joined the central Home Office in 1982. His 1997 report on a review of delay in the criminal justice system (also known as 'The Narey Report') won widespread acclaim and many of his recommendations were implemented. He came back to the Prison Service in 1997 as Head of Security Policy and later as Director of Regimes before succeeding Sir Richard Tilt as Director General in 1998. A down-to-earth Middlesbrough man and a strong manager, he was determined to ensure that the programme of improvement already started would continue and he lost little time in communicating that to the service. Martin committed the service to providing decent treatment for all prisoners in conditions consistent with that objective. He recognised that if the service were to address the problem of re-offending we had to do something about the fact that the levels of literacy and numeracy of most prisoners leaving prison were below those required for most jobs. The main focus of education resources was therefore directed at basic education.

Martin was promoted to Permanent Secretary in 2003 and became the first Commissioner for Correctional Services in England and Wales with responsibility for HMPS and the National Probation Service (NPS), oversight of the Youth Justice Board (YJB) and policy responsibility within the Home Office for correctional, rehabilitation and sentencing issues. He was later appointed Chief Executive of the National Offender Management Service (NOMs), integrating into a single service prisons and probation. He was awarded the Chartered Management Institute's Gold Medal in 2003, an annual award to an individual who has demonstrated outstanding achievements through his leadership. He is now the head of Barnardo's, the leading children's charity.

Phil Wheatley had served as a prison officer and was also a very experienced operational Governor. He had been my tutor when I attended the Staff Course at the Prison Service College in Wakefield way back in 1973. I had also worked with him when I was Principal of the Prison Service College in Northern Ireland. Phil, though a tough, plain speaking Yorkshire man, was intellectually very able and had the capacity to take a massive workload in his stride. He had previously been an Area Manager and the Director of the High Security estate. His experiences of managing at all levels gave him a realistic perception of difficulties in the field and the pace at which change could be achieved. Phil's ability to read situations ensured that he would not be fooled by bluffers. The combination of Martin and Phil was formidable and in addition to giving the HMPS a very clear focus, would demand and achieve high standards in all areas of the work of the service. Phil would later succeed Martin as DG.

AN OPPORTUNITY SPURNED

During our appraisal interview in May the Governor of Blantyre House had assured me that he was willing to learn from his mistakes and, where unsure, would seek advice. It later emerged that he seemed to have no intention of paying any heed to my instructions and appeared to be actively seeking the support of his local Board of Visitors in this.

It was customary for selected prisoners at the prison to assist at fetes in the local community at the invitation of the organizers. On many of these occasions the prisoners concerned were not supervised by staff. It also became the practice for some of the prisoners' families to turn up at these fetes. In the summer of 1998 Martin Narey attended the Goudhurst Fete in a private capacity and found that, contrary to the Blantyre House rules, prisoners assisting at the fete were drinking alcohol. He was so perturbed by this and the inappropriate behaviour of some of their family members that he raised the matter with me. Martin was clearly concerned that some of these individuals were out of place at these events and that their behaviour was reflecting badly on the service. He was also concerned that though the Governor assured him that all prisoners returning from weekend activities were breathalysed, clearly some were not.

A short time after the May meeting with the Governor, his Deputy contacted Area Office seeking guidance on whether a group of prisoners could attend a fete to assist the organizers. He was told that provided their families were not attending and that arrangements were made for adequate supervision, there was no reason why they could not attend. He seemed content.

However in mid-June the Governor wrote to inform me that in accordance with my instructions he had declined three requests from the community for prisoners to assist with fetes. He went on to state that he was reviewing other activities the prison was involved in and would either terminate them or discuss them with me. Most of his letter related to Prisoner K and continued to argue that there was confusion over the instructions issued about temporary release. The position had already been made clear both verbally and in writing but he seemed unable to accept it, preferring to rely on the prisoner's version. He went on to state his intention to allow him (Prisoner K) to attend his son's birthday party and would allow him to go home for six hours accompanied by one officer, unless instructed otherwise. This he claimed was in accordance with what I had told the prisoner in the presence of Brian Hales. He was well aware of my position but seemed unable to say 'no' to the prisoner. If the temporary release had to be refused then he seemed to prefer it to come from me.

The letter concluded by him telling me:

> In essence I am leading Blantyre House in a different direction. Activities that have been undertaken here for several years are now stopped. This has caused uncertainty amongst both prisoners and staff. Within that context I am restricting the regime in a way that I have not done before and in accordance with your advice.

The prison's business plan had just been signed and required him to maintain the regime. The issues raised with him related to his failure to properly manage aspects of the work of the prison, to comply with HMPS instructions relating to temporary release and his judgment in matters of public safety. There was no reason why this should have any adverse impact on the regime. The DG and the DDG were both fully aware of events and were in accord with the line I was taking with him.

Shortly afterwards I received a letter from a member of the BOV challenging my intervention to stop Prisoner K's trips home and rehearsing the usual arguments. The contents of the letter suggested that the board member had been well briefed at the prison in that it reflected the same sterile arguments in support of Prisoner K and a familiar 'spin' on events reflective of the loaded accounts given by the Governor and Hales. The board had also communicated with the Chief Inspector of Prisons, Sir David Ramsbotham, seeking his support. He in turn wrote a personal letter to Martin Narey raising his concerns at being told that 'the Governor's freedom and ability to conduct the regime at Blantyre House is having restrictions imposed upon it'. He went on to indicate that if the restrictions were real he would bring forward an inspection to 'bring these concerns to public notice.'

Martin Narey was invited to meet the BOV about a week later. At that meeting, held on 24 June 1999, they complained about me and the constraints I was placing on the Governor and expressed fears that the ethos of the prison was being destroyed as a result. Martin tried to reassure them that rather than threaten the ethos of the prison, my actions were protective of it and the Governor. He also made it clear to them that he was aware of the situation and fully supported the action I had taken. Following this meeting he responded in writing on July 16 to the chair on all the points they raised. He also briefed Sir David Ramsbotham about the situation.

The YJB came into existence under the Crime and Disorder Act 1998 and took over responsibility for the treatment and custody of young offenders aged under 18 years. Because of the limited availability of secure accommodation outside the Prison Service estate it was necessary for them to contract out some of their custodial needs to the Prison Service. The YJB purchased these places and specified the nature and content of the regime. There was a requirement for these children to be kept separate from older offenders. The number of places required by the YJB from the Prison Service increased considerably over a short period of time and prompted the DG to develop contingency plans to accommodate a further increase should it be needed. When developed, the planned strategy was based on phased action to meet increased need as or if it occurred.

I had not been involved in this process but in June 1999, prior to Martin Narey's meeting with the BOV, I was informed that Blantyre House was listed as an option for the later phases. As a definite decision had not yet been made, the details were to be kept confidential. However the subject did arise in a discussion with Martin about the Governor's future. If Blantyre House was to become a juvenile custody unit then we both agreed that Eoin would be an ideal person to manage it but, if not, then he should move when a suitable opportunity arose.

The Blantyre House facility was ideal accommodation for a secure juvenile unit and had housed children in the past. It was therefore understandable that it was listed. Though I was keen to keep it as a resettlement prison the fact that its role could just as successfully be carried out elsewhere in the estate diminished the case. When the DG met with the BOV he briefed them, in confidence, on this matter. Later the Governor was also briefed on the same basis.

The Prison Service Standards Audit team visited the prison at the end of April 1999 and their report graded security 'deficient'. Following these audits Governors were required to produce time-bound action plans to correct any deficiencies. Each plan had then to be approved by the Area Manager. Common standards applied to all prisons by type, and security standards were related to the security classification of the prison. The prison's business plan and the agreed searching strategy identified all areas where standards could not be achieved and a written derogation was granted by the Area Manager. Though this was a category C prison the nature of its role allowed a proportionate reduction in security procedures. These had already been agreed and derogations issued. An action plan was produced by the Governor in late July that contained elements that were unacceptable to me in that they fell short of the standards that we had already agreed. The Governor was instructed to produce an improved plan.

OPENLY CHALLENGING AUTHORITY

Between May and November of 1999 Eoin was absent from the prison each time I visited, which was unusual. Governors knew in advance of my visits and tended to be present on such days. Prior to May he had been away during two of the previous three scheduled visits. On each occasion I was told that he was either at

Cambridge or on leave. Though I do not question the reasons for his absences his pattern of attendance was in stark contrast to those of his peers who also attended Cambridge. Where their commitments or annual leave clashed with scheduled visits they would discuss it in advance and if possible the visit would be rescheduled. His absence from the prison at other times made efforts to contact him increasingly frustrating and on one occasion led me to improperly vent that frustration on one of his staff.

After his departure from the prison an audit of his attendance between May 1999 and May 2000 was carried out. The audit revealed that of 267 possible working days he was recorded absent from the prison on 125 days, 35 of which were recorded as annual leave and 31 attending Cambridge. Of the remainder 22 days showed him attending meetings and conferences but most worryingly the reason for his absence on the remaining 37 days could not be explained. Though it is possible for some unexplained absences to be justified it compared badly with the attendance patterns of his in-charge peers whose attendance history was subjected to similar scrutiny. Most of these had much heavier workloads. The audit's findings in my view went some way to explaining my frustrations.

During a scheduled visit in August I rejected the security audit action plan because it failed to meet the basic standards already agreed in the prison's searching strategy document and the Governor was instructed to produce a revised plan. A meeting was to be arranged within two weeks to finalise the plan but due to difficulties in contacting him this did not occur. This matter was again discussed and rejected in his absence on a visit in mid-September when I discovered that no progress had yet been made. The Governor was on duty during a visit in mid-November and the plan was again discussed. Most issues appeared to be resolved but he argued that he could not carry out basic search procedures at the prison gate due to a lack of resources. He seemed unable to understand the importance of searching prisoners entering the prison on their return from periods of absence or to have any awareness of the possible consequences, having regard in particular to the fact that 50 per cent of the prisoners in the prison were not yet security cleared to leave the prison.

It was obvious that he had deployed staff away from these duties to undertake less important tasks and I ordered him to implement immediately an interim arrangement whereby all prisoners entering the prison from any outside activity were given a 'rubdown' search and scanned with a metal detector. Later he would be required to carry out random strip searches on them at a relatively low rate of five per cent. The Governor agreed to implement these minimal interim security procedures, if somewhat grudgingly as it appeared to me.

All Governors carried out annual reviews of the work of their prisons to ensure maximum efficiency in the use of staff. These reviews enabled unnecessary tasks to be identified and dropped and provided an opportunity to develop more efficient ways of carrying out the essential work. It was also the only effective way of proving a need for additional resources. This annual review was known as re-profiling. It seemed that a re-profiling exercise had not been carried out at Blantyre House for a number of years and the Governor was ordered to undertake one immediately. An effort was made to get the services of a specialist team but this was not successful because of their prior commitments. He was advised that if necessary he could seek the help of a fellow Governor, Mike Conway, who was particularly skilled in this work. However assistance of this kind should not have been necessary as the process was relatively easy and was being carried out in most prisons each year without difficulty.

By then I was also becoming concerned that some of the recommendations of the Smith Report had still not been implemented. These mostly related to controls on the use of vehicles and mobile phones by prisoners but also included concerns about the suitability of some London based work placements. These concerns were also discussed with the Governor in September and he agreed to review the situation.

He had kept Prisoner K at the prison, ignoring advice to send him back to a more secure prison. Though Prisoner K was in my view not in need of resettlement and was manipulating staff, the Governor could not see this. In September he would reach the stage of his sentence where, if in a normal prison, he would become eligible for consideration as a possible candidate for a resettlement prison. On the basis of his criminal record, personal circumstances and the absence of credible evidence that he was making any effort to change it was unlikely that a sentence review board in any other prison would have recommended him for Blantyre House. But if they had, he would still not have been eligible to participate in any outside project until March 2000 at the earliest. Phil Wheatley, the DDG, was aware of the impending review and instructed me to ask our police liaison section to check if there were any particular police concerns before any review could be completed. I advised the prison to delay a decision until I received a reply. The section head had indicated that an answer would take a few weeks. Before a reply was received I was made aware that the prison was making direct approaches to the police liaison section, pressing them for a quick reply. In fact the Governor seemed to be aware of the content of the reply before my office received it. The police had no particular concerns other than to point out that Prisoner K was a career criminal. With the approval of Phil Wheatley the prison was told that they could proceed with the review. As all previous advice regarding this prisoner had been ignored I cautioned managers at the prison to give careful consideration to this exercise. Predictably this was also treated superficially and he was immediately allowed to attend a course in recreation studies and work at a sports centre.

The investigation mentioned in *Chapter 5* into the activities of Principal Officer Catton, following the ATM scam that led to his dismissal also concluded that he was not alone. Although the evidence was insufficient to support charges, intelligence identified other individuals at the prison who were suspected of being prepared to arrange places at the prison for career criminals and others who were willing to pay. A reliable source identified at least seven prisoners who had got to the prison in this way prior to the 1998 audit and the number of this type of prisoner still getting there suggested that a problem might yet exist. Chaucer investigators had detected corrupt staff at other prisons who were dismissed or had resigned from the service but they had considerable difficulty in penetrating the culture at Blantyre House.

However there was a continuous flow of intelligence alleging that some officers were still active in receiving payment for places. This information was coming from various unconnected sources and followed a consistent theme in terms of cost and method of payment. It also indicated that the network included individual officers in at least two other prisons. Chaucer had obtained a deposit slip for £750 paid into the account of a middleman allegedly as half payment for a move to Blantyre House. This was passed to the police. At least one officer named by intelligence sources as a link in another prison was subsequently suspended in connection with other allegations of serious corruption and faced criminal charges in the courts. Information of this kind continued to come in until the spring of 2000.

This, of course, is not the only form of staff corruption. In some cases individuals are corrupted by prisoners without realising it. This occurs through conditioning by prisoners who gradually erode the parameters of control and discipline to an extent that the line between staff and prisoners becomes blurred. In most circumstances this can lead to an over-identification with the prisoner to a degree that the officer becomes unable to maintain a professional perspective in the relationship. The manipulative nature of some of the prisoners at Blantyre House, its role in the system and the length of time most staff had been there made many of them vulnerable to conditioning. This was evident in the behaviour of some of them in individual situations and on occasions collectively and at all levels. Without doubt many of these individuals would be horrified at the suggestion that they had been corrupted in this way but it is unlikely that a dispassionate analysis of events at the prison would support them. The ability of some dominant prisoners to influence decisions and seemingly to exercise power over staff, including the most senior managers, was an obvious feature of the culture at Blantyre House. The roles of Prisoner A and other prisoners in controlling the 'charity work' fiasco and their ability to continue exercising power in the prison, well after it was brought to an end, speaks for itself.

Normally reliable intelligence sources inside the prison also alleged misconduct by individual members of staff that included: trafficking of alcohol into the prison, falsifying search records, drinking alcohol with prisoners in the prison where it was prohibited, ignoring the movement of contraband carried by individual prisoners into the prison when the officer concerned was on duty at the prison gate, and numerous allegations of individual prisoners being warned in advance, through their mobile phones, of gate searches before they returned to the prison. It was also alleged that a small number of prisoners were 'set up' to provide an excuse for their transfer out, thus facilitating the transfer in of other prisoners. There was also intelligence, considered reliable, alleging misappropriation of prison property and the use of prisoner labour for personal benefit. Though there was insufficient evidence to take action against the small number of officers concerned the consistency of the reports and the normal reliability of the sources gave credence to much of the intelligence. Furthermore some evidence did exist that suggested an inconsistent approach in the transfer out of some prisoners even if their alleged misconduct was true.

Toward the end of 1999 information was received from a source within the National Crime Squad (NCS) that a named serving prisoner (Prisoner C), who had also been a leading player in the 'charity work' debacle, was believed to be involved in a conspiracy to import cocaine and was under surveillance. Though the individual concerned had been an associate of Prisoner A there was no suggestion that he (Prisoner A) was linked to this alleged conspiracy. The Governor was made aware of this information.

Within weeks the Chaucer Unit received information, from a normally reliable source, relating to alleged activities of Prisoner K when on temporary release. Later reports from other sources seemed to confirm the information which, though unsubstantiated, suggested that he was involved in unacceptable activities. He had also got himself a girlfriend and it was alleged that he was breaching the conditions of his temporary release license by meeting her when he was supposed to be at work.

An allegation of a similar breach of his temporary release licence was made against another prisoner on the same project as Prisoner K. On December 31 this man was removed from Blantyre House for breaching his licence by leaving his place of work to meet his 18-year-old girlfriend and for having a mobile phone. In the circumstances the Governor acted correctly in removing him from the prison. Whether he was aware of the allegations about Prisoner K is unclear but following his departure from the prison one of his staff alleged that he knew that Prisoner K had an unauthorised mobile phone and had given him permission to obtain and use a car.

In the period between November 1999 and May 2000 both staff and prisoner intelligence sources at the prison consistently commented on Prisoner K's growing influence over staff and other prisoners in the prison, referring to him as 'The Main Man'. Some speculated about the nature of his relationship with a couple of individuals at middle and senior management level and the source of his apparent influence over them. From my perspective the Governor's protective stance in relation to him was consistent with that which he had shown in relation to Prisoner A and other career criminals. It seemed to be born of a belief that they were genuine in their commitment to 'go straight' and the notion that trust was the key factor in the reformative process. He too seemed to have been a victim of the conditioning process. He was later to admit that he had a 'special relationship' with some prisoners because 'he had to protect them from the Area Manager'.

Prior to Christmas Chaucer received information that another named career criminal at the prison was running a large scale drugs operation in Kent. The information indicated that he was managing the operation when on temporary release and from the prison by mobile phone. It was alleged that he was assisted by a relative and two serving prisoners at the prison in running this operation. The fact that this individual had a history of this type of offence gave greater credence to the intelligence. Because of increasing concern about the Governor's judgment in matters of confidentiality and to protect the sources, he was not briefed on this intelligence. The police were aware of this information and the situation was being monitored.

THE LOBBYIST

After being briefed by the DG in June 1999 about the possible change of role of Blantyre House to accommodate juvenile offenders, both the BOV and the Governor seemed unhappy with the proposal. Though nothing specifically was said it soon became obvious that someone had breached confidentiality. A series of letters from MPs and other pressure groups began to come into HMPS Headquarters and to the Home Office lobbying against any change of role. From the consistency of their content it was fairly obvious that whoever briefed them was well informed. As the inclusion of the prison in the contingency plan was known only to a small circle, most of whom had no vested interest, it was not difficult to identify potential culprits.

On the basis of the information I was receiving, from sources in the prison, it appeared that the Governor was using every opportunity that arose to present a case in support of maintaining the status quo at the prison. He was allegedly claiming that research supported the view that the regime at Blantyre House was more successful than that of any other prison in HMPS and should be preserved and protected from the threat of a possible re-role and from the constraints being placed upon him by the senior management. It seemed that a key element of the case being presented was a comparison of re-conviction rates for the prison with the average for the service as a whole. By the autumn of 1999 the same sources were saying that he had developed a polished statistical presentation on the work of the prison and its increased success under his leadership which was targeted at anyone perceived as having political influence. He was also allegedly bringing former prisoners back into the prison to support his case and testify to the success of the regime. When I pointed out to him that it would be inappropriate for him, as a public servant, to engage in lobbying he firmly denied any involvement in any such activity. Subsequent events that I will describe in later chapters led me to form a different conclusion.

Again sources inside the prison alleged that an underlying theme in some of these presentations was a perceived 'hidden agenda' within parts of headquarters and Area Office by elements opposed to resettlement. My actions in restraining some of his excesses and in seeking to protect the public from them and the DG's support for me seemed to be seen by him as evidence of such an agenda.

Much of the evidence presented in support of the prison and later attributed to the exceptional ability of the Governor and his 'enlightened and successful' regime was pure spin. The performance of the prison during his tenure as Governor, though good, showed no substantial improvement on that achieved by his two predecessors. In reality the development of Blantyre House as a centre of excellence is chiefly attributable to one man. Jim Semple was its architect and during his time as Governor he had developed its regime and general ethos. During the succeeding tenures of Brian Pollett and Eoin McLennan-Murray there were few marked changes to the ethos of the prison though each would have made some procedural changes. However during the tenure of McLennan-Murray controls were allowed to slip and there was an increasing number of recorded senior management failures.

The nub of the arguments put forward by the Governor and his supporters in presenting Blantyre House as a unique and successful prison were primarily based on its reconviction rates in comparison with the average for the service as a whole. The basis of this argument was misleading in the form presented. The lower conviction rates for prisoners discharged from the prison and other prisons of that type were predictable and not necessarily related to the content of the regime. However that is not to say that the regime may not have been a factor in some cases.

The fact is that all the prisoners sent to Blantyre House were hand picked by staff from that prison. Most were at a stage in their criminal careers where they had already decided to 'go straight'. Some had committed only one serious offence and were always unlikely to re-offend. There was also a small but worrying number of professional criminals whose offending behaviour was such that detection and prosecution was not easy for the police and who could easily avoid re-conviction for the limited period on which the statistics were based.

In most prisons Governors have to take all prisoners sent by the courts. In all training prisons except those fulfilling a specialist function, the only criterion is security classification. Many prisoners participate in programmes that successfully help them confront their own offending behaviour, but equally many decline the help that is on offer and choose to continue offending. A major contributor to offending, in its various forms, is drug abuse and the drug culture, this is also a predominant factor in re-offending. An examination of the population of Blantyre House at that time would reveal the presence of very few prisoners in this category (though they in particular had the greatest need for a gradual and supported return to society) and a disproportionate number of professional criminals who were serving sentences for drug importation or supply. As I described in *Chapter 5*, the former Governor seems to have been enthusiastic to ensure that the majority of prisoners selected to go to Blantyre House would not present a risk statistically.

In the autumn of 1999 Jonathan Shaw MP visited the prison. The exact purpose of the visit was unclear to me at the time, but the Governor told me it was to see a named constituent. Prisoner K was also one of his constituents and he, in a later unguarded and recorded conversation, said, 'We invited him down for lunch'. He did not elaborate on who 'we' included. However Shaw met with the Governor who gave him a presentation on the prison. In his report to the BOV meeting on October 5 the Governor informed them that Jonathan Shaw MP had written expressing how impressed he was with the presentation on Blantyre House and he had asked for some statistics. In an interview with Adrian Smith following his removal McLennan-Murray told a different story. He then described how the MP had telephoned him in a 'very agitated' state regarding the delay in completing Prisoner K's security clearance review until a report had been obtained from the police. Shaw is alleged to have been 'agitated' by what he considered 'unnecessary treatment' of Prisoner K. The Governor now stated that he invited Shaw to the prison to 'see [Prisoner K] and reassure the MP that there was no "stitch up" going on'. He did not explain how Shaw and Prisoner K were aware that a police view had been requested when this information should only have been known to senior managers. Neither did he explain why he organized the presentation about the prison with which Shaw was so impressed.

The extent of Shaw's role in events between this visit and 1 March 2000 is unclear but he was active in supporting the Governor and promoting the prison with members of the Home Affairs Select Committee. A source within the prison's management at the time informed me that he asked the Governor to invite members of that committee to visit the prison. Prisoner K later stated that Shaw was responsible for encouraging their involvement. Such visits are rare, though not unprecedented, but if they were to take place they would normally be arranged through the Home Office or Prison Service Headquarters. My office became aware of a planned visit by the Select Committee to Blantyre House, scheduled to take place on March 1, only days prior to that date. A check with HMPS headquarters and the Home Office revealed that neither was aware of it.

The Select Committee visit to Blantyre House

Four members of the Home Affairs Select Committee: the chair, Robin Corbett MP (Labour, Birmingham Erdington); Martin Linton MP (Labour, Battersea); Gerald Howarth MP (Conservative, Aldershot), and Humfrey Malins MP (Conservative, Woking) visited the prison on 1 March 2000. It seems that their visit was carefully planned and orchestrated by the Governor with a view to soliciting their support. He had mustered members of the BOV who were already committed to supporting him, certain ex-prisoners (most of whom had been career criminals) and selected serving prisoners, to present a well rehearsed common account of the unique effectiveness of Blantyre House and the transformation it had made to their lives. This was supported by his equally well rehearsed statistical presentation painting in my view a superficially impressive but misleading picture of the prison's 'unique performance'.

During the visit the MPs walked around the prison talking to selected staff and prisoners, most of whom were serving sentences for drugs related offences, mainly importation. One of them, 28-year-old Christopher Johnson, had been convicted in December 1998 for importation and sentenced to seven years' imprisonment. Though his earliest possible date of release, if granted parole, would have been 2002, he had managed to get to Blantyre House very soon after being sentenced. Corbett was so impressed by Johnson that he agreed to sponsor him in the London Marathon. He clearly did not question why a prisoner who had been sentenced to seven years just 15 months earlier was being allowed to participate in this event so soon after being sentenced, or at all. Johnson was eventually released on parole in 2003, having spent most of his sentence enjoying the privileges of the resettlement regime. A number of these prisoners would later enter into correspondence with Corbett, sometimes in cordial terms, though perhaps this was prisoners courting the HAC, but frequently and to my mind surprisingly with regard to matters concerning the management of the prison.

The four Select Committee members were clearly impressed and Corbett wrote to the Governor following the visit, congratulating him 'on the way Blantyre was presented to them'. He went on to say, 'You will want to know how we will take forward what we learned with you on Wednesday ... I fully expect that we will decide to write to Ministers straight away. Personally I would need a lot of convincing that any alternative use of Blantyre House would be in the public interest'. Though the Governor continued to deny that he was lobbying against the DG, within days of their visit Robin Corbett wrote to the Home Secretary opposing any proposals for a change of role for the prison. From the content of the letter it seemed that he and presumably the three other committee members accepted at face value and without any hesitation the substance of the Governor's presentation. His comments also seemed to indicate that the presentation included issues about risk and the constraints being placed on the Governor to manage risk in accordance with Prison Service policy. However it is not clear if they were told that the Governor was disobeying the orders of his line manager. The MPs who visited were experienced individuals who might reasonably be expected to have questioned why they were getting a hard sell.

ENTER THE CHIEF INSPECTOR

Her Majesty's Chief Inspector of Prisons carried out a full inspection of Blantyre House in January 2000. Prior to their arrival I met with the team leader and briefed him on recent events at the prison and the concerns that the DG, the DDG and I had regarding some of them. Inspections were carried out at that time by one of two teams within the inspectorate. These were each headed by a senior Governor. Generally the Chief Inspector or his deputy would attend for a short time toward the end of the inspection. It was normal practice for the Area Manager and the Governor to attend a meeting with the inspectors on the last day of their inspection.

At that meeting the inspector's feedback was glowing in its praise of the prison. However concern was expressed about perceived confusion over its security status, which they considered to be a cause of conflict between myself and the Governor. He seemed to support the Governor's view that the prison was not really a category C establishment, but in reality the security status of the prison was decided by Headquarters on the basis of the security category of the prisoners held there. In their report they record the fact that 'all prisoners received were category C and went through a six month assessment period before being considered for outside work. Currently 52 of a population of 116 were not cleared'. This made me think that the inspectors had forgotten or maybe did not fully understand the niceties of security categorisation within the Prison Service. If they did they would otherwise have known that as Blantyre House was holding category C prisoners it had to be a category C prison with a resettlement function.

Though only a small circle of people were aware of the contingency plan to possibly re-role the prison, the inspectors made an issue of uncertainty about the prison's future at the meeting. This was an operational management matter at the highest level within HMPS and, in my view, not the business of the inspectorate, at least at this level. If the Chief Inspector had felt a need to comment then he should have done so in private to the DG or the Minister. At the end of the meeting the Governor informed me that staff were aware that the prison was to be re-roled and were distressed. He claimed that they got the information 'in a phone call from an unidentified officer at an unidentified prison up north'. Someone seemed to be putting a 'spin' on the issue to give the impression that re-role was on the cards. Additionally, the remote possibility of re-roling was being made to look like a deliberate attack on the existing Blantyre House regime—and possibly on resettlement generally—by the higher management of HMPS. I met with the staff on duty and explained the actual situation. They were also given an assurance that if any decision was made that affected the future of the prison I would come and tell them personally.

It was no secret that Sir David Ramsbotham had been in fairly regular contact with some members of the BOV at the Prison before the inspection and had already written to the DG complaining of my interventions with the Governor. From the content of that correspondence it appeared that he had already taken sides. Having crossed swords with him on a number of occasions in the past I knew that I would not be at the top of his popularity list.

The Rochester inspection

Only months before the Blantyre House inspection the Chief Inspector published a report on an unannounced short inspection of Rochester Prison that had begun on 31 August 1999, following a bank holiday weekend. A new Governor, Tony Robson, had been appointed a couple of months earlier, but he had been abroad and this was effectively his first day as Governor in the prison. The prison had been without a Governor for many months and was experiencing some problems which I had already identified to the DDG in my visits reports. The new Governor had been briefed and was about to take corrective action. The situation at the prison was no secret and neither was the fact that the new Governor was about to take up his post. In view of this the timing of the unannounced inspection was 'unusual' to say the least.

During bank holidays most prisons operate a 'Sunday routine' and only essential work parties operate. All areas of the prison would normally be cleaned every day except at weekends. Following the bank holiday the area around one wing at Rochester was littered because the young prisoners held in it had thrown paper and other items out of their cell windows. Normally this would be cleaned up first thing on the Tuesday morning but the new Governor understandably wished to meet his staff and address them. To facilitate this the normal routine was suspended until after the meeting. The meeting was interrupted by the arrival of the inspectors and terminated. During their initial tour of the prison they observed the litter in the vicinity of B wing before the cleaning party had been deployed.

As the senior inspectors were experienced prison Governors they should not have been surprised by this. The grounds cleaning party had cleaned up the area as soon as they were deployed and operated as normal for the remaining four days of the inspection. The prison was generally very clean and tidy and the grounds were always well kept with bright floral displays. Though clean, four of the five wings were in need of refurbishment. However the inspectors commented on the litter they saw on the first morning of the inspection.

Martin Narey saw the draft of the Rochester report on a Friday afternoon before the Governor or I became aware of its content and decided to check the facts for himself. He made an unannounced visit to the prison on the following Sunday morning, a time when the prison was most likely to be grubby. He found it 'worn but clean'.

When published the main body of the inspector's report told us much of what we had already told them and was reasonably balanced. But the preface to the report, the section that I have explained earlier is usually read by the media, contained a description of Rochester as 'filthy and vermin infested'. These comments infuriated the Governor and his staff and were incorrect. They also incurred the wrath of the BOV. I too strongly disagreed with that description, as did the DG who had recently visited the prison. On the eve of publication of inspection reports it was common practice for embargoed copies to be passed to the media prior to a press conference at the prison. This enabled the media to raise issues from the report with the Governor and the Area Manager. On this occasion the chair of the BOV also asked to participate.

Though the Prison Service frequently disagreed with some of the inspectorate's published findings and comments the longstanding and accepted convention, custom and understanding was not to say so openly to the media. However on this occasion feelings were so strong that to ignore it would damage staff morale and was inviting others to respond in a less restrained manner. Therefore in response to questions from the media I made it clear that, amongst other things, we disagreed with the Chief Inspector's description of the prison. Television, radio and newspaper reporters who attended the press conference were invited to look around the prison and form their own conclusions. Included in that group was a leading national TV news reporter who interviewed Sir David Ramsbotham and Martin Narey on a main evening news programme the following day. On the day of publication Sir David was also interviewed on local radio and robustly defended his description of the prison. One reporter came back to me seeking further comment on the conflicting views. He was told that his visit to the prison and first-hand experience placed him in a stronger position to make a judgment on its cleanliness than the Chief Inspector who had never been to the prison in person. The interview ended in stunned silence. By then if not before Sir David would have been in no doubt that there was strong disagreement with his assessment of the state of Rochester Prison.

SPINNING OUT OF CONTROL

In the spring of 2000 events at Blantyre House continued to cause concern. We became aware that a number of law enforcement agencies were separately showing a close interest in a number of prisoners there. To avoid the danger of investigations being compromised these agencies often did not tell us of the extent of their interest and frequently did not tell us of any interest at all. The Chaucer Unit sometimes became aware of such matters inadvertently when pursuing other things or via contacts within the investigating agencies. However it was becoming clear that a common factor in all the interest was drugs.

During the early months of 2000 a number of new, separate but well informed prisoner sources were established by the Chaucer investigators. Initially their reliability was viewed with come scepticism but they gained greater credence when sensitive information they passed was found to be accurate, or corresponded with information already received from sources known to be reliable. The information the new sources provided shed fresh light on the prison subculture and the nature of some staff-prisoner relationships. It also confirmed information already received, the reliability of which investigators had been previously unable to grade.

The picture that emerged suggested that prisoner power was being exercised by two separate career criminal groups. The groupings were based on their area of origin, an East London Group and a South-East London group. This reflected the organized crime culture in London. The leaders of these groups and, to some degree, their members seemed to enjoy easier access to temporary release. Prisoner K was the alleged kingpin in the South-East London group. Other prisoners told Chaucer investigators that if they were not members of these inner circles they would have to go through the leaders of either group to obtain an extra privilege such as additional home leave. Favours of this kind were not without cost. It is not unusual in prison subcultures for strong individuals or groups to emerge and exercise a degree of power over fellow prisoners but such behaviour would not be reinforced by staff and should not occur in a prison like Blantyre House.

There had been concern for some time about the integrity of some middle managers at the prison. Information suggested that they had been corrupted and that one was 'in the pocket' of a named prisoner and a career criminal. New intelligence seemed to confirm the earlier information. At the same time investigators were informed that a prominent prisoner at the prison had purchased a car for a named officer as a reward for services rendered. This matter was investigated but it was not possible to obtain sufficient proof to proceed against the officer. However all the indications supported the probability that this did occur.

The intelligence picture now suggested that the situation in the prison was such that the line between staff and prisoners had become so blurred that many staff seemed no longer to be acting professionally. The level of conditioning and the Governor's perception of how the prison should run seemed to intensify the confusion in the minds of many staff. HMPS headquarters, the Area Manager and Chaucer Unit now seemed to be the common enemy while prisoners and staff appeared to be united against their perceived opponents.

Throughout the period from April 1999 the DDG was kept fully informed of the ongoing situation at the prison. He received copies of all visits reports and most of the more sensitive correspondence between Area Office and the Governor. The situation was also discussed at our monthly bilateral meetings. Similarly, the DG was kept informed through regular formal bilateral meetings, copied correspondence and briefings. He also visited the prison and on one such unannounced visit early in 2000 was surprised to find that, though there were a substantial number of prisoners lounging around the prison, there were only three in the education department with four teachers. He told me that what he witnessed led him to conclude that prisoners were being indulged and, it seemed, were not being required to do anything which might reduce their criminality.

Martin Narey knew that I had previously had a high regard for the Governor and wanted to avoid damaging his career. It was because of this that so much latitude had been given to him to enable him to get back in line. The situation might have been complicated for me by the fact that Martin had been a friend of Eoin's for some time. However he could clearly see what was happening and knew that it could not continue. In fact we both agreed that in my efforts to protect him I had been too soft on a number of occasions. Martin had already decided that the Governor should move when a suitable vacancy occurred. But as we both considered him an ideal person to head a juvenile unit if the prison was to be re-roled, we felt he should stay there until a decision was made. Once the Minister, Paul Boateng MP, had asked Martin to retain Blantyre House as a resettlement prison, a move for Eoin was back on the agenda in early April.

The intelligence picture at the prison was already very worrying and the added interest of other agencies suggested that the prison might be being used by a small number of professional criminals as a base for drug dealing or worse. The picture became more alarming when during a routine search by an area drug dog team one dog indicated that it had detected the possible presence of drugs in a plastic bag containing a metal box belonging to an identified officer. The box was found to contain syringes. When asked, the officer explained the dog's interest by claiming that the box was used to store illegal drugs that were found in the prison before they were 'destroyed'. There is a strict procedure in HMPS for the handling, processing and disposal of illegal drugs and the procedure described by the officer did not conform to the standard requirement. During that same search a quantity of cannabis was found in another area of the prison. The dog handlers involved in the search were not based at the prison nor under the Governor's control. After the search they reported to the Area Drugs Coordinator that these matters had been referred to the Governor. The former became concerned, in turn, when he learned that the prison had not reported these events on their drug incident returns as required and drew this to my attention. This event and the fact that the officer concerned was closely involved in administering the voluntary drug testing programme at the prison added to the existing unease.

Prisoner A had, by now, been released from prison. However some staff were concerned that he appeared still to have free rein to come into the prison whenever he pleased. This was highly irregular and undesirable whatever the purpose. Ron Gooday of the Chaucer Unit informed me that, when he asked for an explanation, he was told by a manager that he (Prisoner A) came in to play football but some staff at the prison alleged that he seemed to come and go at will, and did not appear to be the subject of searches or have any restrictions placed on his movements inside the prison.

Following the discovery of the 'charity work' debacle described in *Chapter 5* the Governor was ordered to stop all charity work by prisoners with the exception of one prisoner working in a local charity shop. The Smith Report and the internal audit report had both confirmed the undesirability of what had been happening under the guise of charity work. However, in 2000 staff sources at the prison were reporting that the Governor was again allowing prisoners to undertake charity projects, in direct contravention of orders. Charity work now took a different form and involved prisoners being used as labour in exchange for donations to the prison's Mencap fund. Informants told us that some of the work being undertaken was inappropriate. It involved the exploitation of prisoners and there were no controls on the whereabouts of some of those prisoners involved. In reality there was no requirement for the recipients to make any set donation or one reflective of the value of the work done. In one case it was alleged that apples were offered in payment for 'a lot' of manual work done for a private individual on his property. Because I was no longer confident of getting a reliable answer from the Governor to a direct question about what was happening, independent confirmation was sought which eventually confirmed the information.

In late March 2000 Sir David Ramsbotham produced his draft report on the inspection of Blantyre House. The inspection had been led by his deputy. The main body of the report, usually written by the team leader, was highly complimentary of the prison and the courage of the Governor in taking risks to aid the resettlement of 'prisoners with heavy criminal backgrounds'. However it also contained some accurate cautionary comments which were overshadowed by untested accusations of lack of support and destructive interference by the Area Manager and Headquarters with this 'courageous Governor'. The inspectors did not appear to notice the uncanny similarity in the comments made by the Governor, the staff, the prisoners and particularly the ex-prisoners whom they spoke to in separate groups. All majored on the excellent work being done at the prison where prisoners were treated with respect and allowed to decide what they wanted to do, rather than be restrained by a sentence plan which was the norm throughout the service. Each group spoke in remarkably similar terms of the 'lack of support' the Governor received from the Area Manager. Inspectors did not seem to have considered how ex-prisoners, some of whom had been out of prison for up to two years, could be so well rehearsed in matters such as the relationships of senior managers in the service. Staff and prisoners were never party to discussions between the Governor and his superiors but their remarkably similar accounts were given credence.

On a more cautionary note, the draft report also pointed out that the evidence being put forward in support of the success of the prison was anecdotal and needed further research. It also contained a paragraph which covered, in part, some of the concerns felt by senior managers of the service about the prison and included (executive summary, conclusion, p. 12):

> Any risk taking is inevitably vulnerable to being abused by a minority of prisoners eager to take powerful advantage of opportunities to continue their criminality. In these circumstances risk assessments, monitoring of behaviour and further assessment reviews must be as rigorous as possible if confidence in the work of the

establishment is not to be lost. The following area affecting security needed to be examined further:

- Arrangements for selecting prisoners for Blantyre House need to be seen to have integrity and in this the co-operation of Governors of other establishments is essential.

It would seem that this careful form of words was only hinting at what Sir David Ramsbotham was actually thinking in that at a private meeting with the DG at the time, he told him that he believed that some prisoners were buying places at Blantyre House.[1]

However the draft preface to the report by Ramsbotham himself contained an unprecedented personal attack on me. It accused the Area Manager of imposing inappropriate constraints on the Governor and of attempting to destroy the ethos of the prison, implying that I was against resettlement and pursuing my own personal agenda against the prison and the Governor. I and others were shocked and dismayed by the ferocity and inaccuracy of his comments. Prior to writing this draft preface he did not discuss any of these issues with me or seek my views on them. On receipt of the draft the DG wrote to him acknowledging what was generally a good report on the prison. However his letter (dated 18 April 2000) was highly critical of the content of the draft preface, particularly the criticism of the Area Manager, and stated (para 2):

I need to say from the outset that I cannot accept that and I am, frankly, stunned to read it when I took the trouble some months ago to brief you about my concerns about security issues at Blantyre.

The letter went on to respond specifically to the various points raised and to give an accurate account of my involvement, including instigating and leading the early development of a resettlement policy.

Normal etiquette in respect of draft reports restricted their circulation until checked for factual accuracy. Until that process was completed and a publication date agreed they would not normally be circulated in public. It later emerged that the BOV were given sight of the draft report at the same time as the DG. The minutes of their May 2000 meeting show that the Chief Inspector had also sent the Governor a copy of his suggested press release, for issue on the day of publication, a copy of which was also passed to the BOV. Some board members did not like the wording of the last paragraph of the press release and the chair was instructed to write to the Chief Inspector informing him accordingly. The minutes also show that, surprisingly, at that meeting a copy of a letter from the chair of the Home Affairs Committee to Jack Straw, the Home Secretary, was

---

[1] Source: Martin Narey.

circulated. Because of the inaccuracies in the Inspector's draft report, the full report was not published until the end of July.

In mid April I became aware that the DG had written to the Chief Inspector, in confidence, informing him that he intended to move the Governor of Blantyre House 'in the near future'. The DG discussed this with me at that time but no final decision was made as to when or where he would go. However a series of events in fairly quick succession, in addition to what had already occurred, led him, the DG, to focus on an early move.

TIME FOR DECISIVE ACTION

Prisoner C who I mentioned in *Chapters* 5 and 7 and who had been under surveillance by police in relation to suspected drugs offences was released from prison. A short time later he was arrested and charged with possession of a substantial quantity of drugs with intent to supply.

Information, originating from a law enforcement agency, was received by the DG that a Blantyre House prisoner (Prisoner D) was in contact with a known member of a Columbian drugs cartel and was meeting this individual when on temporary release. The presumption was that this prisoner was involved or about to get involved in drug dealing.

The role of the external security officer, introduced earlier, was to monitor the activities of prisoners on outside work placements and to regularly check out these placements. One day in April 2000 he was parked in the car park of Prisoner K's work placement covertly checking on him. He reported that the prisoner approached his car uttering a tirade of abuse and threats against him. It seemed that he had been tipped off about the surveillance by someone but was so self-assured of his power base at the prison that he was confident that he could get away with threatening and intimidating the officer. Following this incident the officer left the scene as he felt that his continued presence would serve no useful purpose. Prisoner K's decision to confront the officer was probably calculated as it is unlikely that he would take such a risk without good reason. In the early evening, shortly after his return to the prison, Prisoner K was reported to have gone to the Governor's office where they had a private meeting. The discussion is alleged to have continued uninterrupted for a number of hours and late into the evening, according to some officers at the prison. This was an unusual occurrence and some staff members were so concerned about the situation that the matter was brought to the attention of Area Office very quickly.

Only the Governor and Prisoner K know the nature of their discussion on that evening and there is no suggestion that it was improper. However this event and the fact that no action was taken against Prisoner K for the incident with the security officer fuelled concerns about the nature of their relationship. An incident of this kind would invariably have resulted in the removal of most other prisoners from the prison.

During an earlier visit of mine to the prison on 15 November 1999 the Governor had been given a very clear order to implement security procedures at the main gate as an interim measure pending the completion of a work re-profiling exercise. He was then required to increase security measures to partially conform to the service's minimum security standards. On my subsequent visits the new procedures appeared to have been implemented. However in April 2000 Area Office was informed that the basic security procedures were not in operation and that the Governor had taken a decision, communicated to some managers, to ignore and disobey the order. Furthermore he had not carried out the re-profiling exercise. This information seemed unbelievable and members of the area team visiting the prison were asked to check it out. The accuracy of the intelligence was quickly verified.

One of my specialists visiting the prison was the Area Performance Coordinator. His role was to audit the compliance of each prison with Prison Service operating and security standards and to assist Governors to raise standards where necessary. Following a visit he reported some concerns about the management of temporary release procedures. He was instructed to carry out a more detailed audit and report his findings in writing. His report, dated 26 April 2000, highlighted a serious breakdown in the temporary release procedures and concluded that the manner in which decisions to grant temporary release were made ignored mandatory safeguards incorporated in the service's national policy. He also found that as a consequence of this lack of adequate controls prisoners were being released for reasons that fell outside nationally prescribed criteria. His report seemed to indicate that the temporary release situation had reverted to that which existed prior to the Smith Audit in 1998 and seemed to be further evidence that the requirements of the corrective action plan agreed with the Governor were now being allowed to slide back.

During a bilateral meeting with Martin Narey on April 28 the situation at the prison was discussed and he decided that the Governor should be moved without delay. I agreed with that decision. To facilitate the immediate appointment of a new Governor it was desirable if possible to arrange a direct exchange with a suitable individual in an existing position appropriate to Eoin's needs. During his last annual performance appraisal I had talked to the Governor about the possibility of him moving to a position as deputy to a more senior Governor. I felt he would gain valuable experience in such a position and would have the benefit of a knowledgeable mentor. Eoin was not in favour of this at the time but we had to consider it as a possibility. The situation had now changed and there were few alternative options that gave him a better opportunity to re-establish his credibility as a Governor. Though we had differences over his management of Blantyre House, his decision to apply for the position of Governor of Dover YOI in the autumn of 1999, which I also managed, indicated that he was content to continue to work with me. He was not however successful in getting that appointment.

I told the DG that I would be content to retain him within my area as I felt that he had potential and with the help of an experienced senior Governor that potential could be developed. After discussing the options, Martin Narey agreed that he should move to Swaleside Prison as Deputy Governor and Chris Bartlett should move from that position to become Governor of Blantyre House. The Deputy Governor position at Swaleside was at the same grade as the Blantyre House Governor post. All Governors and Prison Officers are mobile grades and can be moved to meet the operational needs of the service. Normally positions are advertised and moves take place on a voluntary basis but occasionally the DG exercises his right to direct a move for operational reasons. This was such a case. However Chris Bartlett was on leave in the USA and it was not possible to inform him until his return early the following week.

The situation at the prison and the intelligence picture that continued to emerge could not be ignored. The new Governor would address many of the procedural problems but the culture that had now developed was likely to be more problematic and the new Governor would need more support at senior management level to restore a professional perspective. A new Deputy Governor had recently been appointed, on the retirement of Brian Hales, and it was felt that he could be relied upon to play his part. The third in charge, Dave Newport, had been there for a number of years and had already displayed some resistance to change. His background in the service was as a tradesman and he had risen to managerial level in that specialist area. As the Manager of Works Services for the three prisons on the Isle of Sheppey was ill and likely to be away for some time, it was decided to deploy Dave to manage this essential service until he retired.

As related earlier, a worrying feature of the intelligence picture was the latitude afforded to certain career criminals and the extent of some of their suspected involvement in criminal activity in the community, particularly relating to drugs. Some intelligence also led us to suspect that the prison might be being used as a base for such activities. The failure to maintain even the most basic security procedures would have allowed prisoners to move contraband in and out of the prison at will without fear of detection. The culture was now such that we did not know what was going on in the prison and we could not rely on many of the staff for an accurate evaluation. What evidence we had led us to the belief that the prison might now be essentially in the hands of prisoners and some corrupt staff. We knew that a small number of the career criminal group enjoyed substantial wealth and might have used it to buy their place at the prison. They knew that the degree of latitude they enjoyed would be greatly curtailed if the Governor was moved and some of them would have real fears about being moved back to secure conditions. Therefore there was a real possibility that if they became aware of the Governor's departure some might well abscond.

To enable us to take control of the prison and check out what was happening without prior warning of the Governor's departure and to ensure that the public were protected from all possible consequences, it was decided that the process needed to be carefully handled. Though neither the DG nor I wished to deviate from the norm in the way the Governor's move was to be managed, surprise was essential. Consequently it was agreed that the handover of control had to be immediate and without prior notice to anyone at the prison. It was also agreed that a full general search of the prison should be carried out as soon as possible after the change of Governor had taken place. As such a search would require a substantial number of staff and strict secrecy, it was obvious that no Blantyre House staff could be involved. It would also need careful planning by an experienced commander.

By the end of our meeting on April 28 the DG confirmed that the Governor was to be moved to Swaleside Prison as Deputy Governor and that Chris Bartlett would be appointed Governor of Blantyre House. The change would take effect on the afternoon of May 5 and later that evening, when all prisoners were back in the prison, a full general search would be carried out. The Director of Personnel was instructed to prepare posting notices for both Governors which were to be served by me at the agreed times. As Operational Manager for the area it was my responsibility to set up and oversee the whole operation. Though I had a week to make all the arrangements, organization was complicated by the fact that a bank holiday weekend fell in between.

Operation Swynford takes shape

Because of the sensitivity of the intelligence and the fact that whoever was to command the operation would have to receive a detailed briefing, I decided to appoint John Podmore as Operational Commander. John was the Governor of Swaleside Prison and one of my most senior Governors. He was also in overall charge of the Chaucer Unit and was already fully aware of all the intelligence issues. His appointment would avoid the need to expand the intelligence loop further. John was an able and experienced man with considerable standing in the service. He had just been informed that he had been selected by the Chief Inspector of Prisons, Sir David Ramsbotham, to become one of his inspection team leaders and would move to that position within a short time. However even without these obvious advantages I would still have appointed him as I considered him the best commander for this operation.

HM Prison Service operates an incident command structure similar to that of the police. All serious or large operations on the ground are led by a Silver Commander. Silver is supported by a series of Bronze Commanders, each taking charge of specific elements of the operation. If the incident involves a hostage situation, concerted indiscipline or a serious loss of control a Gold Commander based at headquarters would take overall responsibility and would advise and support the Silver Commander in resolving the problem. Gold Commanders were invariably Area Managers at Assistant Director level. A Silver Commander was normally the Governor in charge of the prison at the time of the incident.

Bronze Commanders could be in any grade but were subordinate to Silver for the duration of the incident. A search of the scale we envisaged would normally be led by a Silver Commander. Though the duty Gold Commander would be alerted to the event, he or she would not get involved unless there was prisoner disruption or a loss of control. Even then, a request for the Gold Command suite to be opened would normally come from the Area Manager with operational responsibility for the prison

John Podmore was tasked and fully briefed on the Saturday of the bank holiday weekend. Because of the need for secrecy, organizing an operation of this scale would not be easy but he was both reliable and discreet. He was also aware that he could call on the services of any other Governor in the area to assist if required. We agreed to talk again on the Tuesday morning to review and evaluate the outline plan. By the end of our conversation John had begun the process of planning the search operation, which was codenamed Operation Swynford to protect its secrecy and maintain the element of surprise. We knew that if the surprise element were compromised the search would be a waste of time and resources. We were also aware of the predictable speculation that would follow the initial stages of putting the team together and the possibility of leaks. To counter this all staff initially involved in the planning process and Bronze Commanders designate were informed of the need for strict secrecy but with an underlying hint that the target prison was to be Stanford Hill. Blantyre House was not mentioned at any stage.

By Tuesday mid-day an outline plan had been drawn up and detailed preparations had begun. As was the norm in a search of this kind, the assistance of the Specialist National Dog Search Unit was requested and granted. A full briefing meeting involving the senior managers who would participate was called for Thursday afternoon, May 4, at Rochester Prison. Chris Bartlett, who had just returned to duty following a period of leave in the USA, was also told to attend. Prior to the start of the meeting I spoke with him in private and informed him that he was to be appointed Governor. He was fully briefed on the background and the purpose of the meeting that was to follow. During this discussion it was made clear that, for procedural purposes, he should formally request the search. He fully understood and agreed.

The meeting was attended by John Podmore, Brian Pollett (Governor of Elmley prison), Chris Bartlett, Geoff Cooke (Area Drugs Coordinator), representatives of the Chaucer Unit and myself. John Podmore gave a comprehensive briefing on the planned operation to be carried out the following day and the roles to be played by those attending. Bronze Commanders would be briefed the following day and a full briefing of staff involved would occur immediately before the operation began.

The main aim of the operation was to carry out a general search of the residential accommodation, ancillary buildings and the prisoners and to carry out a broad screen drug test of all prisoners on the premises at that time. Our objective was to achieve these aims in as low a key as possible in an attempt to avoid confrontation with prisoners. Brian Pollett was a former Governor of the prison and had good local knowledge. He, together with Alan Shipton, a very experienced former junior governor at the prison, would act as consultants in drawing up the searching strategy and would advise the control and restraint co-coordinator during the initial securing of residential units. The new Governor, Chris Bartlett, would be the regime coordinator. He would be responsible for securing the main gate and the communications system, deploying local staff, carrying out a roll check, maintaining contact with prisoners within the prison throughout the operation and managing the transition back to the normal regime.

Though the aim was to avoid confrontation, an operation of this kind had to make provision for the possibility of an adverse prisoner reaction. There was no secure accommodation at Blantyre House and prisoners could not be locked in their rooms. Sufficient resources had to be available to contain any disruption should it occur. We also needed a secure facility to hold any prisoners who might be tempted to engage in such activity. The general consensus at the meeting was that the search could be completed without major difficulty but in view of the nature of some of the prisoners we could not be certain. It was therefore essential that the contingency plan covered all possibilities. By the end of the meeting the operational plan was agreed and the Silver Commander went away to prepare individual role briefs for his Bronze Commanders and a full brief for all participants. Arrangements were also made for the availability of two secure cellular vehicles to be located outside the prison should they be required. Operation Swynford was now on the starting blocks and the DG was advised accordingly. Martin Narey briefed the Minister in writing a few days prior to the operation and on the afternoon of May 5 Paul Boateng MP phoned Martin offering his full support for the very necessary action we were about to take.

CHAPTER 8

Operation Swynford

At the beginning of April 2000 my area of responsibility was extended to include the five prisons in Surrey and Sussex. With the exception of Coldingly Prison, a well managed, purpose built industrial prison, the performance of the other four fell below acceptable standards. Highdown Prison is a high security local prison designed to hold Category A (high risk) prisoners. Because of its unsatisfactory performance the DDG had been forced to withdraw all category A prisoners from the prison. Similarly Lewes and Downview Prisons were failing to achieve HMPS operating and security standards and were not achieving their own business plan targets in many areas. The large open prison at Ford appeared at first glance to be less problematic than the others but still had considerable room for improvement. My brief on taking charge of the now extended area was to 'sort them out', with raising the performance of Highdown a top priority.

This was a difficult brief that would be demanding of my time. If I was to succeed I needed to spend time in these prisons to identify their performance inhibitors and develop a strategy for corrective action. I also needed to get to know the strengths and weaknesses of their management teams, to assess their ability to deliver the necessary changes. The situation at Blantyre House was taking up a disproportionate amount of my time having regard to its size and the nature of its role in the system. It was against this backdrop that Operation Swynford was played out.

On the morning of May 5, which was to be the crucial day of Operation Swynford, the Area Manager's quarterly meeting with the chairs of each of the BOVs in the area was held in the training unit located just outside the perimeter of Blantyre House. David Cottle, the chair of the Blantyre board attended what was an unremarkable routine meeting followed by a buffet lunch. Though I had good relationships with all the other BOVs in the Area, he was the only member of the Blantyre House board with whom I had any real contact at that time. I have no recollection of ever meeting many of its members and of those that I had, the contact was fleeting. I did not know them as people and they certainly did not know me. Even my contact with David was somewhat limited and occurred mostly at these meetings as he often represented the Blantyre board before his election to the chair.

David was a quietly spoken, polite man who was genuinely interested in the work of the prison. He was not a prolific contributor to meetings but he frequently raised issues with me on a one-to-one basis during the post-meeting lunches. He impressed me as a thoroughly decent man who often seemed reticent in committing himself in case he incurred the disapproval of some of the more dominant or overconfident members of his board.

We talked over lunch on May 5. David Cottle was clearly aware that there were problems relating to the management of the prison and we discussed some issues. During that discussion I did indicate that I might need to talk to him later in the day.

CHANGE OF POWER

After lunch I went into the prison to speak to the Governor and inform him that he was being moved to Swaleside Prison. Though I felt that he had been responsible for his own downfall I still found this mission deeply distressing. In spite of all that had happened I liked Eoin and was genuinely concerned for his future. He came out of a meeting to speak to me and was visibly nervous even before we began to talk. When told of his move and the fact that it was effective that afternoon he was understandably annoyed and demanded an explanation. However it was clear from his comments that a transfer was not entirely unexpected even if the speed of it was.

Chris Bartlett arrived at the prison later in the afternoon and the handover procedures began. I talked to David Cottle by telephone and informed him of the change of Governor. Eoin was not scheduled to report to Swaleside for at least ten days and it was agreed that the handover would continue the following week with the new Governor already installed. Having had it made clear to him that he now had no jurisdiction at the prison, he cleared his desk and continued with the handover before leaving the prison in the early evening.

Obviously if the new Governor was to have a realistic chance of restoring the situation at the prison he needed the support of loyal managers. The Deputy Governor was relatively new and could be relied upon. I also met with Dave Newport that afternoon and told him that he would be moved on detached duty to cover the temporary absence of a senior manager in the Sheppey Works cluster unit. He seemed quite happy. His transfer had immediate effect and it was also made clear that he was no longer employed at the prison. He was replaced that afternoon by Steve Spratling, an able and widely experienced manager with a proven track record.

The most senior member of the uniformed grades had also been at the prison for a number of years. He was the fourth most senior manager and had been a loyal supporter of the Governor. Though he was committed to the ethos of the prison the available information indicated that he had not fallen victim to the conditioning process and would remain a valuable manager for the new Governor. He therefore stayed in his job.

The new management team was now installed and fully briefed. The brief given to the new Governor, in writing, was to comply with HMPS instructions in delivering the requirements of the prison's business plan, already agreed and signed by the outgoing Governor and to ensure that all the recommendations of the 1998 Smith report were implemented. He was also told that Blantyre House would continue as a resettlement prison and that great care should to be taken in introducing changes to preserve its general ethos.

The immediate need was to create an atmosphere of normality and avoid compromising the search that was to follow. Some staff on duty became aware that the Governor had been moved and the news was spreading to the prisoners within the prison. However by this time most of the prisoners on outside work projects had begun to return. There was no indication that plans for the forthcoming search leaked but some of the more sophisticated career criminals would have considered it a possibility even if they were not tipped off.

I left Blantyre House in the early evening and travelled to Swaleside Prison. During that afternoon John Podmore had completed the final planning for the search and briefed all his Bronze Commanders, each of them receiving written role briefs. He would give a general briefing to all staff involved later and they in turn would receive detailed briefings from their respective Bronze Commanders.

CAREFUL PREPARATIONS FOR THE SEARCH

Large searches of this kind were not unusual in HMPS and most of those participating would have been involved in one in the past. This search differed only because it immediately followed the departure of the Governor and did not involve any of the uniformed staff at the prison. However the new senior managers of the prison were involved. This was a general search, not targeted at finding any specific item, as the objective was to get an evidence based snapshot of some key aspects of what had been happening in the prison.

From the initial planning stage we had agreed that the search should be conducted in a non-aggressive but firm manner avoiding confrontation with prisoners. With this in mind John appointed Principal Officer Lisa Rose as Search Team Bronze Commander. Her role was to develop a searching strategy consistent with the overall objectives of the operation, brief and deploy staff to conduct the search and supervise them. Lisa was a highly respected young woman and a very capable operational manager who was the Security Principal Officer at Swaleside Prison. Her good interpersonal skills and calming yet firm approach to both prisoners and her staff were also factors in her selection.

Fifteen prison officers were allocated as searchers under the command of the Search Bronze and would operate in teams in the residential units. They would be supported by the ten members of the National Dog Team with their specialist search dogs, who would primarily be involved in searching the many non-residential buildings and the extensive grounds. These included a football pitch and a secured annex to the prison which consisted of a large field and a horticultural unit to which prisoners had access during daylight hours. The dog team included specialist drugs and explosive dogs that would assist in the residential area search.

Though the intention and hope was that the search could be completed without incident it would have been irresponsible to embark on such an operation without a strategy to deal with any disruption, should it occur. The search was going to involve up to 120 prisoners most of whom had long criminal records, many with a history of violence. Some resistance could therefore not be ruled out but should it occur it was unlikely that all the prisoners would get involved. Therefore the Silver Commander rightly included two Control and Restraint (C and R) units in the team to carry out the operation. These units consisted of 28 officers and two unit commanders.

All prison officers are trained in C and R techniques which are designed to restrain a violent individual without causing injury, using three officers. Another aspect of C and R includes the control and containment of groups of prisoners engaged in disruptive activity. In these situations officers are deployed in units of 14 with one unit commander. Where more than one unit is deployed unit commanders come under the direct command of a Bronze Commander. These units operate in protective clothing.

The two units deployed in this operation would initially be tasked to secure the residential units immediately on entry and maintain them secure throughout the operation. As already intimated, the prison had no cellular accommodation; prisoners held the keys to their own rooms and could move around at will. There were seven exit doors in the residential building that had to be secured. These officers would not be directly involved with the prisoners unless there was any disruption and would mostly be deployed outside the building.

Including the search teams, the National Dog Team, the two C and R units and their commanders, there were 84 staff involved in the operation. These included the Area Drugs Coordinator, six specialist drug testers, the Area Healthcare Adviser, three members of the Chaucer Unit, two search strategy advisers, the new Governor, one of his senior managers, the Silver Commander and his three command room staff. This figure also included the drivers and assistants on the two secure cellular vans on standby outside the prison and a cook to provide refreshments for staff.

The National Duty Gold Commander was advised of the operation early in the day. It was agreed that the Gold Command suite did not need to be opened unless there was serious disorder. I would accompany the Silver Commander as an observer at the beginning of the operation and would decide, on the basis of prisoner reaction, whether the Gold Command Suite needed to be opened.

All the officers involved in the operation were assembled at around 19.00 hours at Swaleside Prison. There they were addressed by the Silver Commander who gave them a general briefing on the operation and what was expected of them. Not until then did they know that the search would be at Blantyre House. As anticipated, rumours had circulated that Stanford Hill was the target prison.

During his briefing John Podmore made clear that this was a general search and that he wanted to complete it avoiding confrontation with prisoners. He instructed officers to be polite but firm in carrying out their designated tasks. Before finishing he invited me to make any additional comments I considered necessary

I again emphasised the need to avoid confrontation and for officers to act professionally at all times. Their attention was drawn to the fact that this was a resettlement prison holding long term prisoners, some of whom could be difficult but who were now accustomed to a greater degree of autonomy and lower levels of control. I pointed out to all involved that the new Governor would be available on the ground and he should be consulted on all matters of local policy. Following my short contribution officers joined their respective sections and received detailed role briefs from their individual Bronze Commanders.

The detachment left Swaleside at 20.00 hours *en route* to Blantyre House. They arrived at the staging point adjacent to but out of sight of the prison at 21.10 hours. The new Governor entered the main gate and took control of that and the prison's internal communications system immediately before the main detachment entered at 21.20 hours. They could be seen entering the prison from the windows of the prisoners' rooms.

THE SEARCH BEGINS

There was no resistance offered but officers reported a lot of toilet flushing by prisoners. Before the search could begin all prisoners had to be returned to their rooms, and counted. There were no toilets in the rooms and as the search was likely to take some time prisoners were allowed to use the toilets and take water to their rooms. This unfortunately provided them with the chance to flush drugs and other smaller items of contraband down the toilets before the search could begin. There is little doubt that some exploited this opportunity. A combination of factors including the insecure nature of the accommodation and the need to avoid an adverse prisoner reaction contributed to this situation. Of course it could have been avoided if we had deployed a much larger contingent of officers to take control more aggressively, risking a violent prisoner reaction. Given that this was a general search primarily concerned with checking out what was happening in the prison, such a heavy handed approach would be disproportionate in the circumstances.

The roll count was completed and all prisoners were in their rooms at 21.32 hours. Two prisoners had still not returned to the prison but were expected at 22.00 hours and 23.00 hours respectively. At 21.35 hours the prison was reported to be 'calm' and there were no incidents reported. At 21.39 hours the situation was under control and the Silver Commander ordered C and R units and the dog teams to withdraw into the grounds. At the same time search teams were deployed to begin their work. Specialist drug and explosive search dogs joined the search at 22.00 hours. At around this time officers in the grounds reported that some prisoners were throwing items out of their room windows.

After the search started the Governor made an unsuccessful attempt to contact the chair of the BOV. He eventually contacted another member, Dr Brian Hugo, who arrived at the prison a short time later accompanied by the chair. The new Governor and Brian Pollett, a senior Governor and a former Governor of Blantyre House were on the ground in the prison. Brian met with and accompanied the board members observing the search. The situation remained calm and no incidents were reported.

Shortly after the search started the Area Drugs Coordinator and his six specialist drug testers began to take and test urine samples from each prisoner. HMPS is empowered to carry out compulsory drug testing. This is normally done on a random basis but where there is reasonable suspicion they can be targeted at any individual. A majority of the prison population have been either regular drug abusers in the community or involved to some degree in the drugs culture. Many try to continue this lifestyle in prison.

Extensive drug treatment programmes are available to prisoners, who can earn additional privileges by participating or joining dedicated drug free regimes. In most cases access is conditional on agreeing to voluntary drug testing. Almost all the prisoners at Blantyre House were on a voluntary test programme and testing was carried out on that basis. Because of this any prisoner testing positive could not be charged under the disciplinary system. The decision to carry out the tests was made to validate the integrity of earlier test results brought into question by an incident during an earlier drug dog search. As most of the prisoners at Blantyre House with connections to the drug culture were suppliers rather than consumers we did not expect many positive tests, even though drugs were frequently found during earlier searches.

The searching of prisoners and their rooms was much more time consuming than had been expected based on the norm for this type of search at other prisons. This was primarily because of the amount of property in their rooms. Because of the slowness some prisoners frequently requested access to the toilets, where they could also obtain water. The search had been expected to finish in the early hours of the morning but this was now looking unlikely. As the prison was quiet and the search progressing in a good atmosphere, the Silver Commander redeployed some of the C and R officers out of 'riot gear' to searching duties. The National Dog Team together with a small number of officers were deployed to search communal areas, the grounds and prisoners' cars.

Geoff Cooke, the Area Drugs Coordinator in charge of the drug testing, expressed concern that some prisoners still to be tested appeared to be consuming large amounts of water and making regular trips to the toilet. He was worried that at least some of them were 'flushing', a practice that I had not been aware of prior to that night. Normally prisoners being drug tested would have no opportunity to do this and would remain under close supervision from the moment they became aware of the test. He explained that the residue of cannabis remains in the body for about a month and is detectable by the dip test that was being administered. However traces of cocaine, amphetamines, benzodiazepines and opiates are only detectable for about three days. As these are water based drugs excessive consumption of water followed by urinating can flush them out of the system much quicker. The excessive consumption of water in a short period of time can also alter the normal constituents of urine sufficiently to falsify a test result. Because of this a separate dilution test was carried out on some samples.

In the early hours of the morning of May 6 Geoff Cook informed the Silver Commander that one prisoner had tested positive with a diluted sample. He was told to test the prisoner again after one hour. When re-tested the result was negative. Why the original sample was diluted is not known for certain. Though it was suspicious, there was no proof that the prisoner flushed out his system in an effort to falsify the test result, but it is possible that he did.

The presence of this fairly large group of officers provided a much higher level of control than was the norm at the prison and gave the new Governor a unique opportunity to take stock of the character of some of the prisoners and recent intelligence relating to them. He met with the Chaucer officers on the scene and received a full intelligence briefing on a number of prisoners and staff. Five prisoners were specifically targeted from the briefing. The Governor took two-and-a-half-hours to digest the information before deciding to transfer three of the prisoners to more secure conditions. The remaining two would stay at the prison. In view of the intelligence his decision not to move all of them was surprising. Following their eventual release one of those retained was quickly in custody again convicted of a serious criminal offence.

Around 00.30 hours on May 6 both members of the BOV left the prison and went home. One of them would later claim that they were encouraged to leave by a senior Governor. This is denied by the Governor allegedly concerned who, as they would have known, was not empowered to tell them to leave and the claim is not supported by the other Board member in attendance. During the time they were inside the prison they acknowledged that the search was being conducted professionally by staff and that the prison was quiet. It is probable that they left because events appeared to be under control. There is no obligation on a board member to stay for the duration of an incident as their participation is always on a voluntary basis and they have no executive role other than as an observer.

During the search of the non-residential areas prison officers were unable to gain access to some areas because doors were locked. In most cases keys were obtained from the key safe at the gate. However the keys to some areas could not be located by the prison's Night Orderly Officer or the officer on duty at the gate. I was present in the Command Suite when senior staff supervising the search informed the Silver Commander that the keys could not be located. All keys in use in prisons are required to be deposited in a key safe, normally located at the gate, when not in use or when the holder is going off duty or leaving the prison, even for a short time. No member of staff in any prison, including the Governor, is permitted to take keys out of a prison. The unavailability of the keys was inhibiting the search and the Silver Commander instructed searchers in a number of cases to force entry. The new Governor was aware of and in accord with the action being taken.

Following the search much was made of the damage caused to doors from forced entry by partisan supporters of the former Governor. They accused searchers of wanton destruction and the Silver Commander of lying about the unavailability of keys. None of these people was present at the time but I and a number of other reputable senior managers were. The Blantyre House staff on duty could not produce the keys and there was a suggestion that the missing keys had probably been taken home by their regular holders. That was speculation, but the keys could not be found and the Silver Commander acted correctly.

In the aftermath of the events of 5 and 6 May 2000 most of those who held keys to these areas vehemently denied taking them out of the prison and insisted that they had been in the safe. A suggestion that a nonchalant approach to the control of keys had developed at the prison was vigorously rejected. Though their protestations were eagerly accepted by at least some members of the Home Affairs Select Committee (HAC), the Chief Inspector of Prisons and some elements of the media, the reality was that their keys could not be found and if they had not been removed from the prison, where were they? In the weeks following the search a number of incidents of keys being taken home by individuals were reported by the new Governor. The casual approach of some middle managers in dealing with these events seemed to suggest that the security of keys was not a high priority to them.

At 01.35 hours the Governor and the Silver Commander met in the command suite to decide the level of the regime that would be provided the following morning. The Governor decided that no prisoners would be permitted to leave the prison but otherwise a normal regime would be delivered. Steve Spratling would be in charge of the prison and he was sent off duty to get some rest.

As the prison remained quiet and the search was proceeding without incident I briefed the duty Gold Commander in London and left the prison. However a log of the whole operation was kept and it shows that five prisoners were removed from the prison and transferred to Elmley prison. Three of these were removed on the instructions of the Governor. One was the career criminal Prisoner K. Of the other two, one was transferred out pending investigation of documents found in his possession.

John Podmore left the command room at 02.53 hours handing temporary command to his assistant Governor, Guy Baulf. He walked around the prison observing the search and talking to staff and prisoners for over an hour before returning to the command room at 04.07 hours to take charge again. During that period he inspected areas where entry had to be forced and was content that the damage done was reasonable in the circumstances and that officers were carrying out their duties in a professional manner.

The National Dog Team reported that they had completed their search of the non-residential and grounds areas at 04.18 hours. Due to the lack of adequate lighting in the grounds their task had been particularly difficult and large areas were searched by dogs and their handlers using torches. It later emerged that the secure annex to the prison had not been searched as the area was locked secure and the dog team were not aware that prisoners had access to it during the day.

The search was completed at 05.00 hours. It was followed by a 'hot' debrief led by the Silver Commander. When this was completed all staff involved stood down. The prison was quiet and most prisoners were asleep. In view of this the Commander reasoned that disruption of any kind was unlikely. The prisons Night Orderly Officer again took charge of the prison and an additional Senior Officer and two prison officers from the search detachment were also in support until the day staff came on duty at 07.45 hours. The Orderly Officer for the day was briefed and the duty Governor, who had been involved in the search until after midnight, came on duty at 08.40 hours. In addition to the normal staffing levels, a contingent of C and R trained staff were on stand-by available to the Governor over the weekend and until he was satisfied that they could be safely stood down. They were not needed.

The search Commander was later criticised by individuals who were not involved and who had considerably less experience than him for not arranging a formal handover and briefing for the Blantyre House staff. The Orderly Officer, who is in charge of the prison, was on duty throughout the search and was fully briefed. The prison was quiet throughout the night and most prisoners were asleep. The Duty Governor coming on duty was fully aware of events, having been involved in them for a number of hours and would receive an updated briefing by telephone on his arrival at the prison. The Silver Commander made a decision based on the situation at the prison and took account of the impact of events on the availability of staff to deliver the regimes of their own prisons on May 6. I do not question his judgment on this matter.

The reported behaviour of prisoners at the start of Operation Swinford suggests that a substantial amount of illicit items were flushed down the toilets. It is probable that significant amounts were drugs. Despite that, the operation made 98 finds of illicit items, the most significant of which included (see also the photographs at pp. 202-3):

- cash to the value of £370.63 of which the biggest find was £120.00;
- 12 cameras;
- 25 incidents of bank cards, including credit cards, bank and cheque books;

- seven mobile phones found in the 15 privately owned prisoners' cars and the five vehicles owned by various employers;
- three mobile phones dumped in waste bins in the residential area. The sim card of one of these phones was missing;
- a quantity of ecstasy tablets and three separate small quantities of cannabis;
- a quantity of hard core pornography;
- a builder's tool kit found in a prisoner's room that contained a full range of tools and which in other prisons would be viewed as an escape kit;
- a quantity of screwdrivers and knives etc.;
- two computer organizers and two televisions;
- a computer tool kit;
- a complete professional tattoo kit;
- a passport;
- various knives (eight in total); and
- four unfitted car radios found in prisoners' vehicles, two of which were found in the boot of a prisoner's car. The remainder were each found in prisoners' cars, one hidden under a seat.

None of the items found should have been allowed to come into the prison even if a small number of prisoners might have been permitted to use mobile phones or tools in connection with their work outside the prison. In most cases the items should have been left at their place of work or stored in secure lockers provided at the gate. Many of the items found were not or should not have been permitted, even outside the prison. About half the prisoners were not security cleared to leave and some of the items found, particularly the tool box, constituted a serious risk to the security of the prison.

The mobile phones found in prisoners' cars could obviously be linked directly to individuals and surprisingly more than one could be linked to the same individual. The three found in the prison had been dropped into rubbish bins, presumably at the start of the search, and could not be linked to any individual prisoner but it would be ludicrous to suggest that they did not belong to prisoners. In one case, it seemed that care had been taken to remove and dispose of the sim card. The phones were passed to Kent Constabulary who checked their sim card histories. The call logs on most of them recorded fairly routine use but one of the phones found in the bins showed that the user had been in regular contact with criminals well known to the police. The phone with the missing sim card was believed to have been dropped by a known career criminal and a Chaucer intelligence target. The sim had clearly been disposed of to destroy incriminating evidence.

The extent to which a professional staff perspective had been lost was highlighted on the morning immediately following the search. The duty Governor, Steve Spratling, who had joined the new management team the previous day, arrived for duty at 08.45 hours. He found Dave Newport in the prison. Dave no longer worked there and so far as Steve and I were concerned, had no business being there.

Steve later described how the Orderly Officer of the day, a Senior Officer in whom Chaucer had an interest, confronted him protesting bitterly about the state in which the Health Care Centre had been left. His behaviour was a particular surprise to the duty Governor who described it as unprofessional and resembling that of an irate prisoner rather than a Senior Officer. They both went to the centre where the Governor noted that some doors had been forced open He saw water and some debris in one area. The Senior Officer was claiming that the water was urine and that the search staff or their dogs were responsible. Steve later stated that he found no evidence to suggest that the liquid was urine and there was no smell. Neither was there any evidence to support the allegation that the searchers were responsible for anything other than the forced entry which was done on the orders of the Operational Commander.

In Steve's view many staff seemed to be acting in concert with prisoners and their behaviour could not be distinguished. Many staff seemed angry that the prison and the prisoners had been searched. Much was made of the damage done during the search by local staff, some members of the BOV and others after the event. In a normal prison situation staff would isolate these areas until they were repaired. Because the search staff did not have an opportunity to re-inspect the damaged areas before they were repaired there remains a suspicion that the damage was exacerbated after the search. Dr Brian Hugo's account of his visit to the prison later that morning and the enthusiasm of some prisoners for him to inspect the damage to the chapel door may lend some credence to this suspicion.

It became clear from an early stage after the search that we had underestimated the extent to which staff, at all levels, had become conditioned and the degree to which their professionalism had been eroded. We knew that some members of the BOV identified strongly with the former Governor but we were particularly surprised at the extent to which some of them appeared to be trying to undermine the efforts of the new Governor and to misrepresent the facts in general.

The new Governor had been given a clear instruction from the start that Blantyre House would continue to function as a resettlement prison and that the general ethos must be preserved. The staff and the BOV were aware of this but many continued to work against him. Middle management grades who should have been actively supporting him and giving leadership on the ground were doing the opposite. The Principal Officer, who was the senior uniformed grade, was considered to be reliable but within days that reliability came into question when Prisoner K telephoned the prison from Elmley. All telephone conversations from high security prisons are recorded. Prisoner K asked for and was put through to a named senior officer. He told that officer to get his illegally held credit card from a locker and other items from another prisoner and pass them to his brother, thereby removing evidence against him. During the conversation

Prisoner K was told that the Principal Officer was present and he asked to speak to him. He made no secret of the purpose of the call and the response was friendly and supportive. There is no record that either officer reported this matter to the Governor and as the credit card was not recovered it seems reasonable to assume that the prisoner's instructions were obeyed. Prisoner K's call to the senior officer and its content seemed to confirm earlier intelligence. Because they lacked recent experience of high security prisons these officers were probably not aware that their conversation was being recorded. As our primary objective at the time was to monitor communications and gather intelligence, no action was taken to avoid alerting targets.

A short time after his arrival the new Governor introduced the search procedures agreed in the prison's searching strategy which the former Governor had failed to implement. Initially all prisoners returning from outside activities were given a 'rubdown' search and a small percentage randomly strip searched. Steve Spratling was the senior manager tasked with implementing these changes. He later recorded a description of an event which seemed to highlight the extent to which a professional perspective had been lost by officers.

> I was confronted by another Senior Officer, Mr Golding, who accused me of destroying the trust upon which Blantyre existed. I explained to him that whilst I was committed to preserving the resettlement ethos of the prison, it was necessary to re-establish certain basic security precautions and that these procedures were common to all prisons including open prisons. The reaction I got was worrying in that he argued that prisoners should not be searched as they could easily throw contraband over the fence if they wanted to get it in.
>
> I countered his views by stating that the proposed procedures were common in all prisons and that searching should be seen as insurance for all who lived and worked in the prison. I added that prisoners were aware that they were not searched and as such could freely walk into the prison carrying contraband under our noses, which could never be an acceptable situation for any prison.
>
> What was bizarre about the exchange of views was that when I asked Mr Golding if he trusted me he replied that he did not. I then asked him if he trusted the prisoners that had recently arrived from Maidstone Prison and were not known to him, to which he replied that he did because Blantyre House worked on trust. My concern was not so much that he did not trust me (I accepted that the circumstances of my arrival were still raw in his mind), but that a culture existed that even new arrivals were given unconditional trust even though they were unknown quantities just beginning a six month assessment period.

The accuracy of intelligence relating to the situation at the prison that led to the removal of the Governor and the search was being confirmed by events. However we had underestimated the extent to which the professionalism of some staff had been eroded and the degree to which basic control elements had been allowed to slide. In fact new managers were reporting that some staff even objected to Blantyre House being referred to as a prison. It was becoming clear that the new Governor and his senior team would have their work cut out to achieve even the most basic changes to procedures to tighten controls and they would need considerable support to restore the professional perspective of many staff.

The events immediately following Operation Swynford were extraordinary to say the least and a warning of how easily the political system is at risk of manipulation (some people might even say subversion) in pursuit of a given ends. The actions of the former Governor were perhaps understandable given his strong belief, however misguided, that what he was doing was right. However the role played by some members of the BOV is more difficult to comprehend, as are to my mind some statements by the Chief Inspector of Prisons. The net effect of misleading, poorly informed, incorrect and frequently second or third hand information served only to inflame a situation in which HMPS was acting in the only proper manner if the risk of a public outcry and of severe censure on other fronts was to be averted. Everything was a matter of balance, careful consideration and professionalism by all concerned. For our pains we were now being made to look like the bad guys.

The search of Blantyre House was but one of a number of large scale searches carried out by HMPS at various prisons over a number of years. The removal of the Governor at short notice by the DG, though unusual, was also not unprecedented. Prior to this operation, similar events had failed to attract media interest unless there had been a serious disturbance, and I have no recollection of the Home Affairs Select Committee getting involved in the aftermath of either the transfer of a Governor or a search. All this was to change.

CHAPTER 9

Aftermath

A review of the search operation, the most recent intelligence and the reports of the HMPS Area Performance Coordinator was carried out by the Area Manager's team on the Monday morning immediately following the search of Blantyre House. What emerged pointed to a recurrence of problems identified two years earlier in the Smith Report of 1998. If this was accurate then we needed to know the extent of these problems and to develop a corrective action plan in conjunction with the new Governor. Brian Pollett was one of my most senior Governors in the area and, as a former Governor of Blantyre House, had a good knowledge of the prison and its operational nuances. Because of this I tasked him to lead an investigation into the management of the prison.

The terms of reference were broadly based and included a requirement to examine all aspects of temporary release procedures, the use by prisoners of motor vehicles and mobile phones, the selection procedure for allocation to the prison and whether prisoners there had identifiable resettlement needs. They also included the arrangements for controlling access by prisoners to cash, credit and banking facilities and the extent to which the prison conformed with security and operating standards commensurate with its status. They authorised the senior investigating officer to examine any other matters he considered relevant to the effective management of the prison.

Within days of the search grossly inaccurate accounts of Operation Swynford were given to the media by a number of sources that were seemingly close to the former Governor and BOV. These accounts were remarkably similar in content and used the same emotive language, describing the search in the language of the prison subculture as 'a raid' and the operation as 'a Rambo-style raid', with staff taking part being accused of wanton destruction. These views were not shared by the new Governor or any of his new senior managers. To the astonishment of many involved this was to set a pattern for other people, with no direct, actual or tested knowledge or intelligence concerning the events of May 5 but with what seemed to be an agenda to damage the senior management of HMPS and the Area Manager in particular. The strategy, if that is what it was, appeared to be to repeat consistently what was being passed on in the hope that it would gain credence in the media, regardless of whether the tale held water. This proved remarkably successful especially as the targets of this disinformation were constrained, as senior public servants, from making any public response.

The former Governor met with the DG on May 9 and discussed his transfer and the search. Martin Narey gave Eoin McLennan-Murray a wholly clear explanation of events and explained the reasons as to why he was being moved. At the ex-Governor's request the DG agreed to allow him to take up a non-operational post instead of going to Swaleside Prison as originally directed. Eoin was clearly concerned about how the circumstances of his move would be perceived by his peers. He was also concerned that Brian Pollett, a former Governor of Blantyre House, had been tasked to carry out an investigation into the management of that prison. Although it was normal practice for Area Managers to task one of their more senior Governors to carry out such investigations, he and officials of the PGA argued that the investigation should be led by an Area Manager. The DG did not accept their argument.

The record of that meeting shows that the former Governor claimed that he had not been given any briefing on the recent history of the prison on his appointment as Governor which was wholly incorrect. He also wrongly stated that he had only been given a three word briefing by me which he later, somewhat implausibly, claimed was, 'Don't fuck up'. All Kent Governors were given a full briefing when taking up post and a handover from their predecessor and it was no different in his case. He was made fully aware of the ATM scam described in *Chapter 4* and was the Governor in charge during the ensuing internal disciplinary investigation and the subsequent dismissal of Principal Officer Catton.

A few days after this meeting the first evidence of a media campaign emerged in an article by Martin Bright in the *Observer*. Relying on factually incorrect second-hand accounts of the operation and the number of staff involved, the article went on to imply, quite inaccurately, that the former Governor had been operating an 'experimental' regime and repeated the prison's performance data out of context as proof of its success. As the data being quoted in such detail was not in the public domain it surely had to have come from a source close to the former Governor. Contributing sources—some of whom, at this stage, may have acted simply as conduits and in all innocence, but who with hindsight might think that they should have checked matters out thoroughly before nailing their colours to the mast—were identified by the correspondent as Lynne Bowles of the PGA, a part time chaplain at the prison, Harry Fletcher of the National Association of Probation Officers and Alan Rogers, a former prisoner at Blantyre House with convictions for drugs and firearms offences who was known to be a friend of McLennan-Murray. Rogers saw the events as evidence of a conspiracy to destroy the whole ethos of the prison. The contribution of the part time chaplain fell short of a conspiracy theory but may well have passed for expert opinion concerning the workings of HMPS.

Most national newspapers briefly reported with varying degrees of accuracy on the search. But the *Observer, Private Eye*, some Kent based local papers, and some radio and television newsrooms followed up on the story seemingly based on the inaccurate accounts being leaked to them by what appeared to be supporters of the former Governor, officials of the PGA and others.

On May 16 the Prisons Minister, Paul Boateng MP, and the DG of HMPS, Martin Narey, attended a pre-scheduled hearing with the Home Affairs Select

Committee (HAC), mainly to give oral evidence about drugs in prisons. Members of the committee were obviously already aware of the search and the transfer of the Governor and the matter was raised at that hearing. Martin Narey gave a brief account based on the initial reports, including his views on the quantity of items found during the search. Both he and the Minister agreed to provide the committee with an interim report on the investigation into the management of Blantyre House.

Based on the comments of some HAC members it seemed obvious that they had already been given a similarly inaccurate account to that already in circulation, the source of which was unclear but it was certainly not HMPS which was yet to report via the DG and was the only repository of full and correct knowledge and information. Thankfully, the implementation in 2005 of the Freedom of Information Act 2000 has enabled access to previously unpublished documents that identify some of the sources of the committee's misinformation. However a substantial amount of evidence, believed to include unpublished written evidence and records of discussions with Sir David Ramsbotham, individual members of the BOV, officials of the PGA and others who might be said to have vested interests, has been withheld using Parliamentary privilege. Though I myself am aware of the existence of ten unpublished files, the contents of only one of these has been released. The clerk to the HAC is withholding access to further information having refused to confirm whether or not these files exist. Following a requested review of that decision, the Freedom of Information Officer (FIO) at the House of Commons upheld the original decision not to release what might—in terms of my reputation and career—be misleading and highly prejudicial information.

I had sought access to the information contained in files that I knew existed, the numbers of which were identified by me when making the request. Having been refused access, I requested a review of that decision or at least that I be given access to any memoranda, statements, correspondence or notes of meetings, interviews and discussions, including telephone conversations in which comment was made about me either by name or as Area Manager. In her reply denying all access, the FIO stated: 'This information related to the substance of the Committee's enquiry ... and was therefore protected by the [section] 34 exemption and was rightly withheld'. Her reply also refused access to the named files that I had requested and concluded:

> Providing this information would reveal which reports the Committee may have taken into account in reaching its conclusions and lay it open to allegations about how it conducted its inquiry. This would contravene the Parliamentary privilege of 'exclusive cognisance' whereby proceedings of the House or its Committees should not be questioned outside Parliament ... and that confirming which of the named reports were in the files would infringe the privileges of the House of Commons.

This explanation does not bear scrutiny and seems to be no more than a device to give such inquiries carte blanche. In short, Select Committees are a law unto themselves and accountable to no one in terms of how they chose to operate. Their proceedings do not conform to the rules of natural justice which govern other public enquiries, judicial and quasi-judicial proceedings including disciplinary investigations in a workplace. Furthermore there is no avenue of redress if an individual is defamed, maligned, mistreated or harmed by the workings of a Select Committee.

The information that *was* disclosed reveals that letters were sent to Robin Corbett (chairman of the HAC) on May 8 and 15. One was from Alan Rogers, whose most recent convictions were for possession of a Class A drug with intent to supply, and three firearms offences. He had served the last three years of his sentence at Blantyre House. Rogers had been released about 18 months prior to these events and said that he was working as a drug counsellor. By his own admission he was 'an active criminal and drug user for 20 years' prior to his last conviction. Said to be a friend of Eoin McLennan-Murray's, he had been involved in the visit to Blantyre House by members of the HAC that I described earlier. He had, so it was said, also participated in other presentations by the Governor.

In his letter Rogers stated that following the earlier visit by Corbett he 'felt reassured that Blantyre's future was secure'. He then went on to outline an account of the events of May 5 and 6 that was wholly inaccurate. He talked of over 100 prison officers in 'combat gear' storming the prison and behaving in an abusive and destructive manner, ripping prisoners' rooms and possessions apart and keeping them awake all night being drug tested, in an attempt to provoke an adverse response from prisoners. This was of course absolute nonsense. But the version he gave was to become familiar in the months to come concerning the transfer of the Governor and the search. He had no direct knowledge of these events and quoted as his sources HMPS staff who had not been present and who were well outside the intelligence loop!

Rogers then expounded a conspiracy theory accusing me of 'taking [my] revenge and destroying the careers of two men who developed and defended a regime with a "long proven record"'. He went on to suggest that the intention of HMPS was to dismantle Blantyre House by stealth. This, as I have already explained earlier in this book, was also incorrect. It seemed that his letter, as with many that were to follow from various individuals, was drafted in a way that would set a pattern or template for what would follow. It also contained a call for the HAC to enquire into the affair and to exonerate the former Governor.

Rogers went on to draw Corbett's attention to the, as yet unpublished, Inspector of Prisons' report, claiming that it was being suppressed because it was favourable to the prison and critical of 'regional management'. This too was incorrect as the report could not be suppressed by HMPS. However it was the subject of discussion between the Chief Inspector and the DG on matters of factual accuracy. Either Rogers was just guessing or he had somehow obtained improper access to an unpublished draft which had been given a restricted circulation within HMPS and the Home Office.

To compound matters, Corbett responded to this letter in warm and supportive terms. It was to be the first of a sequence of correspondence between them throughout the summer and autumn of 2000. In a letter to Corbett in mid-May 2000 Rogers returned to the issue of the inspection report and stated that he had been told by the Chief Inspector's liaison officer that HMPS were causing the delay because they were insisting on changes that the Chief Inspector did not want to make. HMPS can only object to factual inaccuracy and quite rightly cannot (and would not wish to) *force* the Chief Inspector to make changes even when they are factually inaccurate. Corbett was to table questions in Parliament relating to the report and Rogers asked him to copy the Minister's reply to him. I have no way of knowing whether any of the correspondence between them has been withheld by the HAC under Parliamentary privilege. The remaining discovered letters focused on critical comments about the new management team, untrue slants on changes being implemented and testimony by Rogers as to how Blantyre House helped him as an offender.

During the earlier visit by the HAC to the prison Corbett was in contact with a prisoner named Chris Johnson and sponsored him in the London Marathon (see *Chapter 7*). Johnson was a 28-year-old man who was convicted and sentenced in December 1998 to seven years' imprisonment for importation of drugs. Immediately following the transfer of the Governor and the search he too wrote to Robin Corbett in a similar vein to Rogers. Corbett's reply was not disclosed but in a follow up letter dated May 21 Johnson was thanking him for the copy of a transcript of evidence he had sent him and suggesting that 'certain people were being economical with the truth'. A further four letters from Johnson were discovered but none of Corbett's replies, though in a letter dated June 15 Johnson thanked him for 'the recent text and for keeping me informed of the relevant developments'. Throughout all this correspondence HMPS, its DG and senior staff were kept completely in the dark.

In the weeks following the search and on the basis of this same line of disinformation we became aware of intensive briefing by friends of the former Governor soliciting support from individuals in positions of power. As already noted, certain prisoners and former prisoners were also engaged in attempting to influence the perception of events, in some cases through their solicitors, MPs and directly with the chair of the HAC.

As a result of these by now almost surreal briefings a number of prominent individuals—by now themselves taken in by the only story in circulation—were also corresponding with the Home Secretary and the DG expressing their concerns at the events of May 5, the removal of this 'progressive' Governor and the ending of the 'experimental' regime at the prison. None of this was true. Even to refer to the regime as 'experimental' was, at very best, a curious use of the term because the general approach had been in existence for many years before McLennan-Murray became Governor and continued after his departure.

Some members of the BOV were also strong supporters of the former Governor and to my mind seemed to be actively trying to undermine his successor. It is also now clear, from sources within the prison, that certain BOV members were in regular contact with the former Governor, the Chief Inspector and members of the HAC—and were effectively and erroneously briefing against myself and the DG. This in turn led to a split in the board and eventually to the resignation of some members who found such behaviour unacceptable. I believe that some members had been in contact with the Chief Inspector regarding their disagreement with some of the constraints I had placed on the former Governor. This led me, rightly or wrongly, to suspect his involvement with them in a degree of politicking behind the scenes. Added to this, his as yet unpublished report seemed to be evidence of a determination to place the blame on me, even though he had been made aware of the facts during face to face and also via written briefings from Martin Narey.

Simon Hughes MP, the Liberal Democrat spokesman on home affairs was, so I am told, seen leaving Sir David's headquarters a few weeks after the search. That in itself was of little significance as the Chief Inspector reports to Parliament on matters within his remit. However it was significant that immediately following this Hughes wrote to the Home Office exclusively relating to the search at Blantyre House. From the contents of his letter it appears to me that he had been given a questionable account of the search and the events leading up to it. His letter seemed to question the accuracy of the intelligence and the integrity and motivation of Chaucer Unit staff. But most interesting of all was his request for the Home Secretary to ask the Chief Inspector to investigate the circumstances surrounding the search, as his 'independence' would be valuable in ensuring confidence in any findings.

At the time when he wrote his letter Hughes was probably aware that a full investigation was already underway and was thus implicitly questioning the integrity of the HMPS officers who were conducting it; had he known it or stopped to check matters further, without any solid basis for doing so. Simon Hughes' letter to the Home Secretary was copied to Sir David.

Jonathan Shaw, the MP for Chatham and Aylesford, had been quick in responding to Prisoner K's call for support some months earlier and was alleged to have been involved in encouraging the HAC to visit the prison and support the Governor. Based on a prisoner's recorded telephone conversations, I found it difficult to believe that he was not also operating behind the scenes following the search and removal of his 'friend' Prisoner K from the prison. However, again there is no concrete evidence that he was. Nevertheless, given the serious drug problems that exist in the Medway towns and in parts of Shaw's constituency many of his constituents might rightly be concerned at his willingness to use his time and influence to assist a man whose past criminal activities might have contributed to these problems.

As the HMPS investigation into the management of Blantyre House was continuing, led by Brian Pollett, the DG came under mounting pressure to stop it and appoint an Area Manager to lead it. Supporters of the former Governor questioned Pollett's independence and, by inference, his integrity. Some officials of the PGA even attempted to get an Area Manager of their own choice appointed. I had no concerns about the outcome of the investigation if properly carried out and therefore I was quite content for the DG to appoint a more senior and independent investigating officer if he so wished; in the circumstances I would actually have welcomed it. Martin Narey eventually agreed and appointed Adrian Smith, the Area Manager for London, to take the lead in the investigation. Adrian was appointed because he had carried out a similar investigation at the prison in 1998, was independent of me and had a detailed knowledge of Blantyre House.

The pressure being generated publicly by supporters of the former Governor and for all I knew more covertly by others seemed to be having an unnerving effect at the highest levels of HMPS. Though everyone at HMPS was clear that the action taken had been appropriate, there seemed to be a fear of antagonising members of the HAC. Though some prison officers at Blantyre House seemed to be trying to undermine the efforts of the new management team to implement some pressing changes, I was discouraged from assisting the Governor and advised to 'take a back seat' for a time. When Adrian Smith was tasked to lead the investigation he was also discouraged from recommending disciplinary action against the former Governor. The HMPS investigation continued and I directed my attention to my other prisons.

LESS DIVISIVE BUT EQUALLY IMPORTANT MATTERS

Whilst all this was going on in the background I turned my attention to other important but less controversial and exasperating matters.

Highdown

My major concern at that time was Highdown Prison which came under my control in April 2000. This high security prison was performing so badly that the DDG had removed all Category A prisoners, as their retention would have presented a risk to the public. The purpose built prison was expensive to run and Category A accommodation was urgently required. When I took over responsibility for Highdown I was given a clear brief to deal with this problem.

From my initial visit it was clear that this prison had the potential to be a centre of excellence in the high security sector. Junior and middle ranking officers were well motivated and the staff-inmate relationship was excellent. Unfortunately the prison lacked fully effective leadership and direction. As a consequence operating and security standards had fallen and continued to fall. Attempts had been made to correct the problems but all had failed and the prison was now 'treading water'. The Governor was an intelligent and experienced man with a quiet and thoughtful approach to management. It seemed to me that too much unnecessary thinking was contributing to high levels of inertia and this was the nub of the problem. It was going to be a hard slog to get the prison's performance back to an acceptable level and under the existing management it would take a long time—a luxury I did not have.

I met with the management team toward the end of my first visit and in fairly frank terms made it clear that their performance was not good enough. Each Functional Manager was told that they would be held accountable for the performance of their respective departments but that they were also collectively responsible with the Governor for the overall performance of the prison. It was obvious that change would have to be driven through and that this would require me to get more actively involved. Members of my area team carried out a detailed standards audit and their findings and those of the recent security audit formed the basis of a corrective action plan which I was determined would be implemented without delay.

From the start I felt that the Governor, though very able in many ways, did not have the leadership qualities necessary to achieve the level of change I required. He was a decent man but lacked a 'cutting edge' and inspirational leadership skills to change the culture that had developed. We discussed my concerns and the options open to us. Understandably he wanted to be given the opportunity to try to achieve the necessary change and I agreed to allow him to stay with the understanding that I would provide some specialist support and more actively involve myself in the management of the prison.

The corrective action plan had very tight time bound targets and to emphasise the point I invited the national security audit team to re-visit the prison in six months. A task of this magnitude would, in normal circumstances, take at least two years but, again, that was a luxury I could not afford. The management team also recognised the urgency of the situation and most of them responded well. Though there was the occasional backsliding, steady progress was made in effecting change up to a point, but consolidation was problematic. However, when they visited Highdown the audit team recognised the improvement that had been made and graded the modules audited as 'acceptable'. My performance target was nothing short of 'good' and there still remained a lot to achieve but we celebrated our success so far.

The next step in the process would be more difficult and it seemed a good time to bring in a new Governor. The existing Governor had done well but he now needed a change. By mutual agreement he moved on to a new job. There was also a need for some changes to the management team and carefully selected new blood was introduced that would strengthen it. In selecting a new Governor I knew that the prison needed a strong leader and 'heavy hitter' who knew his business and who could relate to the officers and prisoners alike and take them with him. With the approval of Martin Narey and Phil Wheatley I selected Ted Butt who at that time was a successful Governor at Coldingly Prison. Ted and I had remarkably similar management styles and we got on well from the start. As a result of his appointment I was able to spend less of my time concentrating on Highdown and more on the rest of my prisons, though Ted and I continued to work closely together. Through his skilful leadership the prison made swift progress and within the target timescale met the necessary performance and security standards to return to its Category A role. Highdown successfully achieved a performance rating of 'good'.

Lewes
Unfortunately Highdown was not the only problem prison to come under my control in 2000. Lewes Prison had similar performance related difficulties but its security profile was marginally lower. It too had failed a standards audit and was falling short of its performance targets. Though it had a very experienced staff, as I walked around the prison for the first time I would not have been surprised to hear the theme music from the BBC television series *Heartbeat*. The culture that I found was clearly of another era and though the trappings of the modern Prison Service formed part of the façade, in reality, nothing had changed for years. They would have to change now and quickly. Clear targets for improved performance in all areas were set.

Lewes appeared to have been bypassed by the changes introduced in the rest of HMPS where, after some initial resistance, Governors, staff and trade unions had adapted to a performance led culture. These changes gave improved performance and better value for money but also led to considerable improvements to regimes for prisoners. Programmes were focused on confronting prisoners with their offending behaviour and equipping them to return to the community with a better chance of remaining law abiding. Many programmes were targeted at drug abuse and improving literacy and numeracy standards to a level that would enable prisoners to develop the necessary skills to find a job. Though Lewes was delivering some of these programmes it had not made the cultural adjustment necessary to bring it in line with that of the wider service. The prison was clearly overstaffed, yet a full regime was frequently not being delivered because of restrictive practices and inefficient deployment. Change is never easy to achieve and resistance at Lewes was very strong.

Initial analysis of the situation also led me to the conclusion that there were serious management problems. The management team lacked cohesion and some of its members were ineffective either through lack of motivation or lack of competence. The problem was compounded by the fact that the Governor had been there for too long. He had been in charge for many years and prior to that had been the Deputy Governor. Most of his senior operational management experience had been there and he therefore lacked the broader perspective that comes from wider experience. Because of this he was part of the culture of the prison and as such, part of the problem. His efforts to implement change seemed to be inhibited by a subconscious desire to preserve the status quo. Though he was an able man I knew he could not deliver the necessary change and we discussed this frankly. I felt that as a manager he was more a safe pair of hands than an innovator and we eventually agreed that he would undertake a new challenge in charge of another prison with a well established high performance record and a good management team. He did extremely well there.

Like Highdown, Lewes needed a strong Governor and the support of an able management team. I had earlier picked Paul Carroll as Deputy Governor of the then troubled Canterbury Prison and he had played a vital role in assisting the Governor to sort it out. When I picked him for that job I believed that he would develop into a very able Governor and his subsequent performance proved me right. Canterbury was now operating well and I felt Paul was ready for a new challenge. He expressed an interest in the Lewes post and I was happy to nominate him to Martin Narey, who appointed him.

When Paul Carroll took charge I gave him a clear brief and together we set a corrective action plan. The first step in achieving change was to build an able management team around him. This necessitated the removal of some of the existing team, none of whom wanted to go. However between early retirement and transfer out this was achieved and they were replaced by hand picked managers who would complement the Governor and who individually were very able. The team was also supplemented by specialist support from Area Office.

Within a very short time Paul was proving the wisdom of his appointment. He had come up through the ranks and had learned the business well. He presented as a tough, straight talking, no nonsense individual with a clear vision of where he was going and an iron determination to get there. However this façade hid an extremely intelligent and articulate individual with good interpersonal skills that enabled him to take staff and prisoners with him on his journey of change. Over the next 18 months he would transform Lewes Prison.

In undertaking their difficult tasks both Ted Butt and Paul Carroll would require my ongoing and active support. I had hoped that the rest of my new prisons would be operating more effectively but that was not to be.

Ford
Ford Prison is a large open establishment which in the past had attracted negative media attention. The prison had a capacity for about 500 prisoners and a large commercial horticultural operation, as well as commercial engineering, laundry and textile operations, and a multifunctional contract workshop. There was also an extensive education programme and other vocational training facilities which together with housekeeping work and outside resettlement work

projects occupied the prisoners. The various commercial operations were income generating, receipts from which formed part of the prison's operating budget.

The Governor in charge was Ken Kan a bright, articulate, pleasant young man and a former army officer. On my first visit I met with his entire management team to introduce myself, explain my method of operation and my expectations of them. It was my normal practice at each prison to require all functional managers to submit a report on the performance of their areas of responsibility to their Governor a week prior to my visit. The Governor would copy these to me with an overall assessment before my visit. As this was my first visit I sought verbal assessments from them. Some showed little knowledge of their areas and seemed unable to cope with performance details. It was clear that the Governor was not served well by some of his senior team. I knew that he had inherited many of the problems and would need some help in addressing them

I had real concerns about the management of the budget and the accuracy of some performance data returns. However after visiting the prison a few times I also became increasingly concerned about the effectiveness of the management of the activities department which was responsible for all prisoner activities including work, education and resettlement projects. There was clearly a lack of coherent thinking in deciding priorities and a tendency to over-react to criticism in any area at the expense of others. As a result I became sceptical about the accuracy of performance data. The Governor undertook to deal with these matters. In discussion with him, we agreed that two members of the management team should be moved or offered early retirement as their performances were below par and were unlikely to improve. Both resisted but eventually agreed to retire early. This enabled the Governor to bring in new blood to revitalise his team.

Shortly after Ford joined my area I met with officers from Sussex Police Service at their request. From them I became aware that an auxiliary officer at the prison was under investigation and had been suspended from duty for many months. As the details given described corrupt activity by this officer and possibly others yet to be identified, I referred the matter to the Chaucer Unit for examination. On the basis of their interim report I had sufficient concerns about the financial management of the prison to ask the headquarters Internal Audit Department to carry out a full audit.

Their findings confirmed my concerns and led me to commission a full disciplinary investigation led by another of my senior Governors, Colette Kershaw (now sadly deceased). She was supported by Chaucer investigators and financial specialists from headquarters Audit. This later became a joint investigation with Sussex Police Service and quickly led to the suspension of both the Head of Finance and the Industrial Manager. The auxiliary officer admitted that he was guilty of theft and received a police caution. He resigned before being dismissed from HMPS. Both managers were later charged and found guilty of serious offences under the Code of Discipline for Prison Staff.

The Head of Management Services, who had overall responsibility for the supervision of these managers and for the financial management of the prison, resigned before he too could be charged with neglect of duty. These events enlarged the task faced by the Governor but with help and aided by his improved management team he succeeded in regularising the situation.

THE BLANTYRE HOUSE INSPECTION REPORT

Back at Blantyre House some middle managers, it seemed, were doing their best to stir up discontent amongst staff and prisoners. Though they were well aware that the prison would continue in its resettlement role they consistently suggested otherwise and effectively undermined the morale of their colleagues. New managers brought in following Operation Swynford expressed disgust at the subversive behaviour of these individuals. Firm management action should have been taken against them but the Governor decided to 'ride it out'. It seemed that the activities of these individuals were hardly spontaneous and may have been orchestrated from outside of the prison as their comments seemed to tie in with statements being made by other supporters of the former Governor.

The final report of the Chief Inspector of Prisons' inspection in January had still not been published by June. The DG had welcomed the draft report in March but had challenged what he had objected to as an unjustifiable personal attack on me in its preface. Sir David Ramsbotham had been reminded by Martin Narey that he, Martin, had already spoken to Sir David of his concerns about the situation at the prison so that he was fully in the picture. The purpose of producing a draft report is to enable any such factual inaccuracies to be identified and corrected before publication. Normally the DG would correspond with the Inspectorate to identify any matters that HMPS considered to be inaccurate. It was then a matter for the Chief Inspector to decide whether to make an amendment. In the event of a major disagreement between the DG and the Chief Inspector on a point of accuracy, the Home Secretary would adjudicate. To my knowledge disagreements never got to that stage. Because Sir David's reports enjoyed Parliamentary privilege he could not be held accountable under the ordinary law. Rightly or wrongly many people within HMPS who were on the receiving end of his criticisms felt that he sometimes relied on this fact to make comments which were hasty, loose, unfair or that lacked an everyday context of managing prisons and prisoners.

The Inspection Report on Blantyre House was eventually published on 26 July 2000. The preface to it had been rewritten and the baseless attack on me contained in the first draft had been removed. It would, of course, not have been removed if the Chief Inspector had known it to be true. The published preface rehearsed the praise already recorded about the prison by the DG and his predecessor, Sir Richard Tilt. It went on to criticise 'some parts of headquarters' and specifically the Area Manager and the Standards Audit team for regarding it as a category C prison with a resettlement function (which, of course, is what it was as explained in *Chapter 7*). The remainder of the preface was rightly complimentary of the prison's performance and critical of any uncertainty about its future. It praised the courage of the Governor in taking risks, but on a more cautionary note pointed out, 'Unfortunately, evidence that the admirable Blantyre House regime is being successful remains largely anecdotal'. This seemed to contrast with the strong claims being made by the former Governor and his supporters as to the efficacy of the regime and, to a degree, the views being expressed by Sir David, in what I took to be a personal capacity.

As was the norm in all prisons, a pre-publication press conference was scheduled for mid-morning on July 26, the day before publication. On that morning it became clear that the event was in danger of being hijacked by supporters of the former Governor. The unpublished and now withdrawn preface to the report was leaked to BBC Radio Kent. The General Secretary of the PGA, David Rodden, a friend of the former Governor, took part in an early morning current affairs programme. He gave an account of what had been in the original draft and described the decision of the Chief Inspector to redraft it as 'quite astonishing'. He implied that pressure had been placed on him to do so. Ann Widdecombe MP was also interviewed. As a former Prisons Minister, now in Opposition, she had a good knowledge of HMPS and knew me. She was much more cautious and balanced in her contribution and challenged some of Rodden's comments as being spurious. The interview ended with Rodden calling for the HAC to take the unprecedented step of involving themselves to investigate this matter. Draft inspection reports would not normally be circulated to Rodden but he clearly was given a copy by either by the Chief Inspector's office or one of the small circle of people who received copies. Whatever and by whomsoever the misleading draft report had also been leaked to the press, including Radio Kent.

I received no prior notice of Rodden's participation in the Radio Kent interview nor the leaking of the draft preface. Neither was I asked to participate or respond. As I was a member of the PGA and a former chair of the Prison Governors Association in Northern Ireland it might reasonably have been expected that the General Secretary would, at least, alert me in advance of his intentions and seek my views on these matters. Though his office was within three minutes walk of mine, he never spoke to me or sought any explanation for the events of May 5 and 6. It seemed that, like others, he had made his mind up without considering the full range of perspectives. Furthermore the DG has publicly stated that the President of the PGA was offered a confidential briefing on this affair prior to this interview but failed to take up the offer. During the programme, Rodden incorrectly implied that the DG had failed to respond to requests for an explanation. The PGA's actions in this matter, including their input to the subsequent HAC hearings, was considered by many people to be reprehensible and led to a number of more senior HMPS managers reviewing their membership of the association.

By the end of that day it seemed that the leaking of the unpublished draft preface to the media was part of a more coordinated plan involving supporters of the former Governor and possibly the chair of the HAC. Perhaps it was a coincidence that the leak, the radio interview, the disruption of the press conference and the announcement by Robin Corbett that the HAC would investigate all happened on the same day, but in the light of what has since been discovered, such a view seems hardly credible.

The press conference was well attended by all sections of the media. Some members of the BOV and, unusually, ex-prisoners were also there. Though it remains unclear whether copies of the original draft preface had been leaked to some of the reporters present or whether they had picked up on the Radio Kent report, they seemed to know its content in detail. In the circumstances it was not surprising that media attention was diverted away from the substance of the published report and on to what they had been led to believe was a cover up. Most questions related to the unpublished draft preface, the search of Blantyre House or the removal of the former Governor. As most of these events were the subject of an ongoing formal investigation or related to decisions or action taken at a higher level, I could not respond in detail to many of their questions. Predictably this led to a degree of hostility from some reporters. This in turn seemed to please some members of the BOV who were in attendance and I recall observing two of them smiling at my discomfort. In the circumstances it was not surprising that most of the media reports contained comments from the unpublished draft rather than the published document. However one perceptive journalist saw through it and questioned what was happening in a manner critical of his colleagues.

At the time I had welcomed the announcement by Robin Corbett that the HAC would investigate the reasons for the removal of the former Governor and the subsequent search of the prison, though I was surprised that they were getting involved in an HMPS operational management matter. In the months following the search I had been regularly criticised by supporters of the former Governor, some staff and prisoners at the prison, the Chief Inspector and a variety of other people including MPs. In some cases critics were briefing the media with inflammatory and untrue accounts or—taking a charitable view— genuinely held but largely fallacious opinions. Some of these were published in national newspapers as fact.

The main thrust of their story—that is what it had by now become—was that the former Governor's removal was a result of longstanding conflict between him and the Area Manager, who they claimed was a 'hardliner' opposed to the resettlement regime and who intended to destroy the whole ethos of the prison. The former Governor was presented as a courageous and enlightened character who had achieved unique success in terms of reconviction rates, in comparison with all other prisons within HMPS, mainly as a result of the regime, the level of trust he placed in prisoners and the risks he was prepared to take with them. The former Governor's own data (later to be the subject of an academic dissertation by him and considered as part of the unpublished evidence received by the HAC) were used to paint a distorted picture of the prison's success and without being placed in context. There were no independent evaluations. The former Governor may well have genuinely believed in his presentations and later academic dissertation, but both seem to have been grounded in enthusiasm rather than sound comparative research.

In reality, I was a more experienced prison governor, a firm believer in the value of resettlement prisons and resettlement units and had been instrumental in setting them up in other places. I was also the person who two years earlier had taken the lead in the development of a national policy on resettlement to ensure that such regimes were protected. As Area Manager I had set the business plan for the very prison on which its whole ethos was built. The conflict that existed between the former Governor and myself was not, from my point of view, related to the resettlement concept. It was related to his failure to obey orders and national instructions, lack of judgment in matters of public safety, political acceptability and the propriety of his 'special relationships' with a small number of individual prisoners who enjoyed inappropriate latitude far beyond the scope of national instructions.

As a senior civil servant I was unable to respond publicly to any of the criticisms against me. Some of the more influential critics, including Sir David Ramsbotham, would have known that the main decisions for which I was being criticised were made at a higher level within HMPS, and also that my hands were tied in terms of making any wholesale public defence.

The Smith investigation was ongoing and though I was confident that its findings would clarify the situation, the prospect of an investigation by the HAC was even better. Having been a public servant for 37 years at that time and having faith in the system I believed that such an investigation would get to the truth. Neither the DG nor I had any idea of what was going on behind the scenes or the extent of communications between the chair of the HAC and the supporters of the former Governor. The extent to which other HAC committee members were involved in what had now become a charade is unclear.

Trustingly at first and in ignorance of what was actually going on, I saw the involvement of the HAC as something of a relief. Though I tried to maintain a façade of normality, the ongoing campaign and media interest were creating considerable stress for both my wife and myself. We had become accustomed to the extreme stresses of life in Northern Ireland, even to the extent of the constant threats to our lives. Together we had survived certain death at the hands of terrorists by the grace of God and got on with our lives. But those events had taken their toll on our health. We were now much older and less able to absorb the knocks. On top of this our youngest son, Nigel, was terminally ill in a Belfast hospital. He was a young prison officer in Northern Ireland who had been diagnosed with primary progressive multiple sclerosis following a serious assault on him by a large group of prisoners, all serving long sentences for terrorist offences. His deterioration was swift and his consultant neurologist warned us that due to his incapacitation he could die at any time from one of the many chest infections that afflicted him. We were therefore regularly travelling to Belfast at weekends and at times of crisis for Nigel.

Following Robin Corbett's announcement of the HAC investigation I focused my attention on the other prisons in my charge and in supporting their Governors. Only a few of them knew the reasons for the events at Blantyre House and they knew not to discuss them with other colleagues not already in the confidential intelligence loop. Some were obviously curious and concerned for the welfare of their former colleague, but without exception, they gave me their full support. Throughout this period all my prisons continued to do well and as an area we remained a top performer. I knew I had the full support of Martin Narey, Phil Wheatley and the other members of the Prisons Board who knew the real facts. Martin Narey had already made it clear to other people, including Sir David Ramsbotham, that he himself had ultimately taken the decision to remove the former Governor and that he had approved the follow up search. We were all confident that all the action taken was justified and that the HAC would eventually see that.

We also knew that various people in what had now become the former Governor' camp were continuing what had to all intents and purposes become a campaign by word of mouth and that in some cases was seemingly and mysteriously being reinforced via secretive correspondence with the HAC (that I and HMPS were being pre-empted from seeing on dubious grounds of Parliamentary privilege!). The more that this occurred, the more it began to feel that the 'other side' might, by sheer repetition and numbers, actually prevail: that I would become the scapegoat, possibly with calls for my dismissal. The compelling nature of these events, the momentum that they created and their effect on the perceptions of the general public can be judged by the fact that the story even began to gain credence with a few of the other HMPS Area Managers, none of whom had been briefed on the facts of the case. Some of them were clearly distancing themselves from me, giving me the cold shoulder, at a time when their support would have been particularly welcome.

As I have already intimated, the HAC and the Speaker of the House invoked Parliamentary privilege in respect of most of the files relating to this matter when access was sought under the Freedom of Information Act 2000. The limited number of documents that were released points to a constant flow of unpublished evidence which given their eventual findings—of which more later—can only be presumed to have influenced HAC members. However the accuracy of this evidence was never tested. These events also demonstrate the naïveté of at least some HAC members who would credit prisoners, ex-prisoners and non-members of HMPS with a level of knowledge and expertise concerning things that, in most cases, they could have known nothing or little about.

There also seems to be little doubt that there was regular contact and unpublished correspondence between some members of the BOV and others with at least one member of the HAC between the date of the search and the publication of the HAC's report. This input seems to have influenced the committee to a degree that they appear to have prejudged the situation, ignored compelling evidence and approached the public hearings with closed minds. The decision to withhold relevant files only served to fuel suspicion of some irregularities in the conduct of their investigation. Though it is known that there was contact between some committee members and certain members of the BOV, the only unpublished evidence released was that of David Smith, who regrettably died shortly after the hearings.

The documents that were disclosed reveal that shortly after the events of May 5 Ralph Dellow began corresponding with Robin Corbett. Dellow was a tutor in the prison's Education Department. Education services were provided under contract by Kent County Council who were his employer. He had been at Blantyre House for many years and had been a leading light and a trustee of the Blantyre House Vocational Fund, a local charity which provided funds to assist prisoners attending courses at colleges in the community. Dellow was not an employee of HMPS and knew little of its operational management but he worked closely with some members of the BOV and the former Governor in his capacity as a trustee of the charity.

In what seems to have been his opening letter to Corbett, copied to Ann Widdecombe MP, Simon Hughes MP and Harry Fletcher of the National Association of Probation Officers, Dellow jumps from complaining about changes made by the new Governor to blaming me for persecuting the former Governor. Between the search of the prison and the end of the public hearing by the committee he wrote to Robin Corbett on at least eight occasions. The evidence also suggests that Corbett probably disclosed to him and others a copy of the interim report by Adrian Smith into the management of Blantyre House and he may also have disclosed the final full report.

The interim report on the investigation into the management of Blantyre House was completed and copied to the HAC in July 2000. I was not given sight of the document at that time. The initial findings were highly critical of aspects of the prison's management, particularly temporary release procedures, control of the working out schemes, 'charity' work, use of vehicles and mobile phones by prisoners, the selection and allocation process and security standards.

On July 20 Dellow wrote to Robin Corbett thanking him for sending him, Dellow, a copy of the interim report. This letter was also copied to Sir David Ramsbotham, Ann Widdecombe MP, Simon Hughes MP and Archie Norman MP. It went on to say, 'After gathering information from a number of sources I have tried to answer the criticisms contained in the report from a "more meaningful perspective"'. Having thanked Corbett 'on behalf of my colleagues who are unable to speak for themselves without the help of MPs like you' he went on to respond to each of the concerns raised in the interim report, dismissing them as irrelevant or justifiable because of circumstances. Though plausibly presented, this document misrepresented the reality of the situation.

In a further letter dated August 20, copied to each member of the HAC, Dellow writes, 'You have a large file concerning the raid on Blantyre House Prison on May 5/6. I feel therefore, it may be useful to draw together much of the information in, "a factual report". I have my own motives for preparing this report, but I hope it does reflect a fair view of the events. The report is separate from the evidence I shall send to you'. Attached to that letter was a ten-page document entitled 'A factual account of the events of the raid upon Blantyre by Prison Service personnel on the 5/6 of May to now?' Dellow explained that the purpose of his report was 'to draw together all the information that has been circulated since the raid'. He acknowledged that 'facts are subjective and therefore will be qualified by knowing that witnesses could be produced to verify the fact or that it is documented, or the information is in the public domain, such as the media. I shall pose questions where the question would not be as obvious to an inquirer not associated with the establishment. The source of the information will be bracketed at the end of the statement'.

Dellow's 'report' contains an account of events based on selected quotes from the local media, a mixture of fact and fiction regarding the removal of the former Governor and the search of the prison. Much of its content was inaccurate and based on the version of events already circulated to the media by supporters of the former Governor. On a number of matters his stated source was an already published inaccurate account. He went on to suggest a long list of questions that should be put to the Area Manager, the DG or other senior managers in HMPS. Many of the questions were reasonable, but presented in the context of his version of the truth, which detracted from their impartiality.

Dellow was not present at the search and could not have had any knowledge of my relationship with the former Governor, nor the reasons for his removal. Neither did he have even the most basic understanding of operational management in HMPS. But he seems to have been given considerable credibility, at least by Corbett. In subsequent correspondence prior to the HAC hearings and later, prior to their report being published, he majored on criticism of me and the new Governor, and on his perception of the impact that recent management decisions were having on the regime of the prison. Again much of what he said misrepresented the facts or was simply untrue. The separate evidence which he referred to in his letter was not disclosed to me.

Dellow was not the only member of the Education Department staff to correspond with the committee. The Education Manager, Francoise Fletcher, and the Curriculum Leader, Janine Sterling, produced a joint paper giving a critical account of the search and the impact of the new management team on their work. Other education staff both at the prison and from colleges as far away as Norwich offered the benefit of their wisdom to the committee. The extent of their input can only be measured by the limited disclosure of evidence.

The degree of hostility they appear to have felt towards me, the new Governor and the senior management of HMPS may have had deeper origins than the events of May 5 and 6. They were employees of a service provider contracted to deliver a new and specific curriculum by HMPS. The new specification was focused on literacy and numeracy skills, and aimed to raise the competence of prisoners to a level that would enable them to achieve at least the minimum requirements to get a job on release. Performance targets were set for each prison and funding was provided accordingly based on clear criteria set by the DG. There was no longer much scope for the plethora of recreational educational classes that had traditionally been delivered in prisons, the value and substance of which was debatable. Not only was the curriculum being set for them but their performance was now being monitored and contracts tightly managed. Many education managers resented this and argued that they as professionals knew better.

The period between the search and the public hearing continued to be one of intense activity for supporters of the former Governor. Prisoners at Blantyre House were also being encouraged to play their part. A member of the BOV, not known as a supporter of mine, told of his surprise at observing a named senior officer address a large group of prisoners in the prison's main dining hall and tell them that if they wanted 'to save the prison' they should all get writing to the HAC. Putting aside the questionable nature of a serving prison officer doing this openly in front of his charges, it does serve to illustrate the extent to which such a neatly compartmentalised view of the world had emerged, despite the evidence. The extent of the HAC's response can again only be estimated by the unpublished evidence that has been released, which shows that a further five prisoners sent letters, in a few cases more than one.

J R Illingworth had been convicted of importing drugs and sentenced to nine years' imprisonment in 1997. By June 1999 he had made his way to Blantyre House. In his letter to the HAC he states: 'I was in Swaleside for around three months when I first heard of Blantyre House and the good things they done there. I made it my goal to get there and had it made part of my sentence plan'. He would spend more than half his effective sentence there. His plan was to work as an HGV lorry driver. This would give him the freedom to move around without the possibility of his movements being monitored by the prison. However the change of Governor and the recommendations of the Smith Report led to non-static work placements of this kind being stopped. He was upset at the constraints being placed on him, which he attributed to my attempt to 'kill off the Blantyre ethos which had been so successful over the years'. His letter was high in praise of the former Governor who had already allowed him to work as the prison van driver, which also enabled him to move around unsupervised in the community.

Charles Darnell was a 46-year-old man sentenced to eleven years' imprisonment in May 1997 for supplying drugs. Incredibly he managed to get to Blantyre House by November 1999 where he too would serve more than half of his effective sentence. Documents were found in his room during the search that seemed to relate to financial transactions. As he was unable to establish their relevance and having regard to his criminal record, the Silver Commander decided to confiscate them pending further investigation. Darnell was moved to a more secure prison pending the outcome. It later transpired that the documents were legitimate and they were given back to him. He was returned to Blantyre House.

In his letter to Robin Corbett he gave an emotionally descriptive but less than accurate account of the search and events following his removal. He went on to accuse the Minister and the DG of dishonesty in relation to the facts, and played down the relevance of items found during the search and their significance to the security of the prison and public safety. He also set about discrediting the findings of the ongoing Smith investigation, suggesting that their motive was 'to damage the reputation of Blantyre House and in particular the former Governor' and accusing them of 'attempting to tarnish the reputations of certain staff members and criticising accepted and proven security measures'. Clearly anticipating some of the investigation's findings he tried to minimise their seriousness. He also accused Smith of a breach of the Rehabilitation of Offenders Act 1974 because his investigators examined the propriety of the motor insurance cover held by prisoners using cars. They had done so and found that a number of prisoners had knowingly failed to disclose the facts of their situation, potentially invalidating their motor insurance. If so, these prisoners were effectively driving without insurance and thus committing offences on a daily basis. It is surely perfectly reasonable to raise such an indefensible state of affairs.

K Forrester was a 50-year-old man sentenced to seven years in prison in late July 1998 for importing drugs. Within a year of this he had made his way to Blantyre House where he would spend more than three years, mostly out in the community. Forrester had hoped to join the growing number of prisoners who worked as lorry drivers. But the decision to stop all non-static work placements appeared to anger him. He too wrote to Robin Corbett rehearsing much of what had been said by the others and giving the same misleading account of the search that had been consistently spread. He described the search staff as 'storm troopers' wrecking and 'intimidating inmates to cause a riot' and though he knew nothing of the availability of keys during the search, he assured Corbett that they had been available but that the searchers had preferred to force entry. Making frequent use of the phrase 'the powers that be' to refer to the new Governor, myself and the DG he repeated the now familiar, but untrue, charge that our objective was the closure of the prison.

Another correspondent was John Delaney who had been sentenced to 14 years' imprisonment in 1995 for importing drugs. He arrived at the prison in July 1998 from Maidstone Prison. His son was already serving a sentence at Blantyre House at that time and had been one of the group of prisoners involved in the 1998 'charity work' debacle. John Delaney's move was of particular interest to Chaucer investigators at the time. This 55-year-old drug importer would eventually spend almost four years of his effective sentence there enjoying all the associated benefits. Following his arrival he attended a photography course at a College in Tonbridge and joined a local company called Frontier Pictures Ltd on 'work experience'. He later joined this Company on a full time basis describing his role as 'being fully involved in many aspects of the film work and eventually being solely in charge of their newly established Mobile Office Division'. His letter bemoaned the new Governor's decision to discontinue this work placement, criticised his handling of the situation and compared him adversely with the former Governor.

The committee does not appear to have tested the accuracy of Delaney's allegations but his work placement was examined by the Smith team who recorded (Smith Report 2000, annex 7. para 3):

> This particular placement gives cause for concern as the terms of the licence allow travel anywhere within a 15 miles radius of Wadhurst. The prisoner is rarely at the office but is always 15 minutes away. There is no contact to establish where the prisoner is, or why, other than contacting the prisoner direct by mobile phone. This makes realistic checking impossible. The prisoner has also invested in a project with the film company to supply and equip a 'people carrier' vehicle with the necessary equipment for film companies to examine footage, either on site or when travelling between locations.

The Governor was therefore quite correct in his actions and Delaney's account to the HAC was disingenuous.

Nicholas Charles Bertram wrote to Robin Corbett on at least two occasions. He is a convicted murderer who was sentenced to life imprisonment in Cornwall in 1983 when he was 24 years old. He wrote in praise of the former Governor describing him as a visionary faced by 'an older witch burning mentality'. Writing with apparent authority on the 'conflict' between myself and the former Governor he described it as 'clear to all. Each encounter would send shock waves through Blantyre House. The result would send inmates running to the office trying to find out if the work placements in London had been stopped'. I have no recollection of ever meeting Bertram but he would have known nothing first-hand about my relationship with the former Governor. His letters also contained the now familiar misleading account of the search which he described as 'akin to the Normandy landings'.

The telephone conversations of all prisoners in category B prisons are recorded and monitored. Prisoner K had been moved to Elmley Prison following the search and in view of the earlier intelligence on him was closely monitored by Chaucer Unit operatives and the prison's security department. Shortly after his arrival there he obtained access to a personal coded charge account that enabled him to circumvent the prisoner payphone restraints. We can only speculate as to why he would need such a facility. His account was kept in credit for him by a close friend outside. This illicit arrangement was discovered almost immediately and all calls, including those of other prisoners he allowed to use the facility, were monitored and recorded. These included calls to officers at Blantyre House, prisoners, ex-prisoners, members of the BOV and others. Prisoner K also knew some of their private telephone numbers as calls were made to their homes. During one call he claimed to have written a ten-page A4 sized letter to Robin Corbett and received a reply. Neither of these documents was disclosed to the author.

The tone and content of some calls demonstrated the extent of Prisoner K's influence and the nature of his relationship with some key staff at Blantyre House and at least one member of its BOV. In one call he told an ex-prisoner that he had spoken with the former Governor. There is no record of such a call from the prisoner's phones but it could have been illicitly arranged for him by a middle ranking officer who security staff suspected had been corrupted and who, they also suspected, was passing information to Prisoner K relating to Blantyre House and the ensuing investigations. The same officer is believed to have discovered and alerted him to the close monitoring of his calls.

David Smith was a member of the BOV from 1996-2000 and in 1999 its vice chair. Sadly he is now deceased. He was convalescing after heart surgery at the time of the search and the removal of the former Governor. I met him briefly once in 1998 when I briefed him on the findings of the investigation into the management of the working out scheme and the 'charity work'. I did not know the man and would not presume to judge him on the basis of our limited contact. In his statement to the HAC he did not demonstrate such constraints in criticising me. He wrongly stated that I had pressured the Governor to revert to a more traditional Category C prison regime, which he cited as the cause of the perceived conflict between us. Like many other people he overlooked the fact that I set the business plan and objectives for the prison. Having been in post for over five years, much longer than the former Governor, I could have made changes if that was my intention. His paper to the HAC also contained the well rehearsed account of the search and some fundamental inaccuracies.

Adrian Smith's report on the management of Blantyre House was by now completed and available to the HAC. A large section of David Smith's paper to the committee seemed to relate to its findings. His comments suggested that it had been copied to him. It is also probable that many other people including prisoners, ex-prisoners, and individuals outside HMPS were sent copies by the HAC. When I sought access to this report under the Freedom of Information Act it was one of those documents in respect of which disclosure was refused on the grounds of Parliamentary privilege. However I have obtained a copy.

David Smith's comment on the report was initially to question the integrity of Adrian Smith and members of his investigation team, stating (previously unpublished evidence to HAC dated 20 September 2000):

> Those charged with producing the report are cronies of the Area Manager and are themselves implicated by the findings of the report. Both are, and were Governors of 'sending establishments' and therefore equally guilty of the finding that 'unsuitable prisoners' were being sent to Blantyre.

He went on to make allegations against one senior member of the investigation team before attempting to dismiss most of the report's findings and defend the indefensible with delusions or half-truths. In dismissing the former Governor's failure to carry out instructions from his line managers he suggested that as he had raised these matters with the BOV he had a 'dispensation'. As the board had no executive or management function they had no power or authority to interfere between the Governor and those to whom he was accountable but it demonstrates that he and some of his colleagues did not feel constrained by the nature of their role. He concluded with an equally invalid account of the situation in the prison under the new Governor that included:

> The prison is being Governed by the Area Manager through his team of 'yes men' the result will be 'yet another uninspiring' C category prison not performing any differently to the rest and frankly more expensive to run, so will be closed once the D category men can be relocated.

This is little more than name calling. On reflection, sadly, it seems to characterise much of the hot air that was emanating from the former Governor's supporters at the time. David Smith was closely associated with at least three other BOV members who were known to be active in their support of the former Governor. However for most of this period he was ill or convalescing after surgery. It thus seems reasonable to conclude that most of his account is based on hearsay. Given that his evidence is so one sided and inaccurate, it is entirely possible any unpublished evidence submitted by his BOV colleagues may equally be so.

THE SMITH REPORT

When supporters of the former Governor got sight of the Smith Report into the management of Blantyre House it was understandable that some of them would want to discredit it. However, an independent reader would find it a thorough and balanced report on the situation at the prison. In essence, Smith found that little had changed at Blantyre House since his 1998 investigation. Much of the corrective action plan agreed between the former Governor and myself, based on his original recommendations, had either not been implemented or had been glossed over and allowed to slide. Despite very clear instructions putting an end to 'charity' work the Governor had allowed it to begin again in a different but equally unacceptable form without any reference back to his line manager. Smith found that clear orders given to the Governor regarding security procedures were ignored and even the most basic security procedures were not in place. The former Governor and his Head of Management Services had escaped formal disciplinary action in 1998 for serious failures in the financial management of the prison through my intercession. Smith found similar failings on this occasion and again recommended formal disciplinary action under the 'serious' section of the Code of Conduct for Prison Service Staff.

Grave concern was expressed about a number of other matters including: the appropriateness of some outside work placements, particularly those a considerable distance from the prison; mobile placements such as lorry drivers; prisoners working for their relatives; prisoners working for ex-prisoners; a prisoner working in his pre-imprisonment employment and some who were clearly self-employed and running their own business while serving a prison sentence. This included a prisoner working as a self-employed chauffeur using his own car to ferry celebrities around on behalf of their agent and doing so without valid motor insurance. In fact an examination of the 22 vehicles being used by prisoners revealed that ten were being driven without valid insurance. Some prisoners had made false statements to obtain insurance and one had dishonestly claimed to be a doctor. Given the risk this presented to the public and the potential for serious embarrassment to HMPS and in turn the Government it is beyond belief that the Governor, in allowing prisoners to use their own cars, did not have proper controls in place.

The report again highlighted that the criteria for selection of prisoners for Blantyre House agreed in the 1998 action plan were being ignored and concluded (Smith Report 2000, 11.1.ii)

> Weaknesses in the allocation and selection procedures for the transfer of prisoners to Blantyre House can result in the inappropriate transfer of manipulative and criminally active prisoners to a relatively unsupervised environment with access to temporary release. This presents a risk both to the public and the Prison Service.

Examination of security procedures at the prison led the enquiring officer to conclude (Smith Report 2000, 15. xxv):

> Several of these had been identified by the 1999 Standards and Security audit at Blantyre House and been included in a subsequent action plan. The most serious of these was the poor delivery of the searching of prisoners returning from temporary release at the prison gate. In November 1999 the Area Manager had instructed the Governor to implement the rub down searching of all prisoners returning from temporary release accompanied by scanning with a metal detector. This level of searching was not in place in May 2000. In November of 1999 the Area Manager had also instructed the Governor of Blantyre House to carry out re-profiling of the work and staff resources of the prison. This was prompted by the protests of the Governor that there were insufficient resources to implement the recommendations arising

from the 1999 Standards and Security audit. By May 2000 no apparent progress had been made on the re-profiling of Blantyre House.

Commenting on the effectiveness of the resettlement prisons as a group Smith states (Smith Report 2000, 17. para. 4-12):

> As far as we can see from statistics (reconviction rates after two years), they are very successful, particularly Blantyre House. However, the fact that their populations are hand picked and atypical for a category C prison will have significant impact on the figures.

Referring specifically to Blantyre House he records (Smith Report 2000, 17. para 5):

> Blantyre House's ethos, according to the previous Governor, is based on trust whereas most of the prison estate relies on checks and controls through process. This ethos discourages checking, particularly the detail, and encourages staff to get 'closer' to prisoners than is usual and adopt a more 'hands off' approach. This also allows more opportunity for prisoners to 'condition' staff and to be more likely to succeed in pushing the boundaries still further, particularly when the ethos encourages prisoners rather than staff to take the initiative. All of this makes tension and conflict within the Prison Service environment described above more likely to occur. The small number of staff, the large amount of work to do and the tight budget exacerbate this.
>
> There is no doubt in our minds that there has been an ongoing tension and conflict between the Area Manager and the Governor for several years over the balance in the regime between meeting individual prisoners' resettlement needs and security, ethos versus risk. The Governor, wishing to rely mainly on trust and leaving much of the initiative with prisoners; the Area Manager wanting the prison to conform to security and other Prison Service requirements, whilst still holding to the resettlement ethos. This seems to have caused the prison to be reined in periodically, causing both uncertainty and a 'yo-yo' effect which has been unfortunate for the establishment and culminated in the Governor being warned that he might be removed from his post.
>
> As we are quite sure anyone reading this report so far will have gathered, it is our view that although Blantyre House had a very committed management team and staff and an excellent re-conviction rate, it is doing so at too great a risk and without having in place the appropriate structures to ensure conformity to Prison Service Standards. Relationships are good, key performance targets are met and prisoners are complimentary about how Blantyre House has helped them. However it does not have in place all the necessary systems and structures to carry out its role, many systems are either not in place or not operated by staff as required. It is often not possible to discover who had responsibility for particular processes or decisions and what audit trails exist are often inadequate. This is particularly the case with security, the use of vehicles by prisoners and the financial arrangements surrounding charitable and subsidiary funds. In some cases this is disappointing, in others deeply worrying.
>
> What is particularly disturbing is the apparent strong belief held by the former management team and most staff of the prison that these omissions are not important. Particularly in respect of security, these leave the prison vulnerable to abuse by prisoners and outside criminal influences. Examples are the lack of proper searching at the gate, inadequate supervision on visits, the lack of searching of visitors, prisoners and staff and a searching strategy which was not adequate to its purpose.

We were also concerned over a number of outside work projects which in our view would not meet with public acceptability. Incidents, investigations and audits since 1995 seem to have had little impact on the way the prison has been managed, with only minimal change appearing to take place, which has then shown a tendency to slip back. We are left with the feeling that management and staff at the prison have been complacent.

There are grounds for considering charging the Governor with failing to carry out the Area Manager's instructions on the searching of prisoners at the gate of the prison. On balance we have decided this could be better dealt with informally. However the apparent financial mismanagement of charitable and subsidiary funds is so serious, particularly as disciplinary action was considered for the same issue after the 1998 audit, that we have felt that we have no alternative but to recommend charges under the 'serious case' procedure for both the former Governor and the Head of Management Services of Blantyre House.

We believe that it should still be entirely possible to have both successful rehabilitation through the resettlement ethos and the proper structures to control risk, although there may be some financial implications. We believe that it is essential that the new management team at Blantyre House deals with these issues together with those outlined above in order to set the prison's future course in the right direction.

Blantyre House now needs to move forward, putting what has gone on behind it, in a way which not only retains its strengths in rehabilitation but does so in a way which has the confidence of the public, Ministers and the Prison Service. It can only do this if it puts in place a comprehensive and effective risk management strategy with audit trails in line with Prison Service requirements.

Commenting on the former Governor's much publicised belief that the Area Manager was opposed to resettlement, Smith says (15, xxxvii): 'It should be emphasised that we believe the Area Manager remains fully committed to resettlement, which should be supported by the necessary security standards'.

During his investigation Adrian Smith and senior members of his team were briefed on the intelligence that contributed to the decision by the DG to take decisive action. As it was not within the scope of his terms of reference he made only brief comment in his report.

THE FORD INSPECTION

In late September 2000 the Chief Inspector of Prisons' inspection team carried out an unannounced short inspection of Ford Prison. Sir David Ramsbotham attended for one day and immediately afterwards contacted the DG accusing me of bullying the Governor (Ken Kan), and members of the management team. He also complained that the prison's resettlement role was being undermined by unnecessary restrictions on prisoners, more severe than those in a closed prison. Martin Narey was already fully aware of the situation at Ford (see pp. 137-139), the action I had taken to assist the Governor to improve performance and the financial management issue which was the subject of a joint police and HMPS investigation.

During the debrief on the last day of the inspection a junior member of the inspector's team told the meeting that she had read my reports on all my visits to Ford and did not agree with many of my supportive comments. Having been told that the reports reflected my observations on the day and were based on considerably greater experience than hers, she was asked to explain her comments. Seemingly irate, she made a response during which some unnamed officers were accused of regularly being drunk on duty. Others were accused of being racist in their dealings with prisoners and some of bullying prisoners to a degree that they were frightened to make a complaint. These were very serious allegations which if true would not be tolerated. Because of this I insisted that the inspectors reveal the names of those concerned and any evidence that they had to support the allegations before they left the prison. They refused to provide the information. When pressed, the team leader accepted that the description of officers as racist was inaccurate. But he insisted that these, still unidentified, officers had a training need in this area. He declined to provide any further information

As they failed, or were unable, to provide the evidence they claimed to have regarding the alleged serious misconduct by staff, I tasked a senior Governor from another prison to investigate the claims on behalf of the Governor. He found no evidence of any basis for these allegations.

When the report was published Ken Kan publicly stated that he rejected any suggestion that he felt bullied by his Area Manager and appreciated the support he was receiving from him. As he was a hardworking and able young man who had inherited many problems there was no reason for me to be hostile towards him.

Most of the in-charge Governors in my area had been selected and appointed by me, including the former Governor of Blantyre House. The qualities I looked for when selecting them were: a commitment to all the goals of HMPS; a clear understanding of these; good management and interpersonal skills; and an ability to give strong leadership to their staff. In the organizational culture of the time a key feature of successful management was an ability to cope under pressure and drive forward change and improved performance. Though all of them were different characters they all possessed these qualities to varying degrees and without exception were robust in their own way.

I think that I was well known in the service as a robust, direct and plain speaking individual with a propensity to use some strong language on occasions to emphasise my point. However I also have a strong and often self-effacing sense of humour. All my Governors were well aware of this when they accepted their appointments, as most of them had already worked with me and I had fully supported them in their professional and career development, as instanced by my support of the former Governor of Blantyre House in his studies at Cambridge University. They were also aware that I was supportive and understanding of failure where it could be reasonably explained. As members of a corporate team and as individual Governors all of them knew that they were not expected to take nonsense from anyone including their Area Manager. All of them were strong individuals who could and did argue their corner when necessary. Visitors attending our area meetings consistently commented on the good humour, camaraderie and frank talking that became a feature of the team, in comparison to the meetings they attended in most other areas.

The accusation by the Chief Inspector of Prisons that I was bullying the Governor was insulting both to me and to Ken Kan and wrongly portrayed my relationships with my Governors. Though we would have had differences of opinion on occasions, I always considered Ken to be an able colleague with whom I have continuing regular friendly contact. As with other derogatory matters that were aimed in my direction, at no time before making these accusations did the Chief Inspector raise his concerns with me or seek my comments. Ken made it quite clear that he did not agree with him either. As an ex-soldier, maybe he should have realised that esprit-de-corps and consistently high performance cannot be sustained through bullying. Neither would my excellent Governors want to continue working in such an environment when they knew they could find similar posts elsewhere in the service. The accusations seemed to come out of the blue but events that followed, within three weeks, at the HAC public hearings caused me to wonder whether they were designed to set the scene.

CHAPTER 10

The Home Affairs Select Committee Investigation

The period leading up to the public hearings by the Home Affairs Select Committee (HAC) on 17 and 18 October 2000 saw intense activity behind the scenes. The situation at Blantyre House, before the removal of Eoin McLennan-Murray, had been carefully examined and documented in the Smith Report. In response to ill-founded allegations regarding the conduct of the search and the behaviour of the officers involved, two separate investigations were carried out and their findings well documented. Though some reasonable criticism was recorded regarding the organization and management of the search there was general agreement that officers had acted professionally and that it had been conducted with good humour. Though claims were made to the contrary by a few prisoners and individuals who were not involved, the investigators' findings did not support the claimants' allegations regarding the availability of keys, wanton damage or unprofessional conduct by officers.

Parliamentary Select Committees enjoy considerable power and are viewed with some apprehension within the senior levels of the Civil Service. HMPS was no different and senior officials there were busily engaged in putting together the necessary evidence relating to the events that had taken place. As most of the decisions relating to the issues in question had been taken by the DG, my role was to check the accuracy of the evidence being submitted in so far as it related to me and the events with which I was directly involved. It seemed that as far as the Minister and the DG were concerned, they would deal with the public hearings and I would not be required to attend. I therefore got on with supporting the new Governor of Blantyre House and managing the rest of my area. Both the Minister and the DG visited the prison on a number of occasions to give support and ensure that they had a clear understanding of all the issues.

Even after the departure of the former Governor, worrying information continued to come in from the police regarding a prison officer whom they believed was associating with known criminal elements when off duty. We were told by the police that the officer concerned had a serious cocaine habit. Though we could identify the individual concerned from the description given, there was little we could do until the police investigation was complete and only then if they were prepared to provide the evidence to support such action.

All able-bodied prison officers are trained to a reasonably high degree in control and restraint techniques (known as C&R), which enables them effectively to restrain violent prisoners. These skills are very much in demand in the pub and night club security scene and, though not officially permitted, prison officers are sometimes recruited for these jobs in off duty hours. Working in this field can bring them into contact with criminal elements, particularly those in the drugs trade, and can lead a few to fall into that culture or develop relationships with those involved.

Before the HAC was scheduled to hear evidence in public, information began to come in from various sources that some of those most active in their criticism of me were boasting with confidence that the HAC would have me removed from post and possibly forced into early retirement. This was slightly unnerving but as the action we had taken was justified there was no reason to give much credence to such rumours. That was to change when a journalist, the identity of whom is not known to me, is alleged to have attributed comments to Robin Corbett, chair of the HAC, to the effect that the HAC would 'sort out' those in the Prison Service responsible for the removal of the former Governor and for the search. Whether the alleged comments were true or not the report was alarming. The HAC had not yet begun to hear evidence in public yet the chair was allegedly predicting its outcome. If true, it was hardly an indication that he was approaching the investigation *de novo*.

Stress levels were raised by this to an unbearable degree but there was nothing I could do. I was not in control of events and probably would not even have an opportunity to be heard as the DG intended to deal with all the evidence in public himself. Having witnessed the treachery of some senior officials in the past and their willingness to sacrifice more junior colleagues to protect their own skins there might reasonably have been some apprehension for me in this situation. However there was not. I had total confidence in Martin Narey's integrity and if I was not to have an opportunity to defend myself then I was sure that he would protect my interests to the best of his considerable ability.

The DG submitted a detailed memorandum to the HAC outlining all the facts of the case and the reasons for the decisions taken. Additional evidence in the form of the reports of HMPS's own investigations was provided on an 'in confidence' basis. It now appears that the contents of at least some of these reports were revealed to people having no right of access to them by someone associated with the committee.

In addition to the profusion of evidence received by the HAC from prisoners, ex-prisoners, the BOV and non-members of HMPS with no direct knowledge of the facts, the PGA also submitted a lengthy memorandum. The content of this document was—to put matters at their lowest level—inaccurate and misleading. It gave an erroneous account of many aspects of the search and played down the significance of the items found. It was dismissive of the intelligence that together with other factors led to the removal of the former Governor, even though its authors knew nothing of its content and sought to undermine the credibility of the Chaucer Unit. However it omitted to inform the committee that, as I explained in *Chapter 6*, the PGA had never spoken to me to ask for an explanation. Nor did it acknowledge that the DG had offered them a confidential briefing, which they declined. Most of this unpublished evidence remains undiscovered under Parliamentary privilege.

A few days prior to the start of the scheduled public hearing of evidence it emerged that *I would* be called by the committee, together with John Podmore, who had commanded the search. We would attend with the DG and the Prisons Minister Paul Boateng MP on the afternoon of 18 October 2000. Though I was apprehensive because of the comments being attributed to Robin Corbett, an inane belief in the system made this a welcome development.

Because of its relevance in explaining why the DG decided to remove the former Governor at such short notice and carry out the search of the prison, it was important that the HAC was briefed on the intelligence. However this could not be done in a public hearing as it would compromise ongoing investigations and could place sources at serious risk. The HAC were therefore asked to hear some sensitive evidence in private. There was no obligation on them to agree to this request but, if they did not, we would not have been able to deal with these issues in any great depth. It was unclear until just before the public hearing started whether they would agree, but they did.

The HAC had already received a very full account of the situation at the prison in the Smith Report 2000 a similar report on the 1998 investigation and other documentary evidence relating to the prison and to the former Governor's performance and disobedience to orders. In the circumstances it seemed sensible that they should hear the sensitive evidence in private first. This would have enabled them to decide how best to proceed and would allow them to probe issues more effectively. They decided to proceed with the evidence in public first and go into closed session at the end.

THE FIRST HEARING

They also decided to hear evidence from a group of prisoners and to facilitate this they convened on the afternoon of October 17 in the staff training facility located outside Blantyre House Prison. They were then to go into public session and hear other witnesses. On that morning, prior to starting, they arranged to visit the prison itself and talk to staff and prisoners. Normal etiquette on such occasions was for visitors to meet the Governor who would greet them and provide a general briefing. Because of Chris Bartlett's relative inexperience as an in-charge Governor, I was asked by the DG's office to attend the briefing with him. This was not an unusual occurrence for Area Managers when important visits were taking place. Chris had carefully planned the visit to meet their needs and prepared a detailed briefing for them. We agreed that Chris would lead and I would only get involved if he needed help or if they wanted me to comment. Though he lacked experience in dealing with visits of this kind, I was confident that he would handle it comfortably.

The members of the committee involved in the investigation that day were: Robin Corbett MP (chair); Ian Cawsey MP; Janet Dean MP; Gerald Howarth MP; Humfrey Malins MP; Paul Stinchcombe MP; David Winnick MP and Bob Russell MP. Arriving at the briefing as a group, there were none of the conventional pleasantries or introductions. They sat down around the table and as the Governor began to speak, a number of them collectively launched into him like a pack of wolves. Shouting him down, they demanded an explanation for management decisions that he and the DG had taken since he took charge. Not allowing him to speak, they were bullying him into reversing these decisions and restoring activities that had been stopped on the orders of the DG. Though Members of Parliament, they had no executive authority to make these demands in this way and as visitors to the prison their discourtesy to the Governor was unbelievable.

Their verbal harassment was such that Chris Bartlett could barely get a word in. He was visibly distressed and clearly intimidated by them. I decided to interject to help him. As I began to speak one prominent member of the committee stood up and, leaning across the table toward me with his eyes ablaze, his face flushed and contorted, shouted, 'You can shut up, we know all about you, we know what you have done and we will deal with you later!' Though surprised by his behaviour, I had already faced the pressures of threats from terrorists without bending and I was not about to be intimidated or abused by such ignorance or that of any of his colleagues. I too raised my voice responding to him and said, 'No, you don't, you know nothing about me; but if you would listen instead of shouting us down you might learn something'. The situation then slightly improved, but from the atmosphere and attitude they displayed it was quite clear to me that many of the HAC members had closed minds, having already prejudged the situation.

During the afternoon they began hearing evidence in the training centre. Six serving prisoners were heard in private but all the other evidence was taken in public. Discovered HAC documents now reveal that all of the prisoner witnesses had been in correspondence with the HAC chair and, in some cases, regular correspondence. Some members of the media were in attendance during the public session. I was not there but became aware of the substance of what occurred from the official record and from colleagues who were.

Their first witness was Alan Rogers, an ex-prisoner and friend of the former Governor (see p. 129). In welcoming him, Robin Corbett gave no clue that he had been in regular correspondence with him before the hearing, saying (HAC 4th Report, Q1), 'Some of us had the pleasure of meeting you and your colleagues when we were here earlier in the year'. They knew, or should have known that Rogers knew nothing directly of the events of May 5 and 6, why they happened or what the senior management of HMPS now intended to do. Though an active supporter of the former Governor, he could offer no more direct evidence than any man in the street. The fact that he had left Blantyre House more than 18 months earlier only served to further underline his lack of direct and actual knowledge of the current situation in the prison.

Robin Corbett began his questioning of Rogers by asking (HAC 4th Report, Q1): 'I wonder if I might start by asking you to give us your views as to how you think the changes that have been made as a result of the raid on May 5/6 have impacted on the ethos of Blantyre House and how you feel prisoners have reacted to this?' Responding to this and a supplementary question Rogers replied (HAC 4th Report, A1):

> To sum up Blantyre House in one word it would have to be 'trust' excessive security is not needed. By that I mean the raid itself and the way they conducted it and the way they searched the premises and kept the prisoners awake all night and drug tested them ... there is no way they can justify what they did and how they did it. That has got to have an impact.

Though the HAC was aware from the reports they had received on the search and the new security procedures that his comments were at worst wholly unfounded and at the very least highly questionable, he was not challenged on any of it.

Rogers went on to tell the hearing that he did not believe my assurance that the prison would continue in its resettlement role, describing it as (HAC 4th Report, A3) 'an alien concept to the Prison Service' and claiming that the objective of HMPS was to destroy the regime and turn it into a young offender institution. Seemingly, afforded the status of an expert on all things related to the prison, he dismissed the possibility that keys were missing from the gate during the search suggesting that the searchers forced entry just to be destructive, and dismissed any suggestion that there was any intelligence to justify the action taken. A total of 44 questions were put to Rogers. Setting the pattern for what would follow that afternoon and the following morning, it seemed that many of these questions were framed in an obvious attempt to lead him (and in turn other witnesses) to say what some members of the committee hoped to hear.

After Rogers, the committee heard from members of the BOV represented by their chair David Cottle, Mrs Molly Tipples, Lady Rosie Clarke, Dr Brian Hugo and Ms Helen Warriner. In the period between the transfer out of the former Governor and these hearings some of those present had been actively involved in crusading on his behalf. A source close to them also alleges that some were in close contact with members of the HAC throughout this period. They also seemed to be doing their best to undermine the efforts of the new Governor to get the prison 'back on track'. Again Corbett gave no hint, in opening the session with them, that there had been any previous contact.

David Cottle, the chair is the only member of the BOV who had had any real contact with me. I found him to be a decent man. However it seemed obvious to me that he was under considerable pressure from a dominant group within the board. The initial questions were directed to him and mostly related to his perception of morale at the prison and changes that were being made to the regime. His responses, though critical in some cases, were balanced and fair. However as the hearing progressed Lady Clarke and Dr Hugo raised their profile. Dr Hugo had accompanied David Cottle to the prison on the night of the search and both remained there until well after midnight before leaving of their own accord, when it was clear that the search was progressing satisfactorily. After giving a brief account of the events of the night Cottle told the committee that the search was being carried out 'in a civilised manner'.

Lady Clarke and Dr Hugo were strong characters on the board and though they had no contact with me were known to be opposed to the changes that had occurred. Molly Tipples was not known to me until later when she took over the chair and regularly attended area meetings of the local BOV chairs. I think she revelled in her reputation as a campaigner and protester over one issue or another. When I got to know her I found her to be a likeable person but with a warped view of authority who tended to think that she knew better.

David Cottle's account of how the search was conducted was clearly not the message that other BOV members wished to put across and Dr Hugo immediately interjected to say (HAC 4th Report, A71), 'We were very impressed with the exemplary behaviour of our men [prisoners] who were behaving extremely well'. He then went on to suggest that they were deceived into thinking that this was just a low key search, but as there was a command suite, which he claimed not to have been aware of, it was much bigger. This was disingenuous in that he should have known that all operations of this kind, in all prisons, have to be properly managed. The person in overall charge of any operation at establishment level is always referred to as the Silver Commander.

Having left the prison of their own accord they then criticised the Silver Commander for not calling them back when it became necessary to force entry into some areas. However his decision to take this action, because keys could not be produced, did not affect the control situation in the prison as no prisoners were involved and it was done with the agreement of the Governor. Commenting on what he saw on his arrival at the prison at 11 a.m. the following day Dr Hugo said (HAC 4th Report, A73), 'There had obviously been a massive disturbance'. He told of visiting all areas, accompanied by prisoners, noting all the damage and later complaining to the Governor. His comments were not challenged though the committee would have known from other formal reports that there had been no disturbance of any kind during this operation.

David Winnick MP, who led most of the questioning at this stage, said (HAC 4th Report, Q80), 'One of the prisoners said that the search was carried out as if it was by stormtroopers'. Dr Hugo quickly responded (HAC 4th Report, A80), 'It was an appalling mess. If our men had rioted, which they did not, it would have been a lovely story for the press'. None of this was correct. The search was conducted professionally and in good spirits. There had been no conflict between officers and prisoners and any damage that was done was reasonable in the circumstances but was now being exaggerated.

Winnick, clearly aware of the alleged conflict between the former Governor and myself, asked David Cottle for his impression of our relationship. He replied (HAC 4th Report, A81):

> There was certainly, I think, a difference. This is subjective but certainly a difference in the way they viewed prisons, resettlement prisons. I think the Area Manager likes control, as do most people in the Prison Service, and when you have a special unit, a special resettlement unit that is actually doing pioneering work, innovative pioneering work, the two do not meld together in the way they should. So I would say there was probably a professional difference. Although we were aware of a difference of opinion in maybe how Blantyre should be run or the way you should run a prison, there was certainly no animosity that we were aware of, or tension, because Mr McLennan-Murray always spoke well of Mr Murtagh as a professional, equally, Mr Murtagh.

He was interrupted before he could finish by Lady Clarke shouting over him (HAC 4th Report, A81):

> Can I just say that the board had the impression that the Governor was being bullied by the Area Manager and he had a strong enough personality to cope with it. Yes we were concerned about his state of health and for that reason we wanted to get in the Director General of the Prison Service. We were worried about the state of bullying of the Governor.

Dr Hugo and Molly Tipples also began to chip in, the latter adding (HAC 4th Report, A85):

> It was not the Governor who came to us saying, 'I'm being bullied', it was Dr Hugo, as a professional doctor, who came to the board and said he was worried about the state of the Governor's health because he felt the pressure being put on him amounted to bullying and he came to us as a board. I and the then chairman saw Martin Narey and said we were worried. He then came down and the results which followed are well known.

Confirming her comments Dr Hugo told the hearing that the chair also wrote to the DG on the subject.

But according to the DG the issue of 'bullying' was never raised with him either in discussion or in writing. However they did complain that the Area Manager was placing restrictions on the Governor's freedom to allow prisoners to get involved in activities that were not acceptable to HMPS. The DG was fully aware of these issues and agreed with the line I was taking. He made that clear to the board face to face with them and later in writing in a very detailed letter dated 16 July 1999. Furthermore only David Cottle had had any real contact with me or knew me but he was shouted down. An examination of all the minutes of their meetings reveals no record of the discussions they claimed took place regarding concerns about bullying. During their evidence inaccurate, imprecise or misleading comments were also made relating to the education programme, the performance of the prison post May 5 and the search.

It was perhaps predictable that Dr Hugo and Lady Clarke were hostile to the events that had taken place or that their account of these events would have a certain slant, but the extent to which they seemed to be prepared to go to undermine me was something of a surprise. I wondered whether it was just coincidence that a couple of weeks earlier Sir David Ramsbotham had been making similar comments about bullying at Ford Prison (*Chapter 9*, pp. 153-155). I became convinced in my own mind that there was some connection.

The HAC then heard from a group that represented the part-time chaplains and the Education Department, including the Education Manager, Ms. Francoise Fletcher, and members of her team, Ralph Dellow and Michael Duff. The chaplaincy was represented by the Reverend John Bourne (Church of England), the Reverend David Adkins (Calvary Church, Tunbridge Wells) and Mrs Brioni Armytage (Church of England). Both of the male part-time chaplains were former police officers. They were questioned regarding the keys to the chapel that could not be found on the night of the search and assured the hearing that they had been placed in the key cupboard. This suggested that the keys were available during the search, but very reputable managers, including the Governor who designed the Blantyre House key control system, were emphatic that they could not be found. None of the chaplains was a member of HMPS and in most cases they had only limited experience of prisons. Their contributions reflected the nature of their role and, I think, a fair degree of naïveté but clearly they gave an honest account from their viewpoint.

Most of this session focused on issues relating to the prison's education programme and specifically to the Education Department. Strangely, though Ralph Dellow had been engaged in extensive unpublished correspondence with Robin Corbett and the HAC over a period of months no hint of this was given by the chair in opening the session. Furthermore, though that correspondence seemed to indicate that, at least, Corbett appeared to credit him with considerable knowledge of all matters relating to HMPS, he was not asked a single question. The formal record indicates that Dellow never said a word at the hearing.

All of the Education Department staff in attendance were employees of the contracted education provider and therefore not members of HMPS. HMPS sets the education priorities and monitors the provider's performance in delivering them. Tight controls were not always popular with many education staff. At that time HMPS strategy concentrated on public value and tended to the elimination of many of the recreational subjects that some educationalists might prefer to teach. The new Governor had concerns about the efficiency of the Education Department and had sought advice from HMPS's expert advisers. At the time of the hearings some changes were expected, which seemed to unsettle the department.

Francoise Fletcher had been in charge of this department for only a few months when the events of May 5 occurred and had had no previous experience of working in prisons or of HMPS. She was a French national living in the UK and a strong supporter of the former Governor.

During the search of the prison at least 14 cameras were found in the possession of prisoners. For obvious reasons, prisoners are not allowed to have cameras in any prison. It later emerged that these cameras had been authorised as part of a photography class being run by the Education Department. Photography classes are rare in prisons but where they occur cameras are kept under strict control and are not permitted to be in a prisoner's possession. Because of his very real concerns the DG ordered that this class be stopped. This did not please the Education Department and its tutor, Michael Duff, who attended the hearing as a witness. Some members of the BOV and the HAC were also hostile to this decision.

Francoise Fletcher's evidence clearly demonstrated her hostility to the constraints involved in delivering an education programme in a prison setting and to the national targets and priorities on which her performance would be judged. This is borne out in response to a question from Janet Dean MP to which she replied (HAC 4th Report, A124), 'Yes I do foresee problems. One of the problems is that the Home Office only monitors results in literacy and numeracy, none of the other subjects, although they are accredited by Blantyre are seen as having educational value and I have been told that the wide range of classes that we run—i.e. art, pottery, woodwork, decorative painting techniques and languages—are seen as having no educational value'.

This was followed by what appeared to be a 'set piece' designed to undermine me. Humfrey Malins MP asked her (HAC 4th Report, Q126), 'Has it ever been said to you about Blantyre prisoners that "these men are all beyond redemption"?', to which she replied, 'Yes, it has' and went on tell him that it was said to her by the Area Manager in circumstances which she described in detail. This was completely incorrect. I never made any such comment. Neither was it a form of words I would ever use—and it was also against my beliefs as a professional prison Governor with many years' experience. I did once speak to her about the behaviour of one of her staff. She appeared to have overlooked that that conversation was witnessed by the Governor who would also know that the offending words were never used.

How did Malins know to ask this question? There is no record of any such allegation in the record of the earlier proceedings or in any of the disclosed unpublished evidence. Was it intended to give credence to the suggestion that the events of May 5 occurred because of the Area Manager's alleged opposition to the resettlement concept? Whatever its origins, it fed my suspicions that some of the evidence given in public was being contrived to get at me.

Jim Semple was a retired former Governor of Blantyre House and the architect of its resettlement role and general ethos. He had been retired for a number of years and was out of touch with the changing culture of HMPS. Jim's contribution to the development of resettlement regimes was considerable and for that he was widely respected. He had submitted a paper to the HAC and gave evidence in person that afternoon. Jim had no knowledge of why these events had occurred and knew little about me but he had clearly been given a slanted briefing based on 'the story so far'.

Most of Jim's evidence seemed to have been read from a script. It outlined the background to the development of the regime and the prison or was reflective of his personal and in truth admirable views on resettlement. But he went on to describe the circumstances of the removal of the former Governor as 'humiliating and disgraceful'. Winnick asked him who should be held responsible for this and he responded (HAC 4th Report, A160), 'the Director General'. Winnick then asked (HAC 4th Report, Q162), 'What would you say about the Area Manager?' His answer must have been insufficiently critical for Winnick who came back with (HAC 4th Report, Q163): 'You see we have heard evidence that the previous Governor was subject to bullying by the Area Manager. This is my concluding question. Do you have any comment on that?' Jim knew nothing of my management style but having had words put in his mouth and heard the earlier evidence from the BOV, replied in quite vague terms that he was told by unidentified managers that they 'found it a struggle under [my] management'.

Six prisoners met with some members of the HAC who remained after others had left. They were offered the right to decide whether their evidence was on the record or not and given time to decide after the hearing. The six were already known to some HAC members with whom each of them had been in correspondence. Five of them were serving long sentences for importing or supplying drugs. They were: Charles Darnell (eleven years for supplying) who claimed to be a former solicitor; K. R. Forrester (seven years for importing); John Delaney (14 years for importing); R. J. Illingworth (nine years for importing); and Chris Johnson (seven years for importing). The sixth witness was Nicholas Bertram (serving life for murder). From their comments it appeared that they had heard all the earlier witnesses.

The evidence of these prisoners was a mixture of whining about improved security, being searched, tighter controls on work placements, the ending of mobile placements that could not be monitored by staff, criticism of the new Governor and new managers brought in with him. Most of their evidence misrepresented the situation or was baseless. The conspiracy theory that the prison's resettlement role was being undermined was also a feature. However it seemed that they were being bestowed with a high level of credibility by those HAC members still present, who were Corbett, Winnick, Howarth and Cawsey. Some observers described the proceedings during that afternoon as 'surreal'. A reporter in attendance is alleged to have said that he had never witnessed anything like it and opined that it was 'an obvious set up'.

THE SECOND HEARING

The hearing of evidence in public resumed the following morning in one of the committee rooms in the Palace of Westminster. The first witness called was the Chief Inspector of Prisons, Sir David Ramsbotham. He was accompanied by his Deputy, Colin Allen, and one of his inspectors, Geoffrey Hughes. Allen had held the Deputy Chief Inspector's post for more than ten years. Prior to joining the inspectorate he had been a Prison Governor. During his tenure in the post the culture of HMPS had completely changed. Hughes had been promoted to Class 1 Governor on his appointment to the inspectorate but had not managed a prison at that level.

The chair initially questioned Sir David about the delay in publishing his report on the inspection of Blantyre House. His detailed response explained the process of circulating a draft, correcting factual inaccuracies, and dealing with any disagreements. He explained that HMPS questioned the content of his draft preface. Assuring the HAC that he alone decided what was finally published he went on to tell them (HAC 4th Report, A223), 'What has appeared in the Preface, and the tenor of the Preface remains as written, although not every detail I wrote in my first draft was actually published.' This was an interesting response as the preface had been substantially altered but his comments confirm that an earlier suggestion that he was forced to change it by HMPS, made in a radio interview by an official of the PGA, was without foundation.

Robin Corbett observed that the nub of the problem seemed to him to lie between risk taking on the one hand and trust on the other. This he felt led to ambiguities in some people's minds delivering a resettlement regime in a Category C prison. He wondered if there were any other similar prisons in the service. Sir David told him that Kirklevington Grange Prison had a similar ethos. However he then went on to say that the difference between them was that the Governor of Kirklevington was fully supported by her Area Manager, wrongly implying that the former Governor of Blanytre House was not. He did not explain that, though Kirklevington Grange in the North-east of England was a resettlement prison, its population was quite different from that at Blantyre House. Neither did he mention that following the events of May 5 I had invited the Governor of Kirklevington Grange to come down to Blantyre House to assist and advise the new Governor in getting the prison back on track; nor that when there she was surprised by the number of defective systems she found and by the lax attitude of many officers. He did not tell them that I, in conjunction with the new Governor and the Governor of Kirklevington, had arranged a rolling programme of attachments for all Blantyre House staff to Kirklevington to learn how that prison operated. Perhaps he was not aware of this.

During Sir David's evidence the issue of resettlement was discussed. There was general agreement with the concept in respect of all prisoners but less so on what it meant in practical terms. Asked by Gerald Howarth (Q.232) what he would regard as being the essential elements of a resettlement policy and what the fundamental implications of such a policy would be, he avoided the question but offered his now familiar functional management strategy as fundamental to the success of a resettlement policy. Pressed further by Paul Stinchcombe (Q.234) on the substance of a resettlement policy he again seemed to parry the question.

Responding to a very perceptive and well framed comment and question (Q.237) from Martin Linton relating to the management of risk and the difficulty in balancing it with an appropriate level of security, he said that he 'could not agree more' but again parried the question. Sir David then went on to talk about Governors as risk takers, the bravery of Governors like McLennan-Murray in taking risks and the response he got from prisoners because they understood and appreciated the trust being placed in them. He stressed the need for Governors to feel and to be supported in taking these risks and accused me of failing to give that support. He drew attention to the evidence heard the previous day that (HAC 4th Report, A239) 'he was not necessarily supported by his Area Manager', and when pressed to be specific replied (HAC 4th Report, A240), 'The evidence you have had, I know, shows that people did not think that trust was meted out to the Governor in the way he might have had reason to expect'.

An unbiased observer might conclude that too much trust and support was given to a Governor who had already demonstrated such poor judgement and persistent disobedience to instructions both from his Area Manager and from HMPS headquarters. He had had numerous opportunities but failed to avail himself of them. Some might also consider it a matter of concern that Sir David should feel able to tell the HAC members what the evidence they heard should lead them to conclude.

But he would go much further and in response to leading questions from David Winnick, said (HAC 4th Report, A250):

> To be quite honest with you, the reported events of May 5 do not seem to me to be fully in line with what I understand to be the way that the Director General wishes the Service to go and the sort of standards that he wished it to achieve in its Statement of Purpose. Therefore I wonder how much of what happened actually was Prison Service policy or whether it was the policy of the Area Manager.

Asked about the accusation made the previous day by Lady Rosie Clarke that the Area Manager was bullying the former Governor he stated (HAC 4th Report, A252), 'I would be inclined to accept their view'.

But most revealing was his reply to Winnick, who asked him when he first knew the former Governor was being moved and he said (HAC 4th Report, A255), 'I knew nothing about it until I heard that he had been removed that afternoon. In fact I did not hear of it until the next week because I was away'.

Could he really have forgotten that the DG had told him in a letter dated 18 April 2000 of his intentions to move the Governor? This was the same letter in which Martin Narey responded to the draft inspection report on Blantyre House and Sir David's attacks on me in its preface. The letter included the comment:

> I am giving you advance notice, in complete confidence, that I intend to replace Eoin with someone who can combine the special ethos of Blantyre with a sharper appreciation of security and public safety issues.

Martin Narey had shared with Sir David the concerns he had regarding the former Governor's behaviour and disobedience yet Sir David gave no indication of this. He went on to criticise the scale of the search, its objectives and its management and, through his deputy, its proportionality. Throughout the hearing he used every opportunity to paint a detrimental picture of me and to imply that I was personally responsible for all these events because of my opposition to the resettlement work being done at the prison. In making these comments he knew nothing of the detailed intelligence or other factors that led to the search. The enthusiasm with which he seemed to denigrate me throughout the hearing and before it may have encouraged Humfrey Malin to attempt the *coup de grace* by asking (HAC 4th Report, Q277):

> In fact, putting it in a nutshell, if the Area Manager of the South East was the same type, perhaps the same person, as the Area Manager of the North East, and one could take out the Area Manager of the South East from the whole equation, if, then none of us might be sitting here today. Do you think that is possible?

Ramsbotham enthusiastically replied, 'I think that is a pretty fair supposition'.

Then Robin Corbett, in what seemed a blatant attempt to discredit the damning HMPS reports on Blantyre House and any intelligence that might support the action taken, asked (Q.278) whether some criticism could be levelled at HMPS because it lacked a more independent element. Sir David obliged in his reply (HAC 4th Report, A278):

> Yes, I make no bones about that and have done so for a while. Personally, I hate things like Chaucer teams which I understand are there for the purpose of investigating alleged corruption amongst members of your own staff. I hate it, frankly.

He seemed to discount anything connected with my operational leadership or supposedly negative views.

The same kind of atmosphere had prevailed during the previous afternoon and earlier that morning, when the chair of the HAC appeared to be friendly and overtly sympathetic to the views being expressed by some of the earlier witnesses and when some HAC members seemed to be keen to lead witnesses and put words into their mouths; behaviour that would not be acceptable in any similar forum outside Parliament. The more the HAC hearings moved on, the more the partisan nature of some HAC members seemed to become more obvious.

The former Governor, Eoin McLennan-Murray, attended the hearing accompanied by Mike Newell and David Rodden, the President and General Secretary of the PGA respectively. The HAC seemed almost fawning in its welcome to them and particularly towards Eoin. Telling of his visit to the prison the previous day, the chair assured him that he still had friends. I suppose that Robin Corbett took this to be little more than a matter of courtesy, but the committee was supposed to be carrying out an impartial investigation. Any judge in a courtroom would have found himself or herself disqualified for such antics. The approach raised questions about how far the HAC was taking its role seriously. An investigation carried out by reputable professionals of HMPS had found clear evidence of grave shortcomings at one of its prisons when the former Governor was in charge. These were well documented and doubly or even triply checked out by HMPS. But they were being ignored altogether by an HAC that seemed to prefer to be duped by the unchallenged and misleading second hand accounts of witness after witness. This pattern would continue.

This session covered a wide spectrum of issues and featured comments and questions framed in the overtly partisan and sympathetic manner that was becoming familiar. These covered the authorising, planning, conduct and proportionality of the search, the removal of the Governor, the reasons for this, and his relationship with the Area Manager, why any intelligence was not shared with him and more. It started with questions relating to the authorisation and scale of searches in prisons and whether the Blantyre search was somehow unique. As Newell and Rodden had not availed themselves of the DG's offer of a confidential briefing, neither knew why or by whom the search was authorised. However this did not inhibit them in expressing their views, which were predictably supportive of the former Governor and critical of me who was portrayed by them and some members of the HAC as an ogre. Though much was made of why intelligence was not shared with Eoin during this session, the matter was never raised with those who did know why.

The issue of security categorisation of prisons and prisoners came up on a number of occasions during the hearings. Sir David Ramsbotham clearly felt that Blantyre House should not be a Category C prison, suggesting that this was inconsistent with its resettlement function. He and some of the MPs appeared to favour a separate resettlement prison category where, presumably, security would be replaced by a system based on mutual trust. Ramsbotham was critical of HMPS's prisoner security categorisation system and—apparently unaware that it had just been reviewed—called for a rethink. His comments and those of some of his inspectors seemed to indicate that they did not fully comprehend the system or the relationship between a prisoner's security category and that of the prison in which he or she is held.

This subject was again raised during the session with the former Governor. Asked if he considered that the security classification of Blantyre House was appropriate in the light of its resettlement role, Newell said that to call resettlement prisons 'Category C' was a misnomer. As resettlement units were operating quite successfully in parts of secure prisons throughout the service this seemed to be a surprising statement. However it appeared to feed a developing notion within the HAC that there should be a separate category for these prisons. This would support an argument that the very basic security demanded by me was unreasonable and would enable them to recommend such a change. But given the status quo, this was putting the cart before the horse.

Janet Dean raised the tricky issue of why my instructions were not obeyed. The former Governor initially denied that instructions were disobeyed but went on to try to justify his failure to do as he was told. Picking up on the debate regarding the suitability of the prison for a Category C rating he argued that the physical defences of the prison were inconsistent with that rating and that he did not have the resources to carry out Category C procedures. He did not explain that full Category C security standards had not been demanded from him and that I was requiring him to carry out only very basic security procedures, most of which were consistent with the norm in open prisons. Neither did he explain that as half of the prisoners in the prison were themselves in Category C the procedures required were at a basic minimum.

Arguing that he did not think the prison should be Category C or that the procedures were necessary, the former Governor admitted (HAC 4th Report, A300), 'I continually resisted these targets because I said they were unachievable' claiming that he did not have the resources to carry out this work. Governors constantly re-profile the work of their prisons to enable them to accommodate new work or to prove a need for additional resources. Eoin did not mention that I had instructed him to re-profile but that he had failed to do so, or that his successor was able to put these procedures in place within days of taking over with the same resources. He insisted (HAC 4th Report, A300): 'I did not disobey the order at all, I set in train a series of actions that we would do our best to achieve it, but my heart knew that we would fail. That is the honest truth'.

His explanation seemed to be at odds with other statements made by him and others associated with the prison. On the one hand he claimed to have been unable to obey the orders because he lacked the necessary resources and on the other he and his supporters argued that as the regime was based on trust, searching of prisoners entering the prison would damage the whole ethos. Whatever his reasoning, some of the staff were very clear that the decision not to comply with instructions was his alone. His explanation was accepted without challenge by the HAC.

Asked to comment on the statement of the BOV that he was being bullied, he replied (HAC 4th Report, A301):

It is a very difficult question really to respond to. Perhaps it is more obvious to people who are outside observing the situation than it is for the participants themselves. I was under a lot of pressure in that my approach and how I wanted to run the prison, I know, was at odds with the Area Manager's. We had different philosophies. He wanted to exert control over me, and it is fair to say I was resisting that control because I could not see any rhyme or reason for it. That sets up a tension clearly. I suppose the line between exerting managerial control robustly and bullying is a fine line. I think if I am able to stand back, having had the benefit of other people's observations, I would say, yes, I was the subject of bullying.

Asked for examples he went on to state vaguely that on occasions the Area Manager had humiliated him in public in that in the presence of other members of the senior management team he had used the expression that Eoin was 'wired up to the moon'. He also quoted an incident which did occur many months before. It had become increasingly difficult to contact him because of his frequent absences from the prison. I had tried over a number of days to speak to him on a matter of some urgency. After numerous unsuccessful attempts to make contact a further call was made but he was still not available. Angry and frustrated by this situation I told the officer receiving the call to pass on to him 'to make sure he is in his office at 08.00 hours tomorrow because I want to see him'. It is probably true that I sounded aggressive and the Governor later told me that the officer was offended by my manner. Accepting that I might have caused offence I offered to speak to her and apologise personally but the Governor assured me that it was not necessary as he had dealt with the matter himself. That he should introduce it now like some rabbit out of the hat was surprising to say the least.

'Wired to the moon' is a saying of mine generally used in jocular terms to express disbelief at what I see as illogical actions or decisions. All Governors and senior managers in the area were familiar with it and knew it was not intended to be offensive. I had a number of well known jocular sayings, many of which were self-effacing. However that is not to suggest that there had not been a number of heated exchanges resulting from the Governor's disobedience and poor judgment as I have described in earlier chapters, and during which he gave as good as he got. Though he sought to portray himself as a victim, our supposedly difficult relationship did not inhibit him from defying my instructions or from applying for another Governor post in the area, where he was content to continue working with me.

Picking up on the former Governor's comments the HAC went on to explore the circumstances of his transfer. Now clear in his mind that he had been bullied, he and the committee began to see bullying in almost everything that happened to him. Gerald Howarth, seeking to extend the level of proof, wondered if the Area Manager had a difficult relationship with any of the other Governors in the area. In carefully vague terms, Rodden told him that he had (HAC 4th Report, A326) 'more calls from Governors in this Area than any other'. He did not offer any supporting evidence or say how he arrived at this conclusion. However his comments were well received by the HAC. Malins pondered (HAC 4th Report,

Q324): 'To be absolutely blunt about it, would you say that the core of the problem was this particular Area Manager? If there had been another Area Manager such a problem as we are now looking into would not have arisen'. In contrast to Sir David Ramsbotham's earlier contribution, Mike Newell's reply was more cautious and included (HAC 4th Report, A324):

> It would be wrong of me to sit here and cast blame in that way. I am not party to the day-to-day events and operations of the particular Area Manager. What I am party to is, standing outside in this particular case, a set of events which are unique in my experience and where we feel, as an association it was a completely disproportionate response to what the problems were in respect of Blantyre House.

Not the reply he expected? Approaching the same question from a different angle Corbett then wondered (HAC 4th Report, Q325):

> It is likely, is it not, that somebody with the Area Manager's background, including at one stage governing The Maze in Northern Ireland, which arguably has to be probably the most difficult prison in the United Kingdom and the subject of terrorist threats while he was working in Northern Ireland, would have a certain difficulty in understanding what Blantyre House was about?

This deeply patronising enquiry prompted a level of agreement.

Clearly Corbett did not consider that my experiences as a Governor of a female prison, two young offender institutions and as Head of the NIPS Training College in addition to my experience at The Maze could have opened my mind sufficiently to grasp the concept of resettlement. Though I had set the objectives and business plan for Blantyre House and had oversight of its management for many years, could I really have difficulty understanding what it and the other resettlement units in my area were about?

During this session the former Governor gave evidence on a number of matters where his account was at variance with my recollection (and record) of the facts, as when he claimed not to have been briefed, on taking over as Governor, on staff believed to be corrupt, or that he was a victim of 'wind-ups' by me. Toward the end of the session Gerald Howarth raised some of the issues highlighted in Adrian Smith's report. He asked about the large group of prisoners who were found to be driving their own cars on a daily basis without insurance, committing a criminal offence on each occasion and presenting a serious risk to the public. Now suitably penitent, McLennan-Murray accepted personal responsibility for this serious failure. But not for anything else.

Perhaps the most astounding exchange of the whole public hearings came in the latter stages of this session when David Winnick asked the former Governor (HAC 4th Report, Q363) what action the Minister should be taking over what had happened at the prison. David Rodden jumped in to advise him publicly not to answer that question but went on himself to say (HAC 4th Report, A364):

The power of the evidence you have received obviously needs to be communicated to the Minister and we advise the Minister to consider it seriously. Over the last 48 hours a number of people have talked about seeing people being interviewed about should X be sacked and should this happen to Y. As an association it is not our place to make those kinds of observations. It is a matter for individual responsibility and for people to consider their own positions. What my President and I would want to reinforce is that Martin Narey as Director General has the very strong support of the Prison Governor's Association in his task. We also believe that Mr Narey is entitled to be confident in the level of support and the quality of support he receives from his colleagues.

These comments seem to suggest that discussions had been taking place between supporters of the former Governor and members of the HAC regarding my dismissal or removal and possibly the DG's. It also seemed that the PGA senior officials were attempting to focus any fallout on to me in the hope that the DG would then step back and sacrifice me to remove the pressure, irrespective of the truth. If true that the HAC might have engaged in such subterfuge then this is little more than an outrage, that calls our public institutions into question.

In the last session of the morning the HAC heard from Mark Healy and Tom Robson who were senior officials of the Prison Officers Association (POA). Neither had been involved or had any direct knowledge of the events of May 5. Because of that it was unclear why they were called. This would soon become clear in that some members of the HAC would try to put words into their mouths giving credence to falsehoods. However Mark and Tom were experienced men who would not be led.

From the start of this session the nature of the briefing given to staff going on the search became an issue. HAC members told them they had heard that search staff were told during the briefing that 'the prison was awash with drugs' and that 'prisoners were in control of the prison'. They clearly were not told this by anyone who was at the briefing. It was totally incorrect. However some of this did appear in the local papers with other disinformation that was being circulated. Though Mark Healy acknowledged that he had heard the phrases he would not be led to say that they were true. Neither would he give credence to a suggestion that search staff were deliberately 'wound up' to go in and provoke a riot. Unlike the earlier witnesses who were not involved in the operation and knew little of the facts, the HAC was now dealing with experienced individuals taking an unbiased view and who would not be led. Mark Healy expressed the view that the true reason for these events had yet to emerge.

Following the evidence of the previous day some supporters of the former Governor were confidently predicting that I would be immediately removed from my post, or dismissed. They attributed this to alleged comments from a member of the HAC. Rumours were circulating and I received a number of telephone calls that morning from Governors and other staff in the area who were concerned and wished to give support. Though I was satisfied that the DG and I had acted correctly in this matter, I was becoming unnerved by the partisan behaviour of the committee.

Just a couple of days earlier I had been told that the HAC would call both John Podmore and me to attend the public hearing. We would attend with Martin Narey and the Prisons Minister Paul Boateng MP. From their behaviour the previous day, it seemed that the HAC were deliberately attempting to discredit the senior management of the service in the handling of this matter and in doing so diverting attention from the wrongdoing of the former Governor. It also seemed to be clear that I was now their specific target.

We entered the oak panelled committee room in the Palace of Westminster immediately after the lunch break, taking our seats in front of the committee who sat in a horseshoe formation. Behind us were representatives of the media and other interested parties including the former Governor, his wife and some earlier witnesses, such as the ex-prisoner Alan Rogers. The hostility of some HAC members was immediately palpable. At this time I had only a general outline of what had occurred during the examination of earlier witnesses but an observer who had been present later stated that their mood changed with our arrival.

This part of the hearing opened with Gerald Howarth challenging me on the content of an internal report on the events of May 5 sent from Area Office to headquarters. He accused me of being disingenuous in relation to a section of that report dealing with the formality of the new Governor asking for the search. He accused us of having planned the search weeks earlier. This was untrue and an accurate account of events was given in our evidence. He portrayed the search as an SAS type raid planned by me in conjunction with 'Your so-called Chaucer Team'. He should have been aware from the evidence already provided to the HAC that the Chaucer Unit was an intelligence gathering and investigative unit with no executive authority. He implied that they were a sinister group in the background plotting against the former Governor. This tied in with the version of events already put about by supporters of the former Governor.

In a somewhat aggressive and sarcastic tone he then moved on to the transfer out of the former Governor and the manner in which it was handled, accusing me of being responsible for the move. Martin Narey made it clear that he had taken the decision to move the Governor some weeks earlier and had informed Sir David Ramsbotham at the time. He also stated that he had decided, on the basis of intelligence, to bring forward the move and to authorise the search. Howarth was not convinced stating (HAC 4th Report, Q462): 'Surely this was not a well disposed move toward somebody to whom you were favourably disposed'.

It seemed to me that the decision of the HAC not to hear the evidence about the reasons for the search in closed session at an early stage in their investigation was absurd. But as a result they could attack the senior managers involved with impunity in the public hearing, knowing that we could not give a full explanation in response to questions because of the sensitivity of some of the intelligence. At the time I felt that some HAC members were grasping the opportunity this afforded them to give credence to a particular version of events that they had already decided on.

The thrust of their questions initially focused on the planning of the search and the circumstances of the removal of the former Governor. They implied that the search and the removal of the Governor was a plot hatched by me in a vindictive attempt to destroy the ethos of the prison and to damage an enlightened and innovative Governor. Though the DG told them that he had made the decision weeks before the search to move the Governor, and that he was aware of the intelligence and approved the search, some HAC members disregarded his evidence, still accusing me of being behind those events. The chair, Robin Corbett, was particularly prone to interjecting with sarcastic and over-dramatic remarks.

The hostile rejection, by some members of the HAC, of any evidence that was not in accord with the account they appeared to be sponsoring was worrying. These events had been well documented by independent investigators yet their reports were ignored or dismissed as lacking credibility. At the start of the investigation I had confidence in the system and the process of natural justice. My subsequent experiences of the HAC and the behaviour of some of its members had undermined that confidence to a degree that I now entered that committee room with trepidation. Unlike a court of law or other disciplinary processes there did not seem to be any adequate provision for me or other people involved in the proceedings to address effectively any incorrect evidence already given. Neither was there an opportunity to address the HAC on matters other than in reply to their questions even if the rules allowed for it. Furthermore as I was heard along with the Minister and the DG I was not in a position to seek such an opportunity. My trepidation soon turned to disgust and I began to view some of those involved with a level of odium that I have seldom felt before or since. But even with these constraints I was not prepared to be intimidated by them and I tried to deal honestly and robustly with all their questions.

Prior to the hearings it had been alleged that a committee member had stated his intention to 'make the Area Manager pay' for the removal of the Governor and for the search. Martin Narey's evidence to the HAC relating to these events contradicted the well publicised misrepresentation of the facts and would complicate their predicted outcome. If they could not discredit me on the facts then it became clear that some people would seek to do this through insinuations concerning my management style and my philosophy as a professional prison Governor and senior HMPS manager.

Much was made of a 'tense relationship' between the former Governor and myself including accusations, in my view false, by Dr Hugo and Lady Clarke that I was bullying the former Governor. This was put to Martin Narey who readily accepted that conflict did exist but that it was related to the Governor's disobedience to instructions and refusal to maintain a proper balance between security and resettlement. In their evidence to the committee some BOV members had claimed that they told Martin Narey of their concerns that the Governor was being bullied. He denied that any such comments were made to him and went on to tell the committee (HAC 4th Report, A477):

> I do not believe he was the subject of bullying. I know Mr Murtagh has a robust management style. Frankly, in the Prison Service that is frequently necessary. I think the evidence shows that it is perfectly reasonable to argue that if anything, on occasions, Mr Murtagh had not dealt with Eoin as firmly as he might. When there had been recommendations as long ago as 1998 of disciplinary action against Eoin the Area Manager chose not to follow that. Mr Murtagh has 13 Governors working for him at the moment, eleven of them have worked for him before and have volunteered to work with him again. That does not suggest an ogre.

They were also told that at a time when it was being alleged that I was bullying him, Eoin was unsuccessfully applying for a job as Governor of Dover YOI, which was also within my area of responsibility. Questioning relating to the relationship was directed at the DG. No questions were put to me about alleged bullying so I did not have an opportunity to comment. However the HAC would later imply that I had not directly denied the allegations.

Humfrey Malins asked Martin Narey if he shared my views that the prisoners at Blantyre House were 'beyond redemption'. At the time I did not know to what he was referring but later discovered that this statement had been attributed to me by the Education Department manager. I intervened and made it clear that I had made no such statement and that as a professional prison Governor I could not function in the service if I held such views. My response prompted a cynical observation from David Winnick that we could not both be telling the truth. When the detail of the statement, made by this very inexperienced service provider, was explained I was able to support my denial with a detailed account of our conversation. She had obviously overlooked that a third party was present, in the form of the Governor, who could clarify what was said. The matter was not pressed further and the HAC did not call the Governor or check the accuracy of her statement, I take this to be a vindication of my position.

Though persuasive evidence was already available to the HAC in the form of independent reports on these events, without the evidence they had yet to hear in private, it seemed to me that they were continuing to try and discredit the senior managers involved. Their attention then turned to the planning, organization and execution of the search and to my colleague, John Podmore. Again it seemed to me that questions were frequently framed in the emotive language of the prison subculture that had been a feature of earlier publicity regarding the removal of the Governor and the search. They were focused on the briefing of staff and the manner in which the search had been carried out. Though it had been conducted throughout in a professional manner by staff it was obvious that some members of the HAC were not convinced, preferring to believe the emotive and untrue accounts they heard from individuals who did not witness the operation.

The HAC claimed to have heard from an unidentified source that during the pre-search briefing the officers involved were told that the prison was 'awash with drugs and under the control of the prisoners'. The source was not identified. I was present when John briefed his section commanders and later at his full staff briefing. No such statements were made. Neither could anything said be interpreted in any way to infer that this was the case. John's evidence to the HAC reflected what I witnessed. It seemed to me that this was not what they wanted to hear. Though all credible sources pointed to a professional operation some HAC members preferred to believe otherwise, using unduly emotive terminology such as 'Rambo raid', 'SAS type raid' and 'wanton destruction'. This too was the language of the criminal subculture, the vendors of which they chose to believe rather than reputable professionals.

By the end of the public hearing it seemed that the HAC were ignoring the abundant evidence in support of the action taken. It seemed that they had adopted a position and were disinclined to contemplate the possibility that it might be wrong or that they could have been misled. By now I was losing confidence in the integrity of the whole process. We seemed to be pawns in a game being played out for their own amusement, the outcome of which had little to do with right or wrong and nothing to do with justice or the public interest.

During the short period before going into the closed session I took the opportunity to use the toilet. It was located immediately off the House of Commons committee room corridor. As I entered I was accosted by an ex-prisoner. A large, heavily built individual, he leaned his face toward mine as I passed him and in an intimidating manner said, 'You fucking bastard, you're a fucking dead man!' This seemed interesting behaviour from a man who was making great play of his newly reformed lifestyle and in whom the chair of the HAC seemed to have such confidence. I had been threatened in the past by much more fearsome characters than this and was unimpressed. The incident was drawn to the committee's attention immediately before the start of the closed hearing but they seemed disinterested.

During the closed session Martin Narey gave the committee a broad outline of the intelligence which had contributed to the decision to transfer out the Governor and immediately search the prison. This included specific accounts of criminal activity likely to endanger public safety and bring HMPS into disrepute. At best it painted a picture of serious abuse, by some prisoners, of the resettlement process and the trust being placed in them by the Governor. It also highlighted a serious failure by the prison's management to ensure that even the most basic security procedures were carried out to monitor the activities of prisoners and to protect the public. I feel sure that if the situation had been allowed to continue and had the media become aware of it, there would have been a public outcry on a scale that might have threatened the positions of all those responsible for the supervision of the Governor, from myself to the DG and possibly to the Minister. Had that occurred I believe that this same committee would then have led the demands for action against the service's senior managers for failing to take the action for which they now criticised us.

The reaction of some HAC members indicated that they were sceptical of the intelligence. Some clearly failed to grasp the seriousness of what they were being told. Others seemed to be trying to play down its impact and to discredit the intelligence gatherers. Nonetheless, by the time we finished the closed session it was difficult to see how they could possibly disregard our evidence. But we underestimated them.

Over the previous six months both my wife and I had been subjected to considerable stress as a result of events. This was compounded by the added pressure of our son's terminal illness. I had hoped that this hearing would have given me an opportunity to respond to the untruths that had been levelled at me in the media and to the HAC. I did not have that opportunity. Leaving the committee room I was angry and disappointed at the treatment we had received. As we walked into the corridor I was even more surprised and irritated by Gerald Howarth MP, one of the HAC members most hostile to me, walking up behind me and placing his arm on my shoulder uttering light hearted platitudes. My anger was such that I had to restrain myself from a response that I would later regret. He obviously realised that I was not amused and moved away.

It seemed fairly clear that the HAC did not want to be convinced by the evidence we had given, just as they seemed to have disregarded the abundance of evidence about the situation at the prison that they had already received. Their report was therefore expected to be critical. As the committee had particularly targeted me during their hearings there was an expectation that this would follow through in their report. As comments attributed to a member of the HAC had suggested that they would seek to have me removed it was also expected that they would try to achieve that end. I was obviously worried by the way the hearings had gone, but I was told by my superiors that I should have no fears as I continued to have the full support of the Minister and the DG who knew that the criticism of me was unfair and baseless.

HARASSMENT

During the weeks that followed the hearings, supporters of the former Governor seemed confident that they had succeeded in reducing my reputation to shreds and ending my career (but there is no evidence or suggestion that the former Governor had any part in this). Whispers, claimed to be based on 'inside information', were regularly circulated predicting my dismissal or removal from my post. These again led to regular calls from well meaning colleagues in HMPS and other services with whom I had close contact offering support and sympathy. I was confident of my position and the support of my bosses but it would be dishonest not to admit that the whisperers' activities were unnerving on occasions.

Unfortunately the harassment did not stop there. Almost immediately after the hearings regular anonymous and abandoned telephone calls began being made on my home number. These continued for almost a year starting with up to six calls each day and eventually tapering off over that period to a few each week. Many of these calls came at periods of the day which appeared to correspond with the times that prisoners had access to the card phones in their prisons. However there is no clear evidence of their origin as all the callers withheld their numbers. If, as I suspect, some did originate from certain prisoners then my home telephone number must have been given to them by a subversive member of staff. These events were reported to the police and British Telecom but the calls continued. My family had become accustomed to this form of harassment as we had experienced it on occasions in Northern Ireland. Because of this we were not particularly upset by it, preferring to take the view that it was the actions of cowards and was costing us nothing as it is they who were paying for the calls.

By this time, I had lived in my then home for over ten years, and had never experienced problems of any kind. Things were about to change. My home was regularly daubed with graffiti, the content of which was mostly innocuous. But it was irritating and obviously detracted from its appearance. Though I removed it after each attack these incidents continued at irregular intervals, even after my retirement. On one occasion, when my wife and I were abroad, the front garden wall was partly demolished in the early hours of the morning. A neighbour was awakened by the noise and witnessed a small group of young men leaving the scene at speed. Of course there is no evidence that any of these events were connected with Blantyre House or the HAC inquiry but the fact that both occurred around the same time led me to suspect a link.

The telephone calls of prisoners in higher security prisons are recorded and regularly monitored by security staff. At 09.39 hours on the morning of November 2, just days after the HAC public hearings, Prisoner K who I have mentioned in earlier chapters made a telephone call to the home of Dr Brian Hugo, a member of the BOV at Blantyre House and one of those who had accused me of bullying the former Governor. The call lasted 15 minutes and 42 seconds and highlighted, at best, a worryingly close relationship between the pair. It is very unusual for any BOV member to give their home telephone number to a prisoner. It is equally unusual for a board member to be involved with a prisoner not held in the prison to which they are appointed. Dr Hugo's experience of HMPS was limited to Blantyre House and it is probable that he was not aware that calls were recorded and monitored. His response to the call suggested that he was not surprised to receive it. As not all calls recorded are subsequently monitored it is possible that he had received similar calls before or after this event.

Security officers at the prison were so concerned at the content of the call that it was reported to senior managers immediately. During the conversation Prisoner K revealed that he had managed to get a full copy of the record of the open hearing and particularly the evidence given by myself, Martin Narey, John Podmore and the Minister. He told Hugo that 'someone' got this information for him from the Internet. Though he did not say who had downloaded this fairly lengthy document and brought it into the prison for him, security staff had already identified a middle ranking officer who they suspected had been corrupted by him.

Prisoner K wasted little time in getting to the point that interested him. He focused on evidence given by Martin Narey that he had spoken to the chair and deputy chair of the BOV at his home and briefed them on the intelligence which led to the events of 5 May 2000. Martin had also told the committee that he had met with the chair of the board the previous Friday. Prisoner K was very keen to find out what they had been told and seemed to expect that Hugo would tell him. Of course Hugo was not brought into the intelligence loop and so had nothing to tell. However he did volunteer feedback on the reaction of the HAC to the evidence given in the closed session, telling Prisoner K, 'And the story I got back, was that the comments passed was that the rabbit that was produced from the hat at the closed session was a rather mean and scrawny piece or something to that effect'. The HAC had agreed to hear this evidence in closed session as it was sensitive and could place sources in danger or compromise ongoing investigations if it was revealed. If Hugo's claim was true then it reflects badly on the HAC, a factor that by then did not surprise me.

Though denying that he had done anything wrong, Prisoner K seemed keen to ensure that the intelligence contained nothing detrimental to him. Speculating that the events might have been partly related to another prisoner, now rearrested and in custody, he suggested that I had 'thrown him in for good measure once Eoin went'. Unable to satisfy his need for the detail of what had been said in closed session, Hugo, in an apparent attempt to reassure him repeated the fact that he had been told that very little had been produced in the closed session and that 'they' were totally unconvincing. Responding to Prisoner K's suggestion that the HAC's eventual report could say that they found the evidence 'behind closed doors absolutely pooh, pooh you know', Hugo expressed the view that they could and would. He went on to tell him that the board had told the HAC that the Area Manager was bullying the former Governor. Prisoner K reminded him that he had already told him that and that he, Prisoner K, had made a similar statement in a long letter to Robin Corbett. This was one of the documents withheld from me.

Seemingly confident that the HAC would 'pooh pooh' the intelligence, their conversation then turned to likely outcomes. Speculating on a rumour that I had already been removed from post, Hugo told Prisoner K that this was untrue and that nothing was likely to happen until after the HAC reported. He reminded him of earlier advice he had given him 'to be patient'. Their discussion went on to cover the role of the Minister in this matter describing him as a 'tricky politician' who was trying to lead it away from me and the DG, especially me.

The content of this call and the fact that Prisoner K had Hugo's home telephone number led many people to the conclusion that the latter's relationship with a potentially manipulative individual was not consistent with his role as a member of the BOV. In normal circumstances it might have led to censure or his removal from the board. However the power of the HAC is considerable and there seemed to be real apprehension at the highest levels about doing anything that would further antagonise them, even if failing to act might undermine the effective management of Blantyre House. No action was taken concerning this and other cases of unacceptable behaviour that came to light, which may have led those involved to believe that they were untouchable. Though Ministers and the senior management of HMPS were very clear as to the correctness of the action that had been taken at the prison the political realities dictated that the HAC would have to be pandered to and some concessions made to them when they eventually reported. This process of cow-towing, a form of face-saving device employed by public servants in the wider interests of public confidence, had already begun in evidence to their investigation and continued up to and beyond the publication of their report.

CHAPTER 11

A Modern-day Witch Hunt?

In my view the perverse behaviour of the Home Affairs Select Committee (HAC) in the conduct of their investigation, their apparent partiality and willingness to accept the evidence of prisoners and supporters of the former Governor without question, was in stark contrast to what seemed to be their disregard of the extensive evidence in support of the action taken by senior HMPS management. This led us to expect a critical report. On 16 November 2000 that report was published. As expected it was highly critical of HMPS and the action taken at Blantyre House.

It was evident that the HAC placed great store and confidence in the views of Sir David Ramsbotham, the Chief Inspector of Prisons, concerning both events at Blantyre House and on aspects of HMPS policy. They also seemed to have total confidence in the views of prisoners and supporters of the former Governor. Though none of these people had any direct knowledge of the facts or of the search, the HAC never felt a need to test—rather than simply accept—their evidence or to allow it to be challenged. Of course there may be things in the undisclosed evidence, but that in itself is deeply worrying to someone like myself and difficult to see how any valid information given in private could affect the true picture as I and other senior HMPS managers knew it to be.

They did not interview any of the staff who carried out the search or the managers who supervised it on the ground. John Podmore, who they did hear from, had been in overall command of the search and had inspected the search area as it neared completion, but he was not on the ground during the operation. If they really wanted to get the facts about forced entry and missing keys why did they not talk to those who had supervised the operation? Perhaps the facts did not fit with the tendentious report they planned to write. But if so then they would also have to discount all the evidence of investigations into Blantyre House presented to them in independent reports and the intelligence presented to them in closed session and which could not be made public due to ongoing investigations, witness protection and a fear of reprisals, among other things.

THE SELECT COMMITTEE'S REPORT

These questions were quickly answered on reading their report. Commenting on the search and the need to carry it out the HAC concluded, in language remarkably similar to that used by Dr Brian Hugo during his telephone conversation with Prisoner K (HAC 4th Report, para. 37):

We were completely unconvinced that the search was a proportionate response to the intelligence which had been used to justify it. We do not believe that the reasons given to us in public justify the exceptional search or the way in which it was carried out. Nor do we find the evidence given in private persuasive.

Then in an attempt to justify that conclusion they went on to cast doubt on the intelligence, recommending (HAC 4th Report, para. 38):

We recommend that there should be an immediate review at senior Prison Service level of the manner in which the intelligence produced by the Prison Service's own Chaucer group and used to justify the search of Blantyre House was collected and assessed and what steps might be taken to confirm the reliability of such intelligence.

This effectively enabled them to disregard one of the main reasons for the search, at least for long enough for them to achieve their purpose. They knew that the review they sought would take some time to complete and there would be little media interest in its outcome as Blantyre House would be old news by then.

Commenting on the conduct of the search (HAC 4th Report, paras. 39, 40 and 41):

We endorse the substantial criticism of the search made in the Prison Service's own internal report. We do not accept that there were insuperable difficulties in finding the keys and reject the claim that it was necessary to use force to enter the chapel and health centre, which are separate from the prisoner accommodation. Neither the Prison Service's internal report nor the evidence we have heard in public and private provide convincing explanations for the damage caused in the search, the use of force to enter the chapel and the health centre, the fact that some areas were searched and others were not, the statement that the search was conducted at the request of the incoming Governor and the alleged demeanour of the searchers. These are minor matters in themselves, but cumulatively they have done great damage to the ethos of Blantyre House in the eyes of the Board of Visitors, staff, prisoners and outsiders involved in the work of the prison. It is easy to understand why all those people are prone to the suspicion that this was the intended — rather than accidental — consequences of the search.

They then concluded:

On the basis of all the evidence we have heard, we conclude that the search was a failure aggravated by the unnecessary damage caused. It was an exceptional operation in Prison Service terms and it was neither planned nor carried out with an appropriate degree of care.

Though not surprising, to those of us familiar with the facts, this was unbelievably disingenuous stuff. Having disregarded the intelligence in such a cavalier manner they proceeded to misrepresent the findings of HMPS's own inquiry into the search by implying that these supported the HAC's conclusions, when its recorded findings included:

(Para. 9.1) The briefings held for staff at Swaleside on the evening of the execution of the operation were good and comprehensive.

(Para. 9.2) The search of Blantyre House was conducted in accordance with the briefing and instructions. The atmosphere during the search was good, the staff searching the residential areas behaved in a professional manner and related well to the prisoners.

(Para. 9.3) There were no specific targets for the search. It was a general search of the residential areas and the ancillary buildings. Finds included various papers, some cannabis, ecstasy tablets and quantities of pornography. [The findings listed here overlooked a number of important items including mobile phones, cameras and tools.]

The investigating officer was critical about a number of organizational matters relating to the operation, including the fact that a field annexed to the prison was not searched and that detailed plans for searching areas of the prison were only produced on the night after their arrival at Blantyre House. However none of these criticisms had any bearing on the contentions of the HAC. Furthermore, the investigating officer, commenting on the issue of the availability of keys, stated (para. 7.5): 'It was difficult to come to a conclusion some three months later as to whether keys were or were not available'. But he went on to say that the box in which the keys were held normally had a breakable glass front but on the night of the search this was concealed by a wood panel. He concluded (para. 7.5): 'This could have led to the confusion about the availability of keys'. If that was the case and the gate officer could not locate the keys then there was no alternative option available to the operational commander but to force entry. The members of the BOV who attended for the first three hours of the search described it as thorough and professionally conducted by staff. The committee heard no other direct evidence from those present and chose not to call any witnesses who could provide a first hand account in reaching their conclusions.

Having criticised the conduct of the search the HAC then went on to question the justification for it. This was a general search of a kind regularly conducted by HMPS at other prisons. As such its objective was to find any unauthorised articles in the prison. The nature or volume of items found in this type of search is not necessarily a valid indicator of the need for the search. The HAC took a different view, confusingly stating (HAC 4th Report, paras. 42; 43):

Some of the items found were significant—especially mobile phones linked to criminals. But it is odd that the search should be justified after the event by the discovery of items not specifically sought in the course of the search. There was a complete mismatch between the objectives of the search, the methods used and the items sought. This was not a normal search and it should be judged by a different standard. We believe the items found fell well below the level of contraband which would justify an exceptional search of this nature. It appears to us that none of the illicit items were found in the areas to which entry was achieved by forcing locks and breaking doors. If this was all the 'emerging intelligence' anticipated would be found, that intelligence did not justify the search. If the 'intelligence' led officers to believe that more would be found either the intelligence was flawed or the search was.

They were clearly judging the justification for and success of the search from the stated viewpoints of the BOV, a career criminal and a few serving prisoners rather than from the evidence of HMPS professionals.

Following his appointment the new Governor had made a number of changes including the introduction of basic security procedures which the former Governor had refused to implement and stopped a couple of unsuitable work placements. He also began to implement the recommendations of the Smith Report of 1998 and had discontinued some activities on the instructions of the DG. The HAC did not seek his views on these changes but they did record (HAC 4th Report, para. 56):

> We accept that prisoners at Blantyre House ought to expect to be searched on return to prison. Although this may not be consistent with the former ethos, it will not seem strange to prisoners arriving at Blantyre House from other prisons. Driving is a basic skill needed for outside work. It is short-sighted to stop driving lessons and photography classes. While we can see the case for more careful selection of future work placements and better supervision of current ones, we can see no sensible grounds for cancelling work placements already being undertaken. It seems ridiculous to do so when the employer is willing to carry on that employment when the individual leaves prison.

The report concluded that there were three factors which led to the removal of the former Governor, the relationship between him and the Area Manager, the lack of an HMPS resettlement policy and confusion about the status of the prison. This was remarkably similar to views already expressed by Sir David Ramsbotham and was in my view an oversimplified and inaccurate assessment. There was no confusion about the status of Blantyre House as a Category C prison with a resettlement role. That is how HMPS classified it. The alleged confusion was created in an attempt to justify the former Governor's failure to obey orders. Furthermore though there was conflict between the Area Manager and the Governor it was entirely related to his disobedience to orders and refusal to carry out HMPS national instructions.

The HAC also seemed to embrace the views of the Chief Inspector in concluding that I was clearly opposed to the concept of resettlement and saw this as a key factor in the conflict with the Governor. Evidence to the contrary was disregarded. Similarly they seemed to accept without question the evidence of some members of the BOV, who had not had any contact with me, that I was bullying the former Governor when they stated (HAC 4th Report, paras. 79; 86):

> We conclude that the relationship between the Area Manager and the Governor had deteriorated to such an extent that the Prison Service should have addressed it much earlier by moving one of them or by altering the chain of command or both.

They went on to express the view:

Even if Tom Murtagh was fully committed to resettlement as practised at Blantyre House—which frankly we find difficult to believe—he failed to convey that impression to some of those who worked near him. In fact, he gave very much the opposite impression to others and to us.

As I had instigated the development of HMPS's resettlement policy and had set the business plan for Blantyre House, on which its ethos was based, it is astonishing that they should take such a view.

Commenting on the effectiveness of the HMPS's management of the situation the committee added (HAC 4th Report, para. 94):

> We conclude that (a) the absence of a resettlement policy, (b) the ambiguity about the security status of Blantyre House and (c) the obvious tension between the former Governor and the Area Manager all reveal serious weaknesses in the management of the Prison Service. This is compounded by the inability to investigate properly what went wrong. The situation should never have been allowed to deteriorate to the point at which the Director General thought the only option open to him on 5 May was to remove the Governor and conduct a full search of the prison.

Having embraced inaccurate assessments of most of their perceived contributing factors they then criticised the DG for decisive corrective action. They now needed someone to blame. Once again they would seem to be influenced by the evidence of the Chief Inspector (page 167) telling them of his great admiration for Martin Narey and suggesting that the events at Blantyre House did not seem to be in line with the standards he, Martin Narey, wished to achieve. This was buoyed up by the account given by Sir David that the HAC seemed to be all too readily embracing. I felt as if I was being set up. But this was foiled by the evidence of Martin Narey himself who, in spite of the pressure being brought to bear on him, insisted on telling the truth. On the day of our appearance at the HAC, Martin was approached by one of the committee who told him that the committee did not want to criticise him, but that they wanted to pin responsibility squarely on the Area Manager, and suggested that Martin should cease to take responsibility for the events. The clear implication was that, if he distanced himself from the search, he, Martin, would have a much easier time when the report was published.[1] They were perhaps disappointed, but still seem to have wanted it both ways (HAC, 4th Report, para. 97):

> We note that Mr Narey has chosen to take full responsibility for these events, but we do not believe he is entirely to blame. The factors that led to the crisis on May 5 started before he became Director General in 1999. We accept Sir David Ramsbotham's assessment that this is not the way Martin Narey wants the Prison Service to go. The burden of salvaging Blantyre House and devising a resettlement policy rests heavily with him.

As well as dealing with the events surrounding May 5 the report also championed a number of ideas and criticisms put forward earlier by Sir David

---

[1] Source: Martin Narey.

Ramsbotham and made recommendations on matters such as security classification of prisoners, functional management of resettlement prisons, the creation of a separate resettlement prison category that fell between Categories C and the D and the duty of HMPS to protect the public by developing longer term targets which measure rates of re-offending. In an effort to enhance the power of the Chief Inspector they recommended (HAC 4th Report, para. 100): 'When something goes seriously wrong in HMPS, the investigation should be conducted independently by the Chief Inspector of Prisons'. They then went further, recommending (HAC 4th Report, para. 104): 'The new inspection arrangements ... should apply to the overall management of the Prison Service.'

The Home Secretary already had powers to ask the Chief Inspector to carry out an inquiry into any particular matters which gave rise to concerns in connection with conditions in prisons and the treatment of prisoners and he had used them when he considered this appropriate. His existing remit also empowered him to report on the impact in the field of headquarters policy and specific senior management decisions. It seemed that he was already taking a fairly liberal view of the boundaries of his remit.

My reaction on reading the report was one of great sadness. From my perspective it seemed that the integrity of Parliament had been subverted. It alarmed me that the HAC could produce such an erroneous report. I had already accepted that they were not interested in the facts and would inevitably be critical but I was not prepared for what I saw in print. Though I knew it was untrue and that I had the support of my superiors, I felt traumatised. I had operated under considerable stress over many years in Northern Ireland and to a lesser degree as an Area Manager in a fast changing and demanding Prison Service and always felt I was coping well. The added stress of the campaign against me following May 5, together with the pressures my wife and I were coping with regarding our son Nigel's terminal condition took its toll. I was unwell, my blood pressure was out of control and though my doctor tried hard to control it, the drugs were having little effect. He told me that I could not continue to operate in this state and urged me to take time off work. I made him aware of what was happening and why I could not take his advice. With his help and the support of my wife I worked through this period. I did not want those who sought to undermine me to see any weakening in my resolve. I always tried to present a confident façade. This saw me through the HAC's hearings and their immediate aftermath. Many colleagues in HMPS were probably not aware of my health problems, but I suspect that those who worked closely with me knew that I was unwell.

The publication of the report did nothing to improve my condition. But I was immediately reassured from the highest level that I should not worry as those who mattered in the service and in Government knew that I had been wrongly accused. I was grateful for that support and the encouragement I immediately received from Martin Narey and his deputy, Phil Wheatley, but most of all I was buoyed up by the warm support I received from my own team at Area Office and the Governors and officers within the Kent, Surrey and Sussex Area. They will never know how much this was appreciated and the strength I gained from it.

Supporters of the former Governor were jubilant and some were again confidently predicting my immediate dismissal or removal from post and some even seriously believed that the former Governor would be re-instated. A few subversive members of the staff at Blantyre House, as I considered them to be, and some individuals on the BOV appeared to see the report as a vindication of their actions and an encouragement to covertly obstruct the work of the new Governor. For a short period the level of anonymous harassment and sniping directed at me that I described in *Chapter 10* also increased.

Shortly after the publication of the HAC's report the BBC *Newsnight* programme decided to feature the story. They asked both Martin Narey and me for interviews. Though I was quite happy to participate I was told that I could not and must not make any comment as the Minister (Paul Boateng MP) intended to respond personally to the report. The BBC were clearly not satisfied with that and set out to find me. I was not aware of this at the time. A couple of days before the programme was scheduled to go on air I attended a meeting with colleagues from another criminal justice agency which finished earlier than expected. After leaving the meeting I decided to pay an unannounced visit to Blantyre House. No one knew of my intention to go there until I arrived at the prison gate.

Within an hour a BBC camera crew and the *Newsnight* reporter Robin Denslow were at the gate and already aware that I was in the prison. Either I was being followed or a member of staff at the prison had contacted them to inform them of my presence. Having been trained in counter surveillance because of the threat from terrorists and being constantly alert to the danger of being followed, I think it is probable that the information came from a subversive member of staff. As I left, Denslow unsuccessfully tried to press me into commenting. Shortly after leaving I received an anonymous call to my car wrongly informing me that the camera crew were in pursuit and going to my home.

The *Newsnight* programme, presented by Jeremy Paxman featured pre-recorded interviews with Lady Rosie Clarke, Dave Newport, the former junior governor moved out on May 5, David Rodden from the PGA, and ex-prisoners Alan Rogers and Paul Collins. Paxman selectively outlined the recorded findings of the HAC in opening the programme and throughout. Lady Clarke who had not been involved in the search incorrectly led viewers to believe that her colleagues who did attend were told to leave before the 'real' search got under way. Repeating the by now familiar conspiracy theory, she saw the whole affair as an attempt to provoke prisoners to react, giving HMPS the opportunity to close the prison. This theme was also reflected, to varying degrees, by other participants. Dave Newport bemoaned the loss of trust that prisoners felt and predicted that the re-offending rate would now rise.

The ex-prisoners Rogers and Collins were filmed in a pub. They were presented as former career criminals now 'going straight' and an example of the success of Blantyre House. Collins had been in the prison at the time of the search and, led by his interviewer, gave a false account describing the search staff as abusive, 'winding prisoners up' and looking for trouble. The performance of these men did little for their credibility. Within a short time Collins was back in custody having committed further serious offences.

The image that these people presented was in stark contrast to the robust performance of the Minister in defence of the action taken at Blantyre House and of the DG in taking these decisions in the interests of public safety. This and his subtle dismissal of the HAC findings must have been intriguing to many viewers who probably realised that there must be much more to this than met the eye. I received many approaches from members of the public expressing that view and asking what really happened. If supporters of the former Governor had expected this programme to further their cause they would have been thoroughly disappointed—as they would be ultimately with the Government's rejection of most of the HAC'S findings and recommendations.

THE GOVERNMENT'S RESPONSE

Because of the power and status of the HAC it seemed that political etiquette demanded, rightly or wrongly, that the Home Office and the Prison Service should pander to their will. It was therefore to be expected that the Government's response would reflect this and concede to at least some of the HAC's findings and recommendations. That response came in mid-January 2001 and though conciliatory in tone was robust in its rejection of many of the HAC's key findings, which included that the HAC was:

- completely unconvinced that the search was a proportionate response to the intelligence which had been used to justify it;
- did not believe that the reasons given in public justified the exceptional search or the way it was carried out, and they did not find the evidence given in private persuasive; and
- [that it considered that] the absence of a resettlement policy, the ambiguity about the security status of Blantyre House, and the tension between the former Governor and the Area Manager all revealed serious weaknesses in the management of the service;

But the Government replied (Gov. reply to HAC 4th Report, paras. 1, 2 and 3):

The Government notes the committee's criticisms of the search carried out at Blantyre House prison on the night of 5/6 May 2000. It accepts that, unintentionally, the search and the simultaneous move of the then Governor of the prison has led the HAC, and others, to doubt the Government's commitment to resettlement and that of senior managers in the Prison Service to the regime at Blantyre House. It does not, however, believe that that doubt is deserved. The Government regrets the damage caused during the search of the prison and has accepted the need for further work on the security classification of resettlement prisons and the overarching policy framework on resettlement. The committee and the Government are agreed on the importance of ensuring that Blantyre House continues to perform well as a resettlement prison. The Government regrets that the committee did not accept the Director General's explanation of the reasons for the search of the prison and remains firmly supportive of the Director General in carrying out his responsibilities. The Government believes that this response should dispel any doubt over its central commitment to resettlement, and its capacity to respond to learning points related to the conduct of the search. While it welcomes the way in which the committee has used Blantyre House as a vehicle for discussion of wider issues, including security and resettlement, it is also concerned that potentially wide ranging decisions on major, and complicated, policy issues should be put in a wider context.

In response to the HAC's recommendation that:

there should be an immediate review at Senior Prison Service level of the manner in which the intelligence produced to justify the search was collected and what steps might be taken to confirm the reliability of such intelligence

a review was commissioned and carried out by a senior team drawn from both HMPS and the police. Many of those involved had worked within the National Criminal Intelligence Agency (NCIS) and were very experienced in this field. After an in-depth examination of the intelligence and the operational procedures of the Chaucer Unit the review team identified improvements that could be made to intelligence handling procedures, mainly related to the technical training of staff and the collation and analysis of intelligence that would have strengthened the credibility of intelligence produced by Chaucer. Responding to the HAC the Government informed them of the review team's recommendations to strengthen the credibility of intelligence and that (Gov. reply to 4th HAC Report, Section 3 (Use of Intelligence) para. 4) 'they did not find that the intelligence, on which the search was based, was unreliable'.

I believe that this was an understatement of the findings of the review team who actually concluded (Report of a Fact-finding Review, Part 5, p.5 in Response to Recommendation 3 of HAC 4th Report): 'It was our view that there was enough information, most of it reliable or from reliable sources to warrant the action taken in this case'. Commenting on the link between the intelligence gathered and the search, the same report records (section 4. 3 p. 12):

There was clearly a great deal of worrying information which pointed to staff corruption and involvement by prisoners in criminal activities whilst working out in the community. There were potential risks to the public and issues which if not addressed may have resulted in criminal activities being committed by serving prisoners from Blantyre House. Staff could have been left vulnerable to corruption and serious criticism levelled at the Prison Service. Not to have acted in these circumstances would have been irresponsible and a breach of our responsibilities to the public and our staff. In our view the scale and volume of information emerging coupled with concerns about procedural security at Blantyre House drove the decision to take special action. We found that there were numerous issues which needed to be addressed and that the decision to search Blantyre House was designed to address all these issues in a general way in order to provide a clean sweep.

Highlighting the Prison Service's determination to deal effectively with the minority of staff found to have acted corruptly the Government informed the HAC that the Attorney-General had recently given approval to the charging of three prison officers with criminal offences under anti-corruption legislation following a joint police/Chaucer Unit investigation.

The strong criticism by the HAC, their questioning of the credibility of the intelligence which precipitated the removal of the former Governor and the search, together with the views of Sir David Ramsbotham in evidence (*Chapter 10*, p. 168) would have a sustained damaging effect on HMPS's efforts to deal with corruption. Though subsequently vindicated, Chaucer investigators who had worked so hard were completely demoralised by this slur on their reputation and the perceived value of their work. Just prior to these events Ministers had become more aware of and supportive of the need to address staff corruption. The DG had already begun the process of developing a Central Professional Standards Unit to coordinate this work. It was initially envisaged that operational intelligence gathering units, similar to Chaucer, with the specialist investigative skills to work in conjunction with the police when needed, would be created in each area (which in my view was necessary). The critical views expressed by the HAC and the Chief Inspector created a political climate in which it became difficult for HMPS to roll out the Chaucer model, or anything similar or obtain the substantial additional funding essential to make it work effectively. Small units were created in each area solely with an intelligence gathering function. Investigations of alleged corruption which, in my view, is a highly specialised and difficult area, now falls to non-specialist staff in individual prisons. Though these officers will do their best, in most cases they may not have the accumulative experience and expertise necessary. However this should not be seen as a critism of senior HMPS managers. The current model is probably the best we could expect in the political circumstances in which it evolved. But without the necessary additional funding and better police cooperation, it will, in my view, not be conducive to dealing effectively with this serious problem.

Consistent with its general stance, the Government did not get drawn into the argument about relationship issues, preferring to re-state the fact that the decision to move the Governor was taken by the DG. However it went on to say that in view of the time he had been in post the move was 'entirely reasonable'.

By this time HMPS was at an advanced stage of developing a national policy on resettlement and would soon complete the work that I had started. The fact that there had not been such a policy was a valid criticism, even if the HAC did not acknowledge that this was already being addressed before their intervention. The Government response accepted their criticism of this omission.

Seemingly influenced by the Chief Inspector's criticism of the perceived confusion over the security classification of Blantyre House, and to a degree, other resettlement prisons, the HAC recommended that such prisons should be given (HAC 4th Report, para 107) 'an intermediate security status (between C and D) which reflects current layout and facilities—pending reorganization of security classification'. In making this recommendation, the HAC appeared to be demonstrating that, like Sir David Ramsbotham, they did not seem to fully understand all the implications of how security classification worked in terms of HMPS policy and practice or the influence it had on the status of a prison. It also seemed that they were unaware that a review of the classification system had only recently been completed. However the Government accepted their recommendation to classify resettlement prisons as 'semi-open' but their recommendation that the security classification system should be reviewed was rejected, as was their recommendation that the three resettlement prisons should be managed centrally.

The acceptance by the Government of the HAC's recommendation on the security classification of resettlement prisons may have seemed, to anyone who did not have a proper grasp of the categorisation process, to vindicate the position of the former Governor and his supporters. However it did not and its consequences would result in substantial change to the make up of Blantyre House Prison's future population in that only Category D prisoners would be eligible to go there. The added impact of a coherent resettlement policy published in the spring of 2001, with its more clearly stated allocation criteria would also ensure that professional criminals would be less able to subvert the selection process at an early stage in their sentences. It would ultimately transpire that those who had publicly professed an objective to protect and retain the Blantyre House model as it was in 2000 would be responsible for changing it so as to reduce risks rather than to encourage risk-taking. Furthermore the security procedures, required by me, which the former Governor had failed to implement, would become the norm for the prison as they were also a basic requirement for all open prisons.

During the interval between hearing formal evidence, the publication of the committee's report, and the Government's reply there was no let up in the campaign by supporters of the former Governor. Amongst other things *Private Eye* and a national newspaper published inaccurate and in my view—and that of my legal advisers who I consulted at the time—sometimes libellous comments directed at myself and the DG. Lord Mayhew, a former Tory Minister and the former MP for the constituency in which the prison is located, also became involved in the debate with a series of questions to Ministers in the House of Lords. This former Attorney-General, reputedly a friend of certain members of the BOV, succeeded in obtaining Parliamentary time for a debate on the prison in the House of Lords.

This took place on January 17, just days after the Government's reply to the HAC. I attended the debate together with a small group of senior HMPS officials. Protected by Parliamentary privilege, a numerically depleted House of Lords rehashed much of the disinformation relating to events at Blantyre House which was by now the common currency of those who supported the former Governor and which had been given credence by the HAC report. This wearisome affair served little purpose other than to prolong the whole saga and undermine the efforts of the new Governor to settle the prison back down to normality.

Though it appeared that attempts to block progress, by elements within the prison, were continuing, they were becoming less successful. New and improved procedures were introduced. The Governor had successfully implemented all the security procedures which the former Governor had either refused or failed to implement. He had achieved all this within the resources he inherited from his predecessor. He also re-profiled the work of the prison to ensure maximum efficiency in the deployment of staff.

Suzanne Anthony, then Governor of the resettlement prison at Kirklevington Grange, accepted my invitation to spend some time with Chris Bartlett at Blantyre House. The objective was to enable him and his staff to explore how the performance of the prison could be further improved and learning points from Kirklevington's experience. Her presence would give some reassurance to staff that the prison was continuing in its resettlement role and support to the Governor at this time of considerable pressure. Suzanne was a robust and able manager and I was confident that her input would be helpful.

Shortly after her arrival she expressed surprise to me at the unprofessional attitudes and mindset of some staff and their lack of understanding of their role as prison officers. Suzanne also highlighted a number of areas where she felt that the effectiveness of the prison could be improved. As many Blantyre House staff seemed to have come to believe that effective resettlement could only be achieved through the regime in place under the previous Governor, they needed to see that there were other models and options that were equally effective. Suzanne Anthony agreed to host groups of Blantyre House staff on attachment to Kirklevington Grange Prison where they would have an opportunity to observe a more structured and objective led approach in a regime that was also much praised by Sir David Ramsbotham. Feedback from officers suggested that the experience had been beneficial and enabled them to re-focus professionally.

Having re-profiled the work of Blantyre House, introduced appropriate management and security procedures and made inroads into implementing the recommendations of the Smith report, the Governor was given a modest increase in resources to undertake new work not previously carried out at the prison. Some supporters of the former Governor wrongly alleged that the allocation of these ring-fenced additional resources vindicated his refusal to implement proper security procedures due to lack of resources. As the new Governor had already implemented all of these procedures with the resources available to the former Governor they ought to have known that this was a fallacy.

In the time between the removal of the former Governor and the Government's response to the HAC report, the new Governor seemed to get little or at best lukewarm support from various members of the prison's BOV. After a while, I gained the impression that a minority of influential members were actively working against him. Every opportunity was taken to cast doubt on his competence and his commitment to the prison. However their intentions were transparent and they were unsuccessful. The conduct of some members also led to conflict within the board itself. Some members resigned, having tried and failed to get the BOV to function to their liking. This course of action was taken by David Cottle who had been chair at the time of the HAC investigation. Through his departure the board lost a dedicated and level-headed member who commanded a high level of respect within HMPS at that time. In the two years between the events of May 2000 and my retirement from the service in May 2002 the board never seemed to genuinely support the Governor or to carry out its role impartially in the best interest of the prison as a whole. Some board members were reported to refer to him as 'Murtagh's man'.

Whilst some supporters of the former Governor had appeared confident that the events would destroy my career that expectation was not fulfilled. In contrast, many of the HAC's findings were rejected by the Government and I was openly supported by the Minister and the DG. Sir David Ramsbotham was allegedly overheard when greeting David Cottle at a reception he, Sir David, was hosting in London, to say, 'We still have not managed to get rid of that bugger Murtagh yet'! One observer reported that David Cottle was visibly surprised by the remark. This function was also attended by leading members of the HAC.

Prisoner K probably received a copy of the HAC report. A formal complaint was made on his behalf about his transfer out of Blantyre House. It challenged the basis of the decision to move him, sought an explanation for it and the intelligence on which it was based. Because of the criticisms levelled at senior managers in the service the complaint was investigated by the independent Prison's Ombudsman, Stephen Shaw. Mr Shaw is a highly respected individual with a background as a champion of prisoners' rights and a campaigner for better prison conditions. As Ombudsman he had a right of access to all prison records including intelligence relating to any matter which he was investigating. This case was no exception. After a thorough investigation, including an examination of all the intelligence, his report concluded that the removal of Prisoner K from Blantyre House was an appropriate response to the intelligence on which it was based.

THE DIRECTOR OF PERSONNEL INVESTIGATION

Surprisingly, I thought, in the wake of the Government's rejection of large parts of the HAC's finding, Eoin McLennan-Murray, whether egged on by others or not, still wanted his pound of flesh. He made a formal complaint of bullying, something that he only seems to have thought about during the HAC inquiry. It did not appear in any of the records and log that he was required to keep as a Governor. He had never mentioned it to my knowledge until then and always gave as good as he got when working with myself and other HMPS colleagues. He also continued to work within my area when, in my book as a 'bright prospect', he could easily have gone elsewhere of his own accord if he did not like my style or thought he knew better than me.

Following a protracted investigation by an independent senior civil servant with no operational experience in relation to prisons, two relatively innocuous strands of his complaint were upheld. I had on occasion used one of my pet phrases 'wired to the moon' to describe his views, and on another occasion I had lost my cool with a member of his staff on the telephone, in sheer frustration, exasperated at his failure to act as I considered a prison Governor should (both events that I describe more fully in *Chapter 10*, the later for which an apology had been accepted at the time). None of my senior colleagues in HMPS nor the other Governors under my command could believe it. I think that they knew that I had conceded these matters to avoid continuing aggravation and further detriment to my health and family life. They were warm in their support, including the DG. Whatever the modern day dictates of political correctness, the demands of any prison encompass security and control and prisons are not places where it is always possible to pussy-foot around. It was to be sure a blot on an otherwise unblemished career record, but by then the energy to resist some of the unfair things that were still being said was temporarily ebbing away as my wife and I turned our attentions to other priorities. Some things in life are more important.

When he was removed from his position in May 2000, Eoin McLennan-Murray, should have taken up a post as Deputy Governor of Swaleside Prison. He had resisted this move and Martin Narey had allowed him to take up a non-operational position. It was now time for him to return to an operational management role if his career was to get back on track. He probably hoped, after all the fuss that he and others had created, that he would be able to move quietly back to an in-charge post. This was not to be and he now had to resume his operational career in the position he had originally resisted as Deputy Governor at Swaleside. This was still within my area of responsibility, and under the direct command of Mike Conway, an exceptionally able Governor who I knew would be an ideal mentor for him. I doubt if this is what Eoin expected but it seemed again to demonstrate issues of judgment in removing himself from the operational service, thereby setting the progress of his career back two years. But he survived, ultimately regained trust and confidence towards himself in his work, and has it would seem lived up to much of the early promise that various people, myself included, discerned in him.

Throughout the period of the HAC hearings and the subsequent investigation into these allegations all the prisons in my area continued to operate to a high standard and remained within the top performing group of prisons. I was lucky to have such a competent and loyal group of Governors and an area team who collectively and individually demonstrated their professional and personal support to me throughout. I am very grateful to them all for that support which saw me through the low points and enabled me to present a confident façade to the world. My area office team were a tower of strength to me. My Staff Officer Stephen O'Connell, himself a fairly direct speaking Irishman, kept me on my toes and ensured that I did not 'take my eye off the ball' with regard to normal business. He made sure that high standards were maintained in the office. But I will best remember his loyalty, friendship and frankness as my closest confidant in the service throughout this period. I am also indebted to many others too numerous to mention.

●   ●   ●

The pace of events after May 2000 seemed to make time fly. I was fast approaching compulsory retirement age. Some of my enemies had been pressing for my removal or early retirement and if circumstances had been different I would have welcomed it as it would have enabled Frances and me to spend more time with our son Nigel. Immediately following the circus that was the HAC 'investigation' I told Martin Narey that, if he thought it would be helpful, I was prepared go early. He made it clear that as I had done nothing wrong and had been wrongly accused he did not want me to leave a day before I had to retire.

It was normal for individuals approaching retirement gradually to slow down but I was determined that this would not happen in my case. I was keen to ensure that my area did not suffer from the short term vacuum normally created by a new Area Manager coming in. My team, who had supported me so well, did not deserve this and I asked the DDG, Phil Wheatley, if he would appoint my successor and allow him to have a realistic handover period to ensure continuity. He agreed and Adrian Smith was appointed to replace me. This pleased me as I knew him to be a very able manager. At the time he was the Area Manager for the London Prisons but he was familiar with the Kent, Surrey and Sussex Area having been a former Governor of Elmley Prison. He had also led both the major investigations into the management of Blantyre House. Though I continued to manage the area until the day before my retirement Adrian had the opportunity to familiarise himself with all aspects of his new command and thus was able to hit the ground running.

Before I left HMPS the resettlement working group, which I had originally set up and was still a member of, completed the development of the service's policy on resettlement. After all that had occurred in the previous year I was also pleasantly surprised to be asked to lead on the development of policy and operating standards for the new semi-open prisons, the novel category into which Blantyre House now fell. In completing this work a wide spectrum of opinion was drawn together and our work was adopted in full by the Prisons Board.

I would reach compulsory retirement age on 12 May 2002. Frances and I were invited to attend an informal dinner with my area team to mark my retirement on May 9. When we arrived at the Flackley Ash Hotel near Rye in Sussex it became clear that this was going to be a memorable evening for us both. The DG and DDG and most members of the Prisons Board were there, as was the new Chief Inspector of Prisons, Ann Owers, together with the heads of most of the other criminal justice agencies within the South East Region. I was also pleased to see a considerable number of former colleagues from all levels. Though I did not see him, I was later informed that Eoin McLennan-Murray had been there for part of the evening. I was disappointed that I did not have an opportunity to speak to him and at least wish him well in his future career.

During the evening Martin Narey, in addressing the gathering, took the opportunity to ensure that no one should be in any doubt about the fact that I had been seriously wronged by recent events. Making it clear that I had been unfairly accused, he thanked me for my loyalty to him throughout this difficult period. However, more touching to both Frances and me, was a humorous presentation by a couple of senior Governors, on behalf of the whole area team, reflecting on life for those working with me, exposing the true nature of relationships and the supportive environment in the area. They made fun of my robust reputation and produced a list of 'Murtaghisms' made up of my pet sayings, including the by now notorious 'wired to the moon' and others less printable. Many of those present who were now in senior managerial positions within the area and beyond had been developed and promoted by me and there were many emotional private conversations and farewells during the evening.

By the end of the night I was emotionally drained and glad it was all over. I could now get on with the many things that we had planned away from HMPS which had been a central focus of our lives for almost 40 years. In the emotional turmoil of the evening I did not fully take in the significance of one particular message of goodwill. However the following morning I realised that this message, passed through a senior official, from at least some members of the HAC, was significant and was probably the best I could expect in terms of an apology. However the fact that the source had not been on the committee at the time of its inquiry made it difficult to evaluate its real import.

Just prior to my retirement I was approached by a reporter and offered the opportunity to reveal the true background to what had happened at Blantyre

House. I felt it would be wrong to breach confidentiality and declined. These events had made my last couple of years very difficult and I was now determined to put them behind me.

We were now able to enjoy more regular contact with our children and grandchildren. We also spent a lot of valued time with Nigel whose condition continued to deteriorate. Though completely disabled and often near to death his phenomenal sense of humour and inner strength were an inspiration to all who met him. I spent a lot of time with him at his bedside and felt privileged to get so close to him. Speech was frequently difficult for him but we developed a means of communication and discussed many aspects of our lives. Nigel's fight for life and his pain came to an end in December 2003. His fortitude was unbelievable. He impacted on all the family. We miss him so much.

A BLAST FROM THE PAST

Just when it seemed that the Blantyre House affair was becoming a bad memory Sir David Ramsbotham, the former Chief Inspector of Prisons, published his book *Prison Gate*. He dedicated an entire chapter to Blantyre House. He repeated the story as he had told it to the HAC and without mentioning key elements such as the fact that he had been briefed by Martin Narey in advance of the plan to move the Governor and about the search. The book criticises, often unfairly in my view, the judgment of various people charged with responsibility of one kind or another, from the Home Secretary down to the DG, and in particular HMPS for their refusal to sack me. The sense is that he is expert in prison management as well as penal policy. The chapter on Blantyre House paints a wholly negative picture of myself. It also adds the gratuitous but incorrect implication that I triumphantly held my retirement party at Blantyre House! A series of extracts from it was published in *The Times* including his account of the Blantyre House affair and the misleading description of my relationship with Ken Kan when he was the Governor of Ford Prison. Like many of my former Governors, Ken remains a friend and regularly keeps in touch with me.

Prior to the publication of Sir David's book his successor, Anne Owers, carried out an unannounced inspection of Blantyre House in January 2003. Her report, published in February of that year, vindicated our claim that the action we had taken was to protect the resettlement ethos. In her introduction she observed (HM Inspector's Report 2003, p.3), 'This report shows that the prison is responding well to these challenges in many areas' and in her 'Healthy Prison Summary' (HM Inspector's Report 2003, para. 1.02):

> Since the last inspection, Blantyre House had undergone considerable and controversial change. There were some within the prison who regretted the changes that had taken place. Nevertheless, the clarification of the prison's role as a semi-open resettlement prison, with security standards appropriate to that status, had provided the stability and clarity that staff and management needed to function positively.

The summary concluded (HM Inspector's Report 2003, para. 1.21):

Blantyre House was a safe and respectful prison. Prisoners were well motivated to comply with the rules, to develop personal responsibility and to benefit from the available facilities.

Reading *Prison Gate* brought some of Nigel's words to mind. At the time of my retirement Eoin McLennan-Murray was seeking a judicial review of the investigation into his complaints against me. In view of this I had retained a mass of documentary evidence relating to all aspects of the affair including private papers made available to me by other people. I decided to seek a legal opinion, presenting all the evidence, the record of the HAC hearings and the HAC report to a leading libel lawyer. After examining the evidence, including the list of witnesses willing to be called in my support, the lawyers offered to take on the case *pro bono* (free of charge). However after considerable soul searching I decided not to put my family through the stress of such litigation so soon after Nigel's death but to heed his advice and to ensure that one day the true story would be told and the record put straight. This would also enable me to focus attention on the deep concerns that I still felt about what seemed to me to be an abuse of its powers and privileges by the HAC, the absence of observed protocols for the conduct of investigations and any means of redress for those who perceive themselves to be victims of such abuses of power and privilege.

REFLECTIONS

It is impossible for someone who has gone through an experience of the kind that I describe in this book to dismiss the possibility that they might have contributed to the situation. In quiet moments when this unfortunate affair comes to mind, I question whether my actions in managing the former Governor could reasonably have led him to believe what he would later accuse me of doing. Did he really think that I sought to destroy all that was good at Blantyre House when all the real evidence points to the fact that this was not so? Could he really have felt that I was bullying him when all the time he was defying me and demonstrating his disagreement verbally and occasionally in correspondence? Would it have been acceptable for the DG and I to have ignored the intelligence coming to us about the prison and Eoin's blatant disregard of orders from his line managers and wider HMPS policy and instructions? Each time I go through this process I reach the conclusion that the answer to each of these questions is an emphatic, 'NO'. Then I ponder, with disbelief, how the HAC got embroiled in what was a fairly straightforward internal HMPS management matter and, having done so, how they behaved.

I remain at a loss to understand the motivation of Sir David Ramsbotham in this affair. Why, in his evidence to the HAC did he 'completely forget' the briefings he had received from Martin Narey (especially the very clear letter he received only a couple of weeks before the removal of the Governor)? Why on that and other occasions, including in his book *Prison Gate*, did he seem to be prepared to try and damage my reputation? I know that many people see Lord Ramsbotham (as he now is) as a crusader for penal reform and a champion of prisoners' rights, but the events as I have described them in this book have quite naturally coloured my own views in that regard. But we cannot both be right and you, the reader, must form your own conclusions.

When, on occasions, I question my wider contribution to HMPS, I am buoyed by the warmth of the support I received from my Governors and team, the honour bestowed on me by Her Majesty the Queen in the form of an OBE, and the consistent acclaim of my line managers throughout my career, including my last performance appraisal report completed after my retirement and all of these events, in which the DG, Martin Narey, wrote:

> This has been another outstanding year for Tom. I consider him to be an outstandingly effective Area Manager with a real grip on each of his establishments. It has been a pleasure on more than one occasion during the year to visit his area meetings. The shared sense of purpose between his Governors and his area specialists is something which I would seek to bottle and export to every area. Tom retired toward the end of the year and the Prison Service will miss him greatly. I shall miss his commitment and loyalty very much indeed.

These comments seem to be a stark contrast to the image that certain other people who knew little of the facts and the HAC tried to paint of me. I hope they more honestly reflect my contribution as a public servant and as a person.

I will leave the reader to be my judge.

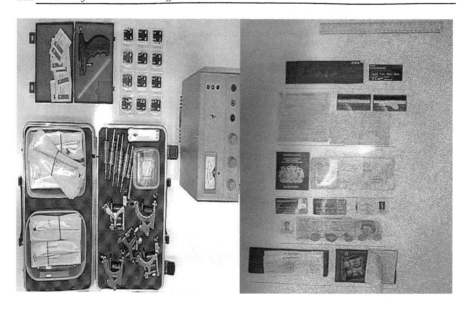

Some of the items found during the search of 5 May 2000

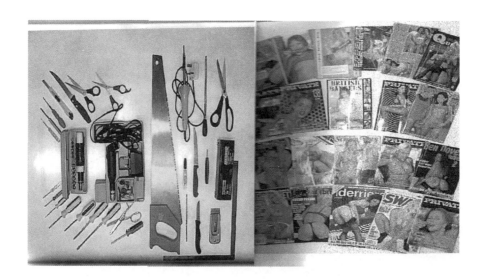

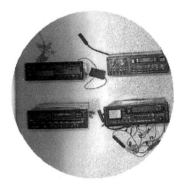

Some of the items found during
the search of 5 May 2000

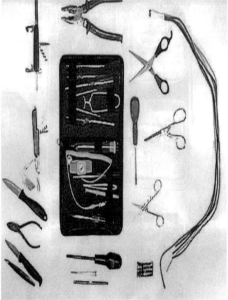

References

Clarkson, W. (2002), *Kenny Noye: Killer on the Run,* London, Blake Publishing Ltd.

Clarkson, W. (2002), *Kenny Noye: Public Enemy No 1,* London, Blake Publishing Ltd.

HM Government (First Special Report), *Reply to the Fourth Report of the Home Affairs Committee, Blantyre House Prison, 2001.*

HM Inspector of Prisons, *Report on Blantyre House 2000.*

HM Inspector of Prisons, *Report on Blantyre House 2003.*

HM Prison Service Internal Audit Department, *Report into the Management of the Special Funds at Blantyre House Prison 1998.* Internal HM Prison Service report.

HM Prison Service Internal Audit Department, *Report on a Financial Audit at Blantyre House Prison 2000.* Internal HM Prison Service report.

Home Affairs Select Committee (2000), *Fourth Report, Blantyre House.* Published by the Stationery Office Ltd on the direction of the House of Commons.

Ramsbotham, D. (2003), *Prison Gate: The Shocking State of Britain's Prisons and the Need for Visionary Change,* London, Free Press.

Ryder, C. (2000), *Inside the Maze,* London, Methuen Publishing Ltd.

Smith, A., *Report of an Investigation into the Management of Temporary Release Schemes at Blantyre House Prison 1998.* Internal HM Prison Service report.

Smith, A., *Report of an Investigation into the Management of Blantyre House Prison 2000.* Internal HM Prison Service report.

Tilley, S., *Report of a Fact-finding Review in Response to the HAC Report, Recommendation 3, Following the Search of Blantyre House Prison in May 2000.* Internal HM Prison Service report.

Windebank, I., *Report of an Inquiry into the Search of HMP Blantyre House 2000.* Internal HM Prison Service report.

Index

accountability 88 131 135 139
Adams, Gerry 30
Aldington Prison 49 64
ambition 24
Amery, Julian MP 33
Andrews, Margaret 72
Anthony, Suzanne 193
Area Drugs Coordinator 106 120
Area Manager 44 46-199
  as Assistant Directors 49
  role 46 90
  selection 49
Area Performance Coordinator 110
Armagh Prison 31-4
Armour, Brian 37 39
army 29
arrest of a prisoner 81
Ashford Remand Centre 24-5
Assistant Directors, Security and
    Operations 34
Assistant Governors 27 30
ATM scam 58 61-5 95 129
Audit Department 67
audits 53 67 70 85 94 107 110 135-6 138
  151-2
see also Smith Reports, standards audit
  unit
availability of keys 69
see also Operation Swynford
avenue of redress 21 131
see also right of reply

bank holidays 103 112
Bartlett, Chris 111-4 116 119-22 125 146
  148 150 158-60 163 165-6 170 174 183
  185 188 193-4
Baulf, Guy 122
Bertram, Nicholas Charles 148 165
Betts, Leah 61
Black, Tony 59
Blake, George 24
Blantyre House 49 58 60-5
  alleged misconduct of staff 96-7
  business plan 64 81 87 92 116-7 149 186
  charity work fiasco 67-76 96 148-9
  control 67-71 107 110 121 126 151-3 165

corrective action plan 75 80-1 87 110 128
  150
culture 75 96 104-5 111 128 176
drugs 69 97-8 111
education department 105 144-6 163-4
  176
ethos 72-3 87 92 99 108 117 125 141 146
  152 160 165 170 175 183 185 198
former prisoners 98 100-1 106-7 129
  131-2 141 157 159-60 177   188-9
general search see Operation Swynford
inspection 101-2
new governor undermined 125 133
performance 81 86-8 101 129 140
possible re-roling 93 98-9 102 106
prisoners' opinions 101 146 158 160
  165-6 183 185
prisoners' purchasing power 69-71 111
  128
prisoners transferred 121-2 147 194
prisoners' vehicles 67 69-70 79-81 97
  105 124 128 144 148 151-2 172 185
regime 75 87 92 98-9 114 122 129 132
  140 142 145 149 190 193 199
re-profiling 94-5 110 151-2 170 193
resettlement function 49 67-8 81 117
  125 139 165-6 169-72 193   198-9
searching 94 106 126 151-3 165 185
security 74 93 110-1 147 151-3 160 165
  170 185 193 198
security audit action plan 93-4
security status 102 169-70 185-6 192
selection process 63 70 73 82 87 99 108
  128 151-2 192
staff not following procedure 95 106
supervision of prisoners 85 87 185
'Terminator, The' 74 109
Board of Visitors (BOV) vi 32 50-2 56 72
  74-6 91-3 98 100 102-4 108 115-6 120-1
  125 127 133 141 144 146 149-50 157
  160-4 170-1 175-6 179-81 183-5 188 194
Boateng, Paul (MP) 20 106 114 129-30
  147 158 174 178 180 188 194
bomb 37-9
Bond, Terry 78
borstal allocation centre 22

Bowles, Lynne 129
Brink's Matt robbery 58-61
Brister, Bill 25
Broad, Ken 43-4
budgets 46 48 51 54-5 57 82-3 138 152
  allocation system 55
Bullwood Hall Prison 57
bullying 153-5
business plans 47-8 50 115
Butler, Eva 54
Butt, Ted 136

cameras 164 185
Cameron, Stephen 58
campaign against standard search
  procedure 32-3
Canterbury Prison 49 64 82-3 137
career criminals 58-63 67-8 71 74 78-9 81
  83-8 91-2 95 97 99-101 105 111 117 124
  185 189 192
see also Prisoners A, C, D, K
Carrol, Paul 83 137
Category A prisons/prisoners 60 115
  134-6
Category B prisons/prisoners 148
Category C prisons/prisoners 76 102 166
  169-70
Catton, Gary 62-3 95 129
Cawsey, Ian MP 159 165
charity activities 67-73 75 96 107 144
Chaucer Unit 63-4 67 74 77-89 96-8 104-6
  112-3 121 124-5 133 138 148-9 157 168
  174 190-1
  right of appeal 78
Chelmsford Prison 54-7
Chief Inspector of Prisons 20 33 44 53-7
  82 101-4 107-9 122 127 133 139-40 187
  197
  remit 53 187
  see also Ramsbottom, Sir David
Chief Officer 24
civil service 33-4 45 55-6 128 142 156
Clarke, Lady Rosie 160-3 167 175 188
clustering 51 56-7
Coldingly Prison 115 136
Collins, Paul 188-9
communication problems 42
Community Care Fund 70-1
confidence in parliamentary system 21
  175 177 187

conflict 52-7 73 104
conspiracy to undermine resettlement
  75 99 129 131 141 164 168 185 188 199
contemporaneous notes 86-7 172
control 29-32 35-6 39 45 67-70 96 113 163-
  4 171
  and restraint vi 156
Conway, Mike 50 95 195
Cooke, Geoff 113 120-1
Cookham Wood Prison 51 57
confidentiality breached 98
Corbett, Robin MP 100-1 131-2 141-9
  157-60 163 165-6 168-9 172 175 177
  180
corporate approach 48 50
corruption 30 39 58 60 63-4 73-4 77-89 96
  105 109 111 138 149 168 180 190-1
Cottle, David 115-6 120-1 160-2 194
Crime and Disorder Act 1998 92-3
criminal conspiracy 58-64 80 97
Criminal Justice Act 1991 47
cult of personality 53
culture 42-4 47-50 55 135-7 166

Darnell, Charles 147 165
DCs Fordham and Murphy 59-60
Dean, Janet MP 159 164 170
Delaney, John 148 165
Dellow, Ralph 144-5 163
Deputy Director General vi 19-20 40 86
  88 90-1 95 101-3 105 134 136
  see also Wheatley, Phil
Deputy Governor 34-6
detainees 25-7 30
Director General vi 20 23 25 40 45 47 56
  76 78 88 90-3 98-9 101-12 136-7 139-40
  142-3 145-7
  see also Narey, Martin
Director of Personnel investigation 195
Director of Regimes 82
Director of Security and Operations
  (NIPS) 25 33 35 38
dirty protest 31 35
discipline 31 138
disciplinary proceedings 71-2 151 153
dismissals 79
Donald, Sergeant John 61
Dover YOI 40-5
Downview Prison 115

draft report on Blantyre House
inspection 107
drugs 99-100 104 106 109 123-4 132-3
crime 61 81 84 97-8 106 147
compulsory random testing 50 120
treatment programme 50 120
Duff, Michael 163-4
Duke of Edinburgh Award Scheme 43

Eames, Brian 40
East Anglia Area Manager 46-9 52 58
efficiency 47 49 51 56 83 94 163
Elmley Prison 49 51
escapes 29 33 35-6 45 50 73
establishment vi
exchange of best practice 48

failures 35 71 99 115 134-7 172 177
family 19 21 38-41 66 142-3 178 199
Farrell, Mairead 31
feasibility studies 51 56-7
Ferris, Jim 35
fetes 91
Fletcher, Francois 145-6 163-4 176
Fletcher, Harry 129 144
flushing 120-1
Ford Prison 137-9 153-5
Fordham, DC 59-60
Forrester, K 147 165
Freedom of Information Act 2000 130
143 149
Fresh Start 41-2 46

Galbally, Jane 83
Gardiner, Lord 30
Gooday, Ron 78 106
Government 20 53
response to HAC 189-94
Governors vi 24 28-9 32 35-6 45-8 51 53
81-3 111
Governor in charge vi 25 31 40 47 50 56
63 103-4 113 135 154
Grant, Martin 58 61-3

Hales, Brian 67 81 86-7 92 111
Hanna, Christopher 39
harassment 178-81
Hayward, Billy 62-3
Head of Management Services 71-2 151
Head of Personnel 31

Head of Security 29-30
health 66 187 195
Healy, Mark 173
Hennessy, Sir James 53
Highdown Prison 115 134-6
high profile management 29 36 45 48 102
high security prisons 31 49 125-6 134-6
Holloway Prison 54
Home Affairs Select Committee vi 19
100-1 109 122 127 129-34 140-5 148-50
156-81 189-95 197
Area Manager's participation 158 175
correspondence with prisoners 101
131-2 146-7 149 157 159 180
evidence in private 158-9 174 176-8 180
183
leading questions 164-5 167-9 172
public hearings 158-78 183
recommendations 183 186-7 189
relationship with prisoners 101
report 182-9
unreasonable behaviour 159 169 172-4
177 182 199
Home Secretary 45 47 52-3 109 132-3 139
187
Howard, Michael MP 47
Howarth, Gerald MP 100-1 159 165 167
171-2 174 178
Hughes, Simon MP 133 144
Hugo, Dr Brian 120-1 125 160-3 175 179-
83
humour, sense of 29 171 197
hunger strikes 31 35
Hunter, John 44 49
Hydebank Wood YOC 36-40

Illingworth, JR 146 165
independence 45 133-4 168
independent monitoring 52-3
industrial relations 36 40-3 46 78
informal discussions 43
informants 79 104-5 107
inspections 52
inspection reports
Blantyre House 107-9 131-3 139-50 166
198-9
Canterbury 82
Chelmsford 54
Ford 153-5
Rochester 103-4

insufficient evidence 105
intelligence 29-30 77 79 96-7 104-6 109
    112 121 126 128 133 143 148-9 153 157-
    8 168-9 174 180 183-5 190-1 194
internal investigations 58 77-89 128-30
    133-4 154
intimidation 27-8 32 36 39 109 159
IRA 31-9

Johnson, Christopher 101 132 165

Kan, Ken 138-9 153-5 198
Kent Area Manager 49-199
Kershaw, Collette 138
key performance indicator vi 50 152
Kidd, Paul 62-3
Kirklevington Grange Prison 60 166 193

Latchmere House Prison 60-1
leadership 28-9 36 39 43 90 134-5
leaks of sensitive information 100 117
    132 140-1 149 157 180
Legal Aid 24
Lewes Prison 115 136-7
Lewis, Derek 47
lies 78 128-9 141 150 164 178
Linton, Martin MP 100-1 167
Lloyd, John "Little Legs" 59 62-3
Lygo, Admiral Sir Raymond 45

Maidstone Prison 49-50 60
Malins, Humphrey MP 100-1 159 164
    168 171-2 176
management style 44 48 56 165   175-6
marked man 33 37-41
May Committee 53
Mayhew, Lord 192
Maze Prison 25-31 33-6 172
McAvoy, Micky 59
McLennan-Murray, Eoin 19 64 70-6 83
    85-9 91-100 105-12 128-34 141-53 197
    199
  absences from Blantyre House 86 93-4
    171
  annual appraisal reports 65 72 87-8
  being bullied 162-3 165 167 170-1 175-6
    180 185 195 199
  disobeying orders 80 87-8 101 107 110
    142 150-3 167 170-1 175 185
98 142 167 171 195

evidence to HAC 169-72
lobbying 98-101
poor judgement 72-3 80 87-9 94
protecting prisoners 81 97-8
relationship with Area Manager 88-9
    105 111 141 145 149 152 162 171 175
    185-6
relationship with prisoners 109-10 129
    131 142 159
supporters 116 121 132 134 139-43 145-6
    150 159-68 173-4 178 188 192-4
transfer 88 106 109-12 116-7 128-30 141
    143 145 152 167-8 171 174-6 190-1
McMullan, Des 35
media 19 38 53 55 84 103-4 122 127-9 137
    140-2 145 159 173-4 177 183 188 197-8
  campaign 129 141-2 192
Mencap 68-71 107
mobile phones 69 96-8 124 128 148 184
motor insurance cover 147 151 172
Mountbatten Report 24
murder 58-9 61 148
  attempt 37-40
Murphy, DC 59-60
Murtagh, Nigel v 19 21 142-3 178 187
    196
    198-9

Narey, Martin ix-xii 19-20 23 82 90-3
    101-12 128-34 136-7 139-40 142-3 145-
    7 153 156-9 162 164 167-8 173-8 180
    185-6 188-9 191-4 196-7 200
  evidence to HAC 175-6
  support for Area Manager 108 143 178
    187 194
National Crime Squad 97
National Criminal Intelligence Agency
    (NCIS) 190
negotiation skills 28
Nesbitt, Keith 72
Newell, Mike 169-72
Newport, Dave 82 111 116 124-5 188-9
Norman, Archie MP 144
Northern Ireland 25-40
Northern Ireland (Emergency
    Provisions) Act 1973 25
Northern Ireland Prison Governors
    Association 36-7
Northern Ireland Prison Service 25-6 28

Northern Ireland Prison Service College 30
Northern Ireland Prison Service Headquarters 34
Northern Ireland Secretary 26 30 33 38
Noye, Kenny 58-63 84

OBE 44 200
O'Connell, Stephen 196
offending behaviour programmes 50 99
Official Secrets Act 21
open prisons vi 49 137 192
Operational Directors 44 46 48 85 87 90
Operation Swynford 112-28 141 160 189
  availability of keys 121-2 147 160 163 183-4
  Bronze Commanders 112-3 119
  C and R units 118-20 123
  criticism of 122-3 147-8 182-5
  damage to doors 122 160-2 183-5
  drug testing 120-1 160
  forced entry 122 161 184-5
  general search 112-4 117-27 161-2 168 174-6 182-5
  Gold Commander 112-3 118 122
  illicit items 123-4 147 164 184-5
    National Dog Team 113 117-20 123
  Silver Commander 112-3 117-23 147 161
  staff briefings 113-4 118-9 173 176-7 184
  strategy 117-9
operational management 28
operating costs 46 51
organized crime 59 61 79
Outward Bound 43
overtime 41 46
Owers, Anne 53 197-9

paramilitary organizations 26 28-39
Parliament 32
Parliamentary privilege 20 55-6 130-2 139 143 149 157-8 193
payment for places 74 95-6 108 111
Pearce, William 53
Pearson, Tony 78
performance 50 66 80 138 196
  appraisal 49 200
based culture 44 47 66 83 136 164
  league tables 50
  monitoring 44 46 146 163

problems 50 134-6
targets 46-50 136 170
personal attacks 108 139 186
Pilling, Sir Joe 47
planning permission 76
Podmore, John 63-4 78 112-3 117-123 158 174 176-7 180
police 58 61-2 64 67 77 79-80 95-8 100 104 109 138 153 156 179 190-1
policy development 52 82
political awareness 28 34 55 89
politics 26 32 35 126 191
Pollett, Brian 58 61-2 64 99 113-4 120 128-9 134
power 21 27 88 105 150 156 181 189
prejudice 23
pressure 66 133-4 162 171 186 193
Price sisters 31
primary carers 83-6
Principal Officers 29 36 62
Prior, James MP 33
Prison Gate 53 198-9
Prison Governors Association vi 55 77 129-30 134 140 157 169-73
Prison Officers Association vi 42-3 46 77-8 83 173
prison
  disciplinary system 46 78
  management 45
  populations 24 27 45 47
  regimes 22-3 36 45-6 51 57 82-3 136
  riots 29-30 32 45
  rules 31-2
  services 51
  structure 30 36 42-3 134
Prison Service of England and Wales 39-40 50 52 189
  code of discipline 63 72 77
headquarters 46 72 98 100
incident command structure 112-3
operating and security standards 54 83 110 115 128 135-6 152
  policy 58 69 101 167 186
  resettlement policy 64 70 82 142 185 191-2 197
prisoners
  'A' 71 79-81 88 96-7 106
  'C' 97 109
  'D' 109

'K' 83-8 91-2 95 97 100 105 109-10 122
125-6 133-4 148-9 179-83 194
drinking alcohol 91 96
education 36 43 90
literacy skills 24 90 146
relationships with staff *see* staff
relationships with prisoners
rights 26 45
status 26-7
supervision 67-8
training 43
Prisons Act 1952 53
Prisons Board 46
Prisons Ombudsman 53 194
professionalism 23 25 53 77 105 122-6
133 193
progressive prisons 23
promotion 24-5 30-1 34 46 72
protecting the public 64-5
psychiatric treatment 22
public confidence 82 153 181

Queen's Gallantry Medal 29

racism 23 40
Ramsbottom, Sir David (now Lord
Ramsbottom) 20 51 53-7 78 92 101-4
107 112 130 139-40 142-4 153-5 174
185-7 191 192-3 194 198-200
theatrics 54
evidence to HAC 166-9
Reader, Brian 59
Rehabilitation of Offenders Act 1974 147
re-conviction rates 98-9 152
remand 24 31 49
re-offending 90 121 189
resettlement vi 36 43 45 49 60-2 74 82 85
108 137-8 152-3 165-7 177 190
resignations 79 138-9
respect 23
responsibility 21 26 64 186
retirement 19 179 196-200
right of reply 56 142 175 *see also* avenue
of redress
risk 64 101 108 142 166 167
assessment 85 108
Roberts, Alexina 76
Robinson, Brian 59
Robson, Tom 173
Robson, Tony 103-4

Rochester Prison 49 51 57 64 103-4 113
Rodden, David MP 140 169-73 188
Rogers, Alan 129 131-2 159-60 174 188-9
Rose, Lisa 117
rumours 157 173 178 180
Russell, Bob MP 159

safety issues 34 41 85 112 147 190
Savage, Jean 62
searches 69
general vi 19 *see also* Operation
Swynford
reception 32-3
rubdown vi
strip vi
secrecy 112-3
secure accommodation 93
security 26 29 51 60 93 114 126
classification 93 99 102 136 169 192
failures 35 39
procedures 32 36 85
Security Minister 34
semi-open prison vi
Semple, Jim 99 165
senior officer 24
Shaw, Jonathon MP 100 133-4
Shaw, Stephen 53 194
Shipton, Alan 114
skills 48-9
Smith, Adrian 66-75 82 100 134 142 196
Smith, David 74 76 144 149-50
Smith Report 1998 68-73 80-2 95 107 110
117 128 146 151 185 193
Smith Report 2000 144 147-53 158 172 183
Special Category status 26-8 30-1 35-6
Special Powers Act 1922 25
Spratling, Steve 79 116 122-6
staff 28-32 35-7 77-89 111 188 193
charged with criminal offences 191
conditioning 96-8 105 116 125 152
disciplinary system 46 151
morale 31 43 139 161
relationships with prisoners 62 74 81
95-8 104-5 125-6 134 149 156
see also corruption, dismissals,
resignations
Staff Officer 84 196
standards audit unit 83 93 139-40
Stanford Hill Prison 49 51 113
steel cladding 76

Sterling, Janine 145-6
Stinchcombe, Paul MP 159 167
Straw, Jack MP 20 109
stress 34 40 47-8 50 142 157 178 187 199
support 108 143 178 187-8 194-6 200
suspensions 138
Swaleside Prison 49 51 56 61 63 111 118

Tate, Pat 61
team approach 42 48-50 154-5
technical ordnance officer 38
teenagers working with prisoners 87
temporary release 62 68-9 80-1 85-6 88
    91-2 97-8 105 109-10 128 151
terrorists 26-7 30 32 34 39 143
threats 28 62 177
Tilt, Richard 78
Tipples, Molly 160-2
Train, Chris 40
training 28 30 36 64 118
Troubles, The 27-8 34
trust 64 68 73 97 126 142 152 160 166-7
    170 189
Tumim, Judge Stephen 45 53 55

unpublished evidence to HAC 130 143-4
    146 149 150 157-8 164 180

value for money 47 55 136 163
vandalism to home 179
views not sought 140 176

violence 29 32 40
visits to Blantyre House 67 86 93-4 105-6
    132 156 158 188
Voicetrack system 83

Walker, Alan 66 85 87
Warriner, Helen 160
Wheatley, Phil 20 25 88 90-1 95 134 136
    143 187 196-7
White, Tony 59
Whitelaw, William 26-7
Widdecombe, Anne MP 140 144
win-win approach 43
Winnock, David MP 159 161-2 165 167
    172 176
women prisoners 31 34 49
Woodhead, Vice Admiral Sir Peter 53
Woolf, Lord 45 47
work regimes 35
working out schemes 43 49 62 67 70 73
    79-82 95 102 109 144 146-9 151-3 190
Wormwood Scrubs Prison 22-4

young offender centre vi
young offender institution vi
    see also Dover YOI
young offenders 22 26 92-3 98
Youth Justice Board 92-3

ALSO FROM WATERSIDE PRESS

Pit of Shame
THE REAL BALLAD OF READING GAOL
Anthony Stokes

With a Foreword by **Theodore Dalrymple**

A REMARKABLE BOOK

This unique work looks closely at the **life and times of Reading Gaol** during the period that **Oscar Wilde** was a prisoner there and contains a number of new insights concerning his classic poem, *The Ballad of Reading Gaol.*

Pit of Shame, by senior prison officer Anthony Stokes, is based on upwards of ten years research and familiarity with the very fabric of Reading Gaol. It also tells of notorious and famous prisoners such as **Thomas Jennings**, **Amelia Dyer** (the 'Reading Baby Farmer') and **Stacey Keach** (the Hollywood actor); of all the hangings that took place at Reading over the years, including that of Trooper **Charles Thomas Wooldridge** - the 'C. T. W.' of Wilde's ballad; the chain of events that led to the rejection of capital punishment by the UK; and of escapes, brutality, corruption, incompetent criminals and other humorous or entertaining incidents.

Anthony Stoke's compelling account also outlines the rich and diverse history of this most famous of English prisons and tells of the many different and intriguing uses that the establishment and its buildings have been put to over the years, before R$ading Gaol's modern-day reincarnation as an innovative and progressive young offender institution. Quite apart from extensive analysis of *The Ballad of Reading Gaol* and fresh information about Oscar Wilde, there are chapters on internment in the wake of Ireland's Easter Rising, Reading's role as a local prison and borstal correctional centre (and later as a recall and correctional centre), and its use by the Canadian military for 'invisible prisoners'. All this is enhanced by fascinating period detail from the archives, newspapers and records, including the old Visiting Committee book, Execution Log, Chaplain's journal, building plans and other, until, now largely hidden sources and materials – making *Pit of Shame* a must for any reader who is interested in **crime, punishment, prisons** and **English literature.**

THE CONTENTS INCLUDE:
Foreword and Preface
The Old Reading Gaols
The New Prison
Punishments of Former Times

Executions
Prisoner C.3.3 Oscar Wilde
The Ballad of Reading Gaol*
The Easter Rising and Internment
Invisible Prisoners
A Pioneering Borstal Correctional Centre
Starting Again with a Clean Sheet
Life as a Local Prison
HM Remand Centre and Young Offender Institution
Reading Gaol Today and in the Future.
*A verse-by-verse exploration with Reading Gaol-related notes.

The appendices include a list of all executions at Reading Gaol, the historic Dietary Requirements and Prison Rules. The **16 pages of illustrations** include photographs and drawings of the prison and the hand-written entry in the Visiting Committee book concerning an ill-fated petition by Oscar Wilde to the Home Secretary; as well as that in the Execution Log for Charles Thomas Wooldridge.

'Here is a detailed history of a single institution that is of wide philosophical significance and that could be read with great profit and enjoyment by the ... general reader ... If I had to recommend a single book about the history of imprisonment in this country, this would be it'. **Theodore Dalrymple** from the **Foreword**

Anthony Stokes was born and educated in Cardiff, South Wales where he joined HM Prison Service at Cardiff Prison in 1988. After training at the Prison Service Training College at Newbold Revel he was posted to Reading Prison in Berkshire where he is now a senior prison officer. He holds a Certificate in Education (further education) from Reading University, is a member of the Institute of Carpenters and a fully qualified prison locksmith. He has been twice commended: by HM Prison Service, after he saved the life of a prisoner; and by the Director General of HM Prison Service, for his part in helping to quell the riot that took place at Reading Gaol on Boxing Day 1992 that is described in *Chapter 11* of *Pit of Shame*. In 2003, his ground-breaking work in setting up a Vocational Training Centre at Reading led to his being nominated for a coveted Butler Trust Award.

I know not whether Laws be right,
Or whether Laws be wrong;
All that we know who lie in gaol
Is that the wall is strong;
And that each day is like a year,
A year whose days are long.

Oscar Wilde (*The Ballad of Reading Gaol*)